FitzSimons on Rugby

FITZSIMONS ON RUGBY

Loose in the tight five

Peter FitzSimons

*with a few words from Nick Farr-Jones
and Sean Fitzpatrick*

ALLEN & UNWIN

First published in 1999 by
Allen & Unwin
9 Atchison Street
St Leonards NSW 1590 Australia
Phone: (61 2) 8425 0100
Fax: (61 2) 9906 2218
E-mail: frontdesk@allen-unwin.com.au
Web: http://www.allen-unwin.com.au

National Library of Australia
Cataloguing-in-Publication entry:

FitzSimons, Peter.
   FitzSimons on rugby: loose in the tight five.

   ISBN 1 86508 132 9.

   1. FitzSimons, Peter—Humor. 2. FitzSimons, Peter—Anecdotes.
   3. Rugby Union football. I. Title.

796.333

Set in 10.5pt Arrus by DOCUPRO, Sydney
Printed by Australian Print Group, Maryborough

10 9 8 7 6 5 4 3 2 1

To my late father-in-law, Ray Wilkinson. He was a good man with a great and pure love of the rugby game—an inspiring example of the breed who built it.

FOUR WORDS

Good lock, exceptional writer.

SEAN FITZPATRICK

FOREWORD

Peter FitzSimons and I go back two decades now and, as with many of my enduring friendships, it was a shared passion for the game of rugby that first pulled us together. From those early days playing for the Sydney University colts team back in 1980 it always struck me that there was something that made Peter stand out from the pack, and that's excluding his sheer bulk. Having now trodden many paths together, I put it down to an exuberance to express himself which has manifested in many ways, particularly through his wonderful writing.

Early in our rugby playing days I learnt to expect the unexpected with Peter. This was a guy who rolled out to training one night with the cushion seats of his mini-moke strapped to his ribs, which he claims he bruised during the previous weekend's match; the guy who exploded out of mauls like a human volcano erupting and when one day I politely enquired if he might lend a little more muscle and bulk to our imploding scrum quipped, 'Nick, when you read in Monday's *Herald* the best and fairest points awarded for today's match, I doubt you will see any points given for "he pushed hard in the scrum"'.

We went on to graduate from those early Uni days to be simultaneously selected to tour Fiji with the Wallabies in 1984. It was a short two week jaunt which culminated in the playing of a one-off Test against Fiji in Suva. And as we nervously awaited the announcement of the team, it soon became apparent that new Wallaby coach Alan Jones had a process of calling into his room players not selected to explain the selectors' rationale. I had been the fourth called up and the fifth and last was my old mate FitzSimons.

In a nutshell Peter did not receive Alan's decision overly well, at least that's how it sounded to the dozen or so Wallabies congregated around the pool at the Suva Travelodge some 50 metres from Jones's room. The big man eventually emerged and made his way over to his mostly sympathetic team mates. Tommy Lawton was the one who broke the silence; 'Jeez mate, what did he have to say to you?' to which FitzSimons immediately replied, 'can't believe it Tom, he's moved me to fullback and made me captain'.

It is this wit that I'm sure endears many of Peter's readers to his writing. But having also been a part of the process that became my biography, I can categorically say that Peter leaves no stone unturned in researching his material. Indeed, out of my biography, I discovered a number of incidents that occurred during the decade I played for the Wallabies of which I had no prior knowledge.

FitzSimons on Rugby is what the rockers would call 'Fitzie's Greatest Hits', or at least, his greatest rugby hits. In a way it is a fifteen year history of the Wallabies and their deeds both good and bad on and off the track, not to mention the various coaches who imparted their individual legacies to the game. And my guess is that, with Peter's style of writing, strangers to the Wallaby teams, players and traditions will be left feeling as though they have an intimate knowledge of some of the characters who made up the various teams and what it is like to be on tour with the tribe, as Peter puts it.

There's no doubt that one Peter FitzSimons could have and should have played more rugby internationals for Australia. But had that occurred maybe his experiences in Italy and deep in France would not have. And for mine, part of Peter's creativity and passion for all things rugby have evolved from these sojourns. This book will give you an entertaining insight into what has now become part of Wallaby and rugby folklore. Happy reading!

NICK FARR-JONES

CONTENTS

INTRODUCTION

Some time ago, on the way back in the bus from a rugby game in Paris which my French provincial club team had lost badly, I was complaining bitterly to our inside centre and captain, Eric Blanc, about where *exactly* I thought his backline was going wrong. Selflessly, I tried to give him the full benefit of every ounce of backline knowledge I had. Why didn't he try having the backs lining up with a flatter alignment, see, with everyone running straighter and trying some loop-the-loop backing-up, like I had long seen the Ellas do?

To his credit, Eric put up with it as long as he could—nodding with glazed eyes here and there—but finally he had had enough. As Paris slipped back in the night, he snorted derisively and let me have it: *'Fitzzeeeee, t'es un avant et tu ne sais rien. Tu vois tous les matchs avec ton cul.'* ('Fitzy, you are a forward and know nothing. You see every match through your arse.')

Charmed, I'm sure.

As you might imagine, we sat in stony silence for some time after that as the wheels on the bus rolled us south and a lot of the guys dropped off to sleep—but it has since occurred to me that there were more than a few wisps of truth in what Eric said.

For despite having played and written about the game for nigh on thirty years now, *detailed* knowledge of all the nuances and technical ins and outs of the game has never been my go, particularly. In fact, I had played for Australia before I had clear in my head the basic difference in the roles of the loose-head and tight-head props—and to this day I keep a lot of such technical rugby jargon in the same spot in my head where I store other newfangled terminology like 'marmalade jam' and 'corrugated iron'.

For me, it was never the game itself that cooked my bacon, but rather everything that went with it—the travel, the camaraderie, the strong sense of *community*, the colour and movement, the simple *zest* for living that so often abounds in passionate rugby people.

All up, the game has been good to me, and I have loved writing about it since the first article I ever had published appeared in the *Sydney Morning Herald* on 25 May 1986. What follows is what I consider to be the best and most interesting rugby writing I've done, drawn from the articles and books I have written—some from the perspective of a player, the rest as a journalist. They are not in chronological order in terms of when I wrote them (and I have occasionally amended them slightly from the form in which they originally appeared), but they are arranged roughly sequentially in terms of the times they refer to.

I hope you enjoy the read.

Peter Fitz
Sydney
June 1999

THE ULTIMATE WORLD XV

Any day now, you'll start spotting them. One by one, and then in swarms, the rugby journalists of the world will start releasing their World XVs—the best team that could be formed from all the players attending the World Cup, etc, etc, et-bleeding-cetera.

It is, frankly, a boring journalistic cliché, and the problem with such lists is they totally ignore the many other fine people who've played rugby throughout the world, and throughout history.

Why, I've got half a mind to release my own World XV, made up of such people, just to spite them. Looky here.

LOOSE-HEAD PROP: *Meat Loaf.* He's big, he's energetic, he looks just like a prop should. And like everyone on this list, he really did play rugby. True. A couple of years ago I happened to be hovering in the darkened wings of the 'Midday' show with Nick Farr-Jones when the next guest, the famous Bat out of Hell himself, appeared at my shoulder. 'Is that Nick Farr-Jones?' he whispered, clearly impressed.

Yes, Mr Loaf, but what would you know and what would you care?

'Are you kidding? I know rugby. I played rugby in the States.' And he did, too.

Growing up in the north-east corner of America where rugby has its strongest hold, he played with one of the college teams that abound there before his singing career really took off. So Meat Loaf's in the team. He's a good guy, he'd be great on the long bus trips with a guitar in hand and I dare say he'd be a damn strong cornerstone for our World XV scrum.

HOOKER: *Charlie Chaplin.* A controversial choice, I know. Hookers are meant to be ugly, squat and mean, none of which Charlie is. But what he does have are those gi-normous feet. Take a look at some of that old footage next time he's on TV and try telling me that they aren't made for hooking in the scrum. He could probably retrieve the ball even when it's under the opposing No 8's feet. And, yes, he did play rugby while at school in England, I am reliably informed by a cabal of rugby journalists in South Africa. Not with great distinction, but he played.

1

I know you're worried about Charlie's fragility in the middle of all the macho mayhem. But don't be. True Chaplin followers know that however big the opposing forwards, whatever their intent to belt the living daylights out of our man, somehow Charlie would manage.

The brutes' fists would connect with each other's noses by mistake as Charlie squeezed his head out of danger; or they'd take a flying kick at him only to slip and fall face-down in the mud. Most likely, Charlie would bend over to tie his shoelaces just as a couple of flying head-butts went right over the top and into a goalpost. Can't you see it? Charlie would straighten up, look quizzically at the carnage all around him and then waddle off to the next scrum, twirling his pocket watch all the way.

TIGHT-HEAD PROP: *Idi Amin*. He's big. He's intimidating. He represented the Ugandan national rugby team in 1956, and should the tough stuff arise, I'd ask you to bear in mind that he was also the Ugandan heavyweight boxing champion for a while in the 1950s. Besides, he'd also be some pretty good protection for Charlie in the front row. Do you think the opposing second-rower is going to come through with a swinging arm, if he has to answer to Idi? I don't think soooooo!

LEFT SECOND-ROWER: *Bill Clinton (c)*. When he attended Oxford from 1968–70 on a Rhodes scholarship, he played rugby for the Oxford Second XV, aka the Greyhounds, in the second row. It is said that what he lacked in skill he made up for in pure bloody-minded enthusiasm. There is even one body of thought that the skills he has applied in American politics were learnt in rugby!

Not *those* skills, the other skills, I mean. I cite an interview he gave to the *New Yorker* earlier this year, when he waxed lyrical about rugby: 'It was pretty tough. I remember we played one of the Cambridge colleges. I got a mild concussion. There were no substitutions in rugby, so our coach told me to go back in. I asked what I was supposed to do, since I was dizzy. He said, "Just get in somebody's way" . . . I just loved it.'

See? He's one of ours, I tell you. So Bill is not only in, but also captain of our side. I know some of the others might get their noses out of joint about this, but this is a team selected in the modern era, after all, and if you're going to have a man in your side with the power to vaporise Russia it seems only fair that he should also get to call 'heads' or 'tails' before the game.

And no, frankly, I don't know what kind of rugby player Big Bill would actually make these days, but BY GOD HE'D BE A GOOD MAN TO GO ON TOUR WITH!

RIGHT SECOND-ROWER: *Malcolm Fraser*. He learnt the game as a lad at Tudor House, the exclusive boys boarding school. When I ran into Mr Fraser in a Johannesburg cafe a couple of days ago and told him he was to be in my World XV partnering Bill Clinton in the second row, he was suitably grateful at the honour done him, but plaintively asked if I couldn't get him a better partner. I'm not sure if he was referring to President Clinton's politics or whether he'd seen him play and was unimpressed. But if it's the former, too bad. This is rugby, damn it, and we all must check our politics in at the dressing-room door. For myself, I didn't like playing in Italy with an avowed anarchist halfback who gave away about twenty penalties a game, but in the end I got used to even that.

BLINDSIDE BREAKAWAY. *Pope John Paul II*. Apparently, His Holiness played rugby for his native Poland. I know, I know, I find it hard to believe too, and it's hard to imagine John Paul II cleaning someone up from the kick-off, but his impeccable rugby pedigree is stated in a 'Did You Know?' section of the 1995 World Cup's official souvenir program. For the life of me I couldn't get the Pope on the phone to confirm it (it was always engaged, and I don't even want to *think* about to whom he might have been talking), but one thing in particular speaks in favour of it being true. He was born and bred in Kraków, the stronghold of rugby in Poland, so it stands to reason that as part of his religious education he got some grounding in the game they play in heaven, no?

OPENSIDE BREAKAWAY: *Che Guevara*. Che was actually a very good breakaway in the early 1950s for the San Isidro Club, in one of Buenos Aires' most salubrious suburbs. He didn't go on to represent Argentina, but perhaps that's only because he had more pressing matters to attend to—like helping Fidel Castro export the revolution to Cuba. The other interesting thing about Che is that even while he was fomenting the revolution with Fido, he spent a short time paying the rent by writing rugby match reports. So I don't care what you say. His combination of rugby and journalism appeals to me.

No 8: *Frankenstein, aka Boris Karloff*. He's perfect. He's big, he's mean, he could single-handedly put the fear of God into an entire opposing pack. And the best thing is 'Frankenstein' would know exactly what he was doing when it came to the finer points of rugby.

Fact is, Karloff, who rose to his greatest fame playing the monster in the 1931 movie, was an absolute rugby nutter. So much so, he not only continued to play when he moved from England to Hollywood in the late 1920s, he was also the founding president of the Southern Californian Rugby Union in 1935. Cranky Frankie's the man.

(*Hey, is this a good team or what? If you look just at the back row, are you gonna tell me that the Pope, Frankenstein and Che Guevara all working closely together couldn't knock over every problem they came across?*)

HALFBACK: *PG Wodehouse*. PG was one of the leading lights of rugby at Dulwich College, London, around the turn of the century. The school still has copies of some of the match reports he wrote for the school magazine, and I fancy he would get on rather well with Che Guevara, chatting rugby and writing and so forth.

The real reason I want PG in the side, though, is his innate understanding of the game. Has anybody, for example, ever summarised rugby better than PG did in this passage from *Very Good, Jeeves* in 1930?

> The main scheme is to work the ball down the field somehow and deposit it over the line at the other end . . . In order to squelch this programme, each side is allowed to put in a certain amount of assault and battery and do things to its fellow man which, if done elsewhere, would result in 14 days without the option, coupled with some strong remarks from the Bench.

PG's a goer, and is just the man we need.

FIVE-EIGHTH: *President John F Kennedy*. A contentious choice, particularly because the only proof I have that JFK played is a single sentence I read in a magazine profile on him many moons ago. It is, though, well documented that his older brother, Joseph, played rugby a lot, so it's not unreasonable to think JFK followed suit.

Whatever, JFK is perfect for the job. There is something of an unwritten law in rugby that the five-eighth has to be a good-looking bloke, with the aspect of one who has never had a glove laid on him, even after years of weaving his magical way through opposition defences.

You gotta understand that when you line up before the kick-off, there are two things guys look at in the opposing team: have they got some big, gnarled forwards, and have they got a good-looking five-eighth? Well, we've got Frankenstein in the forwards; can we ask more than to have JFK in the backs? I think not. He's in.

INSIDE CENTRE: *Richard Harris*. You know him as a blockbusting film star and stage actor, but forty years ago Dick was pressing for selection in the Irish national rugby team until a bad bout of tuberculosis laid him low, never to climb the rungs of rugby again. Instead, he went on to a life of extraordinary achievement with Oscar nominations, Golden Globes, the lot . . . Yet he still misses it, terribly.

'And do you know what?' he recently asked British journalist Peter Jackson. 'I'd give it all up tomorrow, the whole lot, for one Irish cap. Just one. There is hardly a day that passes that I don't think of what it would be like to run out on to Lansdowne Road as one of the Irish team.'

Wait till he hears about his selection in *this* side!

OUTSIDE CENTRE: *Prince Edward*. Just the man we're looking for. He not only played in the Second XV of Jesus College, Cambridge, he's not only attended damn-nigh every televised Five Nations match I ever saw and talked to all the players beforehand, but he's got that inestimable quality so crucial to every world-beating centre—he's got *class*. (Sniff.) High class. Steady Eddie's in, he's captain of the backs, and I don't want to hear any more about it.

LEFT WINGER: *Kerry Francis Bullmore Packer*. Personally, I think this is my most brilliant positional selection of all. Sure, you're thinking

Mr Packer is too big to be a winger, but why don't you try telling that to Jonah Lomu, the sensational 119 kilogram All Black winger? We've got to apply modern theories to this team, and the state-of-the-art theory has it that a huge, fast man out there on the wing creates havoc, and I say Mr Packer is our man. Biographer Paul Barry reports: 'He not only played while at school, he played very well.' And let's face it, there ain't one of us who's at all surprised. Plus, he's got family pedigree, with his grandfather, Dr Herbert Bullmore, having won a single cap for Scotland.

RIGHT WINGER: *James Joyce*. No serious rugby team is complete without at least one whingeing wally out on the wing. The Wallabies have had a genius of one out there for years, and I fancy James Joyce is our man for this team. No-one who's read *Portrait of the Artist as a Young Man*, in which Joyce devotes the five opening pages to the horrified recollections of a twelve-year-old boy playing on the wing for his school rugby team, could possibly disagree. Joyce, of course, played at Belvedere, the Christian Brothers school he attended in Dublin, and could be counted on to hold his own. Best of all, though, with JJ the discipline of the side is assured.

Instead of extra sit-ups or laps of the oval as punishment, try this: 'Frankenstein! You're ten minutes late for training again! Well, you know the rules . . . That's twenty minutes I want you to spend back later, listening to JJ give you a personal reading of *Ulysses*!'

My guess is that Frank, and everybody, would soon get the message and there'd be no further problems with discipline.

FULLBACK: *Sir Edmund Hillary*. I'm proud of this selection, too. For starters, he's a New Zealander, and no serious World XV would be complete without one. He played in distinguished fashion for Auckland Grammar School in the 1930s; he's a fine fellow; and when we put this side up against any of the other fancy-pants World XVs the other journos are churning out, it's not going to hurt any to have as our last line of defence a man who has looked Mount Everest right in the eye and flinched nary a moment.

COACH: *Benito Mussolini*. 'Benny' to his boys in the team. Mussolini was an absolute rugby nut. He saw the game in France in the early 1920s and was instrumental in taking it back to Italy later in the decade, convinced it would go a long way to toughening up a population he wanted strong enough to restore the country to the former glories of Rome. I also reckon his pre-match speeches in the dressing room would be a treat, if we could just persuade a few of the more benign political types to withhold their rage until they got out on the field so as to take it out on the opposition.

REFEREE: *Denis Thatcher*. A great aficionado of rugby is Margaret's man, and apparently not a bad ref, either. So much so he reached the heights of being a touch judge for a couple of Five Nations internationals in the years after World War II.

And where were we? Oh yes . . . Serious rugby began for me at Sydney University in 1980. I arrived at the same time as another bloke who would come to love his rugby, a bloke whom I would end up writing a biography of—from which these and many subsequent passages are drawn.

SYDNEY UNI DAZE

During his first days at Sydney University, Nick Farr-Jones had signed on the dotted line to join the Sydney University Football Club and found himself a few weeks later training with the Sydney Uni Colts side—the under-21s.

Soon he would be trying his very best to make it into the Firsts of the three Colts sides.

The moment came one wet Tuesday night, when the Colts Firsts' coach, Lindsay MacCaughan, gathered the entire Colts squad on Uni's No 2 oval and read out the lucky players who had made it into Firsts: '. . . Jordy Clapham, Peter FitzSimons, Andrew Dunlop, Richard Vaughan, Matt Playfair, Nick Farr-Jones . . .'

Nick was delighted.

'When I didn't make the Firsts at school I had to start wondering if maybe I was already turning into one of those schoolboy athletes who never do anything once they get older, so I was just delighted that I'd climbed back into a Firsts side.'

Even playing for a team so comparatively lowly as a Colts

Firsts side has a certain kudos attached to it in a place with such strong traditions of rugby as Sydney University. Back at the law school in Phillip Street, where he was studying for his degree, Farr-Jones was already walking a good foot taller.

Yo Nick! What are you up to this weekend?

Oh, I'm playing for University.

What team do you play for?

Colts Firsts.

'I was just so proud to tell people,' he recalls. 'To walk around law school and be able to say that I was playing for Colts Firsts was just *fantastic*.' The side announced by coach Lindsay MacCaughan that first night stayed together substantially throughout the year and was in the happy situation of finding that not only did they have a strong player in each position but, more importantly, that a chemistry existed among them which almost always ensured they could do what was required to win. And without overwhelming effort. They did not train particularly hard or long; they did not introduce any stunning new tactical ploys; they did not even go through any massive psych-up sessions before going out to play. They simply didn't need to.

While Farr-Jones was integral to the success of the side, and was a popular enough team member, he was not captain or vice-captain, and certainly not 'one of the boys' in the classic sense. His contribution on the field was robust—the same lad who had been one of the smallest halfbacks Newington had seen in his first year there was arguably the biggest halfback Uni Colts had ever boasted—but off the field he was rarely seen. Too busy attending his various Christian functions.

'It was just one of those things,' he says. 'Pursuing Christianity was really my top priority.'

When at the very end of the season the Uni Firsts beat Manly at Eastwood's TG Milner Field in the Colts' grand final, nearly all the team went out 'on the plonk'. Bar Nick. He went to a Christian function that was being held that night in Miranda.

'I was delighted that we'd won,' he says, 'but given the choice between going drinking with the boys or going to a Christian function, at that time I would automatically choose the Christian function every time.'

The following year, on the strength of the Colts' win, MacCaughan had become the first grade coach, making Farr-Jones his halfback. Alas, the team lost the first four games of the season and the coach was shown the door—with Farr-Jones being immediately dropped by the new coaches, Rupert Rosenblum and Johnny Rouen.

With MacCaughan now banished and, even more galling, first grade starting to win again without him, it seemed for a time as if Farr-Jones' baptism into the big time was to be just that—a brief dip. He never considered for a moment giving up mid-season, but then again . . . If not disgruntled he was still far from gruntled at the manner of his dropping.

Fortunately his reserve grade stint only lasted three weeks.

One Tuesday night in early May he was up in the St Andrews dining room, pushing some food round on the plate to pass the time before reserve grade training started, and the hell with it if he was a bit late, when, 'Someone came racing up to me and said, "Nick, you've got to get down to training. You've been reinstated into first grade!"'

Down in the Uni changing rooms he met briefly with Rupert and Johnny, then raced onto the field to catch up with the others.

This happened to be the very night that Rosenblum and Rouen had decided to put the side into the hands of the one and only David Brockhoff. A former Australian coach who had also been Sydney University's most successful coach, Brock would often make guest coaching appearances with various teams in the club.

As Farr-Jones would find out, the great man's love of rugby in general, and Sydney University rugby in particular, was second only to his capacity to turn wondrous phrases. In his tracksuit, his old towel around his neck and gumboots going clear to the knee despite the warm autumn evening, Brock was in full cry, stabbing the air with his finger as he expounded with great ferocity to the Firsts . . . something Farr-Jones knew not what.

Drawing himself up like Churchill on D-day he got to the point: 'Let's face it, men, it hasn't been a good year. We're second last, and now we play Parramatta, who are on the bottom of the ladder. Fellas, you must have been looking forward to this for a while. But . . . no rubbish! We know how Parra will play and we take none of it! First five minutes, men, we lock the bully out of the gate . . . and then for the rest of the afternoon we play in the field.'

So *that's* the general game plan, Farr-Jones thought. 'Lock the bully out of the gate.'

Fine.

Enough of the generalities. Brock was ready to get specific.

First the instructions to the forwards: 'You have to be everywhere, breakaways. *Everywhere!* No excuses. Cause havoc at the breakdown like sharks in a school of mullet. As for the tight five, all day like wind through wheat. Not scattered rocks here and there, but like wind through wheat. And when you're through the other side we're like crowbars through the Opera House windows. We get in, loot the joint and get out.

'And remember, no height in the lineout is no excuse, we must have the fruit, so every lineout dockyard brawl. Except our 22—row of ministers—no easy penalties.'

To Farr-Jones it sounded a lot like gibberish, though it was perfectly clear to those who knew Brock well.

So to the training proper, and the team run had been going only for about ten minutes when Brock again blew his whistle.

Not happening to know Nick's name, he came up with the instant and logical appellation of 'halfback', as in: 'Oh no, no, *no!* Halfback, listen to me! Listen. No Harbour Bridges [high-parabola passes]. For Christ's sake, no Harbour Bridges or the pigs [forwards] will slit your throat!'

The redoubtable Brock underlined the last threat with a swift movement of his forefinger across his windpipe, and Farr-Jones got the message.

This was no ordinary man.

Twelve years down the track Farr-Jones names Dave Brockhoff as, 'if not the greatest technical influence on my career, at least the greatest spiritual influence'.

WHEN PUSH CAME TO SHOVE IT WAS GREAT

I compose these words on my mental typewriter while I heave away in the middle of the mud heap that is currently Sydney University's No 2 oval. Little matter that the bottom part of my football boots has disappeared into *terra liquida*, that the rain is roaring down, that the wind is screaming imprecations at the devil, that the world beyond this oval has seemingly shut down. My colleagues and I are here on very, very serious business, and goddammit we intend to do it, cyclone or no cyclone.

Once again . . . *ka-thud* . . . we smash into each other, eight tightly bound men against eight others, and once again . . . *ker-splat* . . . the whole thing collapses and my dial goes right into the fetid slush.

This is scrum training. As you may or may not know, the scrum is that part of the rugby union game which involves sixteen fully grown men pushing on either side of a ball to decide who gets possession of it next. Personally, I'd be in favour of tossing a coin, or perhaps having the referee hold his whistle in one hand while the two captains tried to guess which one he had it in . . . but that's another story.

Back in the here and now, we're trying to overcome a problem. Our scrum last Saturday was nothing short of disgraceful and this little session is designed to work out what went wrong. Fortunately, at least a good part of it is talk. Sydney Uni's resident scrum guru, Tony Abbott*, is in full flight. Through the howling gale, I can just make out his words . . . *Turn . . . your . . . wrists . . . tighterrrr* . . .

We hit it again, all turning our wrists tighter (to bind us more closely together) and accentuating the dip in our backs (if I could understand why this was so important *I* could be the guru).

Sure enough, the pressure on us in this scrum is marginally more unbearable than the last one, so we know we must be doing something right. The ker-splat seems to be taking a little longer this time and I ponder, while my face is rhythmically rubbed between the muddy thighs of the prop and the hooker (the two men in front of me), whether I just might get out of this scrum without having to wallow like a little piggy.

But no, the ker-splat makes its appearance soon enough, and we all get down in the mud for a good roll round. Even before we have picked ourselves up, Abbott is off and running, as is his wont, through the sheets of rain to a new scrum position downfield.

Tony Abbott, for the record, went on to become a federal Liberal politician, and is now the Minister for Employment Services.

It is his theory that a good scrum-training session must obligatorily be interspersed with these short sprints so it is as near to a game situation as possible. Ours is not to reason why . . . so we reluctantly stumble after him. By now looking like a pack of mutant muddy wombats, we prepare to pack down a new scrum. But first we must do the ritual shouting.

'Seconds' ball!' yells Abbott (it is the turn of the seconds' halfback to introduce the ball to the scrum). 'Low!' yells the hooker (we must make sure our body position is very low for maximum force). '102!' yells the prop (this is a TOP-SECRET code which indicates to the pack what sort of push we are going to use to try to recover the ball).

All the proprieties observed, we pack the scrum down . . . and try to remember the many things we are meant to be doing with all the different parts of our bodies to maximise the force on the opposing pack. Suddenly . . . *miracle*. Be darned if it is not working. Joy of all joys, pleasure of all pleasures! Somehow, magically, we have gone from being a disparate group of eight individuals, pushing disjointedly, into being fused as one.

Centimetre by muddy centimetre, we can feel the opposing pack giving ground as in unison, in *harmony*, we inexorably turn the screws tighter. The rain has stopped, the wind has fallen, we are as one. The muddy field is a pristine stage on which we can perform our artistry. Is it our imagination or can we hear the strains of Beethoven's Fifth Symphony wafting over us as we push?

Ker-splat! It is over. We wake up in the mud again. Sad, but immeasurably richer for the experience. Nirvana has been reached, for however fleeting a moment.

THE CHOICE

If a good deal of Farr-Jones's rugby education came on the field playing with St Andrews College—where he was in residence on the campus—it was still Uni rugby that was providing him with the week-in, week-out experience of playing the game at a high level. The fact that he was not in a strong team helped stretch his talents to the utmost. In the whole year, University only tallied up five wins, and finally the truth became apparent. Uni was going to finish bottom of the table, and under the rules at that time they were headed for the obscurity of second division.

It was a major disaster for the club, and a minor disaster for Farr-Jones personally. Whatever small hopes he might have harboured of playing representative rugby seemed dashed for at least a year. Even if he were to play terrifically well there would be no-one there to see him and certainly none of the representative selectors.

There was yet one way out of it.

One of his team-mates, me in fact, put the suggestion to him. Why not ditch Uni and come to Manly, where this new guy Alan Jones was taking over? Or go somewhere else, so long as he could keep playing in first division? Otherwise he'd be spending all of 1983 looking at his *Gregory's* street directory trying to find out how to get to obscure clubs he'd never heard of. One thing was for sure, if he didn't go to Manly or some other club, his chances of cracking the big time were *nil*.

Farr-Jones remained unmoved. In the distant past he might have left Cronulla RSL under-6s to go to the Lilli Pilli under-7s, but he'd be damned if he'd leave Uni to go anywhere else.

I moved on. Farr-Jones, ever the loyalist, maintained the faith and stayed, even as Uni went down, down, down to second division.

THE RISE OF ALAN JONES

Jonesy on the blower again.

You've simply got to come to Manly, he said. A player as good as you can't be languishing down in second division. You damn near made the Wallaby side that toured this year—I for one pushed hard for you to go—and if you stay there you'll simply disappear from view and maybe never be heard from again. Come on, we need you, *I* need you. I'm confident Manly can win the premiership if you'll only come across—all the other players are really excited at the prospect you might join us.

He was persuasive alright. At that point I had not even the slightest idea what the bloke looked like, but knew at least that he was a former speechwriter for Malcolm Fraser, and the current head of the NSW Employers Federation—both of which impressed the hell out of me. Of top-line rugby coaching, he'd done little—his chief claim to fame along those lines being that in the previous year he'd coached King's Old Boys to win in the subbies division—but he was pure steely silk over the phone.

What the hell. Not having enough loyalty to Uni to fill a Coke can anyway—wretched brute that I was—I said yes, and attended my first Jones training session down at Manly shortly afterwards, in the last gasp of a Sydney summer.

Right away he was different. His was not an *ad hoc* rugby training that you made up as you went along, but rather it was precisely prepared and slickly executed. Each drill flowed smoothly into the next, every training session having its own cohesive theme. We danced to his whistle, but even that early in the Year of Jones, there was a sense that he seemed to know what he was doing. This wasn't a bloke who thought we might be half a chance to win the competition if we got it right. This was a bloke who said—and *meant* it when he said it—'We are going to win the competition, and this is how we're going to do it.'

The first rule we had to understand, and it wasn't one of those rules of the unspoken variety, was that it had to be 'his way or the highway'. We could discuss things alright, but we were to be under no illusions as to which one of us had the final say. Alan did.

Not to worry. The bloke really did seem to know what he was doing, though I might say in passing there were many of us who were a little bemused at his insistence that we practise even the most basic of football skills. Every training, there was a 'revision' of such things as passing to the left, passing to the right, picking the ball up on the run, catching short passes and long passes alike and doing all of the above when the ball was slippery, heavy and wet. No matter that we were first-graders already, with a small sprinkling of Wallabies: the Jones dictum was that if we couldn't absolutely guarantee that we had the basics right, there was no way known we could acquire the more refined skills.

Did he know a lot about rugby? What I have no doubt about

is that he knew a lot about motivation, about the principles of getting fifteen people together and functioning smoothly. And whatever he might not have known about the game was compensated for by the experts he called in to take us for particular training sessions.

Alan Jones's most fundamental principle of rugby? *Eliminating errors.* 'The difference between professionals and amateurs is that the professional is dedicated to the total eradication of error,' Jones was extremely fond of saying. 'It has nothing to do with how much money you're earning, and everything to do with not repeating the same mistakes.'

And he meant it too. Other coaches would sit watching a game, and gain impressions of how their sides were going. Jones was never like that. He was always scribbling, taking detailed notes on what we were doing right, what we were doing wrong, and how the whole team could be made to function more effectively the following week.

The Tuesday night after the first match of the season, against Warringah (which we won, with no less than *moi* as Jones's man-of-the-match), set the pattern for what would follow the rest of the year.

We arrived ready to rock and roll at precisely 6.30 p.m.—we'd already learnt that when he said a 6.30 start he meant it, and there'd be hell to pay if we were late—and Jones immediately took us into a free dressing room, and handed out sheets to every player.

On those two pages, neatly typewritten, was his analysis, complete with a motivational dictum at the top. The one about the difference between professionals and amateurs, quoted above, started this memo, dated 5 April 1983, and then he got into it, reading it out, and expanding verbally as he went along.

MEMO 1st XV

v. Warringah

- An outstanding debut in discipline, skill and commitment.
- Don't imagine we weren't under pressure early.
- Our attitudes are changing. We must now discipline ourselves to improve this performance and repeat it.

Some Statistics
Tackling
- Some people wrong-footed in defence or too far away from their man.
- Fabulous performance by Wally Meakes (8), Bill Calcraft (6), Ross Reynolds (6), Paul Flemon (5), Steve and Ollie (4).
- Our defence now looks a powerful instrument towards our success. There can be no lessening of the importance we place on it.

Penalties
- Better discipline here, but still not good enough.
- Paul, Ross and Fitzie passed off the ground; Ian had his hands in a ruck; Billy was placed offside when Ross failed to catch a high ball.
- We conceded 9 penalties. They conceded 14.
- Why on one free kick did Tony tap it and pass back to James, who then kicked to the right touchline?
- With a kicker like James Black we must seek many ways to induce opposition error when in attack.

On and on it went in much the same vein, with commentary on scrums, rucks and mauls, lineouts, and 'in general', before he finished up.

A fabulous beginning. We are proud of it. But now let's go full throttle to do it again. We want no big heads, just big scores.
Alan Jones.

Though it was not absolutely obvious at the time, in hindsight there is no mistaking it. A new force had been unleashed in Australian rugby, a particularly intense and creative tornado of energy that would transform the rugby landscape. Treating rugby like a science and not a mere shemozzle, Jones was laying the foundation stones of a truly professional approach on which a lot of subsequent glory was built. I know I'm mixing and straining my metaphors, but hell, I'm trying to get the right one, so try this: that night, an electric generator had been introduced to the game on this continent, where previously all had been wind-driven.

Together with such a very focused approach on the needs of the team came an amazing amount of personal attention. We were all, in our own way, made to feel very special to him. We went out and trained hard that night, and when we returned to the dressing room he gave each of us a personal letter—something he would do often during the rest of the season.

5 April 1983

MEMO TO: Peter Fitzsimmons [sic]

I just thought I would put a couple of things on paper because they are easy to remember. While your performance on Saturday was first class, if you are to represent nationally (and that ought to be your goal immediately), then you must be very constructive and analytical about some of the things you are doing.

- You should see John Lacey and seek an opportunity for further conditioning work and exercize [sic]. You can never be fit enough.
- You should pay close attention to all the ball skill work we do. One of your passes on Saturday was troppo and we lost yards as a result.
- On another occasion when you looked really good you went too far and died with it, or disrupted the developing play.
- Your work on our 25s and their kick-off needs to be more watertight. As a team we have a good deal of work to do on this.

In other words everything you do involves decisions:

- how far to run, when to stop and turn
- when to pass, when to reshape, etc.

I believe you have the capacity to be one of the best second-rowers we have ever had. Think about it now; be modest about it and work towards it. I will help you wherever I can.

Well done so far.

Good luck,

ALAN JONES

The WORK he put into it! The sheer accumulated *hours*. All of this was a mere three days after we'd played, yet every player had a complete analysis of how he had played the game; what he was doing right, what he was doing wrong, what he had to focus on to make himself even more effective. Clearly if we didn't win the premiership that year, it was not going to be because of any lack of energy put in by the coach—and it set a tone that came to transform the entire team.

And you know what? *I think we really might be able to win!* Confidence grew, as Manly continued to win games in an ever more powerful manner. Whatever initial resistance there might have been to the Jones Way of doing things faded fairly quickly as the rewards were there for all to see. We were on top of the table, looking good, smelling fine.

But by gee we saw a lot of Alan. Some of us, anyway. Soon after the season began it became obvious that a kind of Jones Inner Circle had emerged within the team, perhaps five or six players who were constantly invited to his home in Chippendale for lunches, dinners, chats. He was a warm and generous host— and a very good cook besides—and, as one of the foundation members of the JIC, I was knocked out by the opportunity to discuss all kinds of things with him, from Malcolm Fraser to how he reckoned the new prime minister, Bob Hawke, was travelling, to his experiences at Oxford University.

In what I was pleased to call my 'career' outside of football at that time, I was trying to put into operation a few get-rich-quick schemes (all of which were managing to get me poor slowly) and, though he offered, there was little that Alan could do to help me, one way or another. Not so, though with other members of the JIC . . .

Some were in jobs not to their liking, and the contacts that Jones had as the head of the NSW Employers Federation were invaluable to many of them. With Jones championing their causes to the right people, they were able to lift their career boats on the tide of his generous support. Sixteen years on, many can thank Jones for the breakthroughs he provided. His intervention at the right time enabled them to launch careers at a far, far higher trajectory than likely they would have achieved otherwise. He gave them the opportunities, and they grasped them with both hands.

There were casualties though. It was not that being in the JIC was a full-time job, but it could be demanding for all that. The sheer *intensity* of the man was sometimes hard to cope with; he did not brook even minor disagreements easily, and was sometimes slow to understand that you might not be able to accept a social invitation from him sometimes because you had commitments to other friends and family. Inevitably the attrition rate within the JIC was reasonably high, and though you might not have been dropped from the team because of it, there was absolutely no doubt whether or not you were inside or outside the inner sanctum. Sometimes, your passing-out parade could be a quite brutal experience. As I was to find out . . .

One night about midway through the year, we were doing a series of 50-metre sprints for fitness training, and I happened to be having a bit of a chat as we went with the team fullback, Tony McGeoch. I think I might even have been laughing at something Tony had said.

Suddenly it started. A long shriek on the whistle, followed by an explosion of sound.

FITZSIMONS! he barked. WHAT ARE YOU FUCKING WELL DOING? IF YOU CAME TO TRAINING TO HAVE A GOOD TIME, YOU MIGHT AS WELL FUCK OFF NOW! EITHER DO THAT, OR GET BACK TO THE LINE READY TO SPRINT, AND FUCKING WELL SHUT UP.

I was totally shocked. Could this be my friend Alan speaking to me like that? Alan, whom I'd shared so many dinners with, so many lunches, so many chats about all sorts of interesting things. Talking to *me*, like THAT?

I could barely believe it and stood there, gobsmacked. Suddenly though, the light of inspiration went on over my head. The previous year, my coach at Sydney Uni, Brian Burnett, had yelled at me in an equally perplexing fashion—*funny, when I think about it, all through my rugby career coaches have shouted at me for no apparent reason*—and I had immediately taken him aside and let him have it.

Brian, I'd said, there's something you have to understand. I simply won't be spoken to like that. Not now. Not *ever*. I'll overlook it this once, but if you ever speak to me like that in front of my team-mates again, I'll walk.

Brian had quickly apologised, we became friends for life, and everything was hunky-dory thereafter. Why not, I thought, say much the same thing to Alan?

Why not indeed . . .

Alan, I said, there's something you have to understand. I simply won't be spoken to like that. Not now, not ever, and I think you should know that if you so much as raise your voice at me again in that manner . . . I will walk.

I awaited confidently his back-down . . .

. . .

. . .

. . .

And am still waiting, frankly, all these years on. At the time Jones simply narrowed his eyes and waited till the other players had moved back to their marks for the next sprint, perhaps so he wouldn't frighten the horses. Then he turned the full force of his guns on me, and fired right into me, amidships.

Listen Fitzy, he hissed, with a kind of death's head grin that I'll never forget. If you want to take me on, I am more than happy. If you want to take me on, I can accommodate you. And if you want to walk, as you put it, you can do that too and I can assure you I'll be more than delighted to take you to the Manly ferry and put you on it, as well as tell the press exactly why it is that I find you impossible to work with and how I don't think any coach could work with you. But if, on the other hand, on the off-chance you want to stay, I am telling you now to get back in that line, shut your fucking mouth, and do the sprints like I asked you. Your choice . . .

. . .

Oh.

. . .

Shit.

. . .

Oh shit.

. . .

Well seeing as you put it like that, Alan, I think I might shut my mouth after all. My mistake, and I won't be bothering you again. (*Apart from dogging you for the next sixteen years in the press, I mean.*)

We got back to training. We always got back to training. No matter what blues there were, what dramas, what fallings-out, and there were always plenty, training continued apace, all of it pretty much excellent. Personality clashes aside, he was far and away the best coach I ever had by the proverbial country mile. Just as he'd promised, Jones had revolutionised the Manly approach, and taken a club team that hadn't won in the previous thirty-two years and turned them into clearly one of the very best teams in the competition.

There were hiccups here and there, including a terrible mid-season game against St George in the mud where we played diabolically—none worse than me—but the strength of Jones was that he was always able to get the guys to re-group, re-focus, and begin anew with greater vigour than before.

We looked like we really might be able to win it, a thought that made our hearts sing after all the hard work we had put in.

Then why exactly did I briefly contemplate putting my head in the oven? It didn't make sense. On this particular Sunday afternoon in late July 1983 I'd taken my girlfriend, Robyn, to the airport to fly back to Queensland, and then sat in the car outside the Ansett terminal with barely enough energy to drive home. At last, upon arrival at my Manly flat, the greatest wave of depression I had ever felt came along and near drowned me, contenting itself finally to settle all around me. I was hot, then I was cold. I was fevered, then I was shivering.

I had, as it turned out, a particularly nasty dose of glandular fever that put me in hospital for a week, and out of football for five weeks.

By the time I made it back to first grade about five weeks later, I *didn't*, if you get my drift. I thought I was ready to return to the top side, with just a few weeks to go to the semi-finals. Alan didn't. The team sailed on, imperious without me, while I had to content myself with second grade for a few weeks. And they made the grand final too, but I'll get to that shortly.

I wrote the following piece at a time when it was rumoured that the former French coach Jacques Fouroux was trying to launch a rugby circus. It prompted comparisons with David Lord's famous attempts to do the same thing back in the early 1980s.

RUGBY PRO CIRCUS

It was in the middle of the 1983 domestic season and I'd just finished playing a game for Manly at Eastwood's TG Milner Field, when that well-known rugby-man-about-town David Lord came up to me. He had a proposition he would like to make, whereby I could make a lot of money.

Sure, Mr Lord, what is it?

Couldn't talk now, he said, but if I would come to his lower North Shore apartment on the following Monday morning at nine o'clock all would be explained. But remember, he said, we're talking a LOT of money.

Knock. Knock.

Who's there?

Count.

Count who?

Count me in.

Details are hazy now, but I do remember being in the apartment with Mr Lord, a cup of coffee and a contract. The latter guaranteed me something like $180 000 in return for committing myself to the circus for two years. Over that period of time, a lot of Tests would be played all over the world, and I had to be prepared for constant international travel. Lord made it clear that a lot of Wallabies and other international players had already signed, and named some. I can't remember who they were now, but at least it was clear to me that if this circus did get up and running, the regular international competition in which I aspired to play would no longer exist.

Still, I wanted some time to think about it, and told him that before taking such a big decision I really wanted to be dead sure of my ground, have time to talk to my mum and dad and so forth.

'No,' he said, and for some reason I remember this part clearly, 'you either sign now, or we forget it.'

All his previous you-beaut mateyness had fallen away, and he pushed the contract towards me.

I signed.

Maaaaaaate. A slap on the back. You beaut.

I was ushered to the door. The next part of the plan was for all of us who had signed from Australia to meet in two weeks, at the house of the prominent retired Wallaby who was going to be our manager, to have a barbecue and discuss details. Lord said he would be in touch directly to confirm it all. From there, I remember two things.

First, driving in my old, clapped-out Mini Moke—I was fair dinkum on first-name terms with every NRMA man in the area—up Military Road behind a grey Porsche, and thinking, 'Yeah, well I'd love to drive one of those, and as soon as I get the cheque I really think I might BUY one, and damn the expense'.

Second, I remember waiting. And waiting some more. One week passed, and no word. Two weeks passed. No phone calls were returned. A month. Three months. The days got shorter, then longer again as the seasons changed.

Still no word. The Wallabies went away on tour. The stock market crashed. The Berlin Wall was torn down. Paul Keating became prime minister. Still no word. Waiting, waiting, waiting.

Listen, if you're reading this, David, it really is about time you called. Does Jacques Fouroux's circus mean that yours is definitively dead? I hope not, because I've had my bags packed these past eleven years or so, I'm waiting by the phone for the all clear, and I can tell you that the taxi I've had idling outside all this time is starting to get expensive. PLEASE give me a ring.

As to the viability of the proposed new circus, one thing is crucial for mine. The position of Australian coach Bob Dwyer. When I asked him on Thursday night to look me right in the eye and tell me he knew nothing more than rumours about the whole thing, he obliged without hesitation, doing the whole 'looking into the eyes' bit to boot.

Which is important. For if Fouroux hasn't got Dwyer's prior agreement, he hasn't got the Wallabies. And if he hasn't got the Wallabies, he hasn't got the most crucial ingredient of all to make his circus work—the world champions. Without them, there is no circus.

It means that whatever announcement Fouroux makes in November will not be the unveiling of a *fait accompli*, so much as a hauling up the flagpole of a circus flag just to see who salutes. My guess is that this circus is destined for the same fate as the last one.

Back in the then and there, the Manly Firsts under Jones had continued to prosper without me, and made the grand final against the mighty Randwick team.

A TEAM ARISES

It was one of those September days when the sun shines hot and the wind blows cold. In the final two minutes of the Sydney Rugby Union grand final of 1983 out at the old Sydney Sports Ground, Manly—who had last won a Sydney premiership thirty-two years before—were holding on to a 14–12 lead against Randwick.

A great triumph was at hand, but there remained for Randwick one last chance of victory. They were awarded a scrum deep in Manly's territory, and in short order the ball came back on their side and thence to Wallaby five-eighth Mark Ella, who shaped to kick a three-point field goal that would have won the game for Randwick.

Perhaps Ella's most distinguishing feature as a player was that he always seemed to have time—time to read the defence and write a review about it, as the cliché runs. Not on this occasion. With three Manly back-rowers charging hard at him, he was forced to hurry the kick slightly. At first blush it seemed to have been launched straight and true between the goalposts some 35 metres distant.

Just as the entire Sportsground picked up a bead on that small rotating piece of leather and began to follow its path, it started to drift . . . drift . . . drift out to the right, over the dead-ball line and out. With it went the last chance of a Randwick victory and, in its place arose something far more significant indeed.

For in the crowded Manly dressing room afterwards, the man who stood tallest was one Alan Jones, practically unknown in wider Australian rugby to that point. But now, for the first time, Jones really had something solid on his rugby résumé with which to launch himself. In this, his first year of first grade coaching, he had taken a mediocre Manly side and shaped it, cajoled it, *bullied* it into a side capable of taking on and beating the mighty Randwick team, unchallenged as the finest club team in Australia over the previous fifteen years.

After such a victory Jones might have been expected to simply bask in the glory and set about doing the same again next year, with one eye on a representative coaching job a few years down the track. Not the Jones boy, though. Although this former prime ministerial speechwriter has many undoubted attributes, patiently waiting his turn is not one of them. And the man whom he desired to replace, Bob Dwyer, was becoming increasingly vulnerable.

In early 1984 Jones announced his intention of standing against Dwyer for the position of Australian coach. The 1 February edition of the *Sydney Morning Herald* records the very clever stance taken by Jones over his nomination when he said that it was 'representations from players and officials in New South Wales and Queensland' that particularly influenced him to nominate for the position. He continued: 'What else influenced me to make up my mind is rugby being the big game it is, with a large international following, the team needs credibility and I'd be providing that.

'We're entitled to expect of the national team that it should win. That is justifiable on the strength of the personnel we have. I also would want to bring a professional approach to the position. With all that in mind, I have decided to put my name forward.'

By the beginning of the following year, Jones was installed as Wallaby coach, and I was making my first forays into representative rugby.

'MOIDER' IN AUCKLAND

Things always seemed to go wrong for me when I was playing against Auckland. Like the first time, in 1984. It was at Eden Park, and on this occasion my direct opponent in the lineout was that greatest of all great second-rowers, Andy Haden. Not that I was impressed or anything, mind. In fact, from memory I think I announced to all and sundry that come the end of the game I fully intended to be hanging Haden's scalp from the string of my shorts.

And it very nearly happened, *damn* nearly, in fact. The first lineout of the game was our throw-in and, praise the Lord and pass the ammo, our captain signalled that the ball was to be thrown to me. Using our TOP-SECRET code, I indicated to our hooker, Lance Walker, that I wanted a lob ball. And Lance, in fact, threw one that traced exactly the shape of Sydney Harbour Bridge, which is to say it was perfect.

That poor goose Haden swallowed my feint forward, effectively taking him out of the play as he'd hurled his own body forward, and after a quick step back I soared towards the heavens confident as all get-out.

And, YESSSSSSS! Right into my meaty mitts. I pulled it down, knowing that I already had both hands not only on the ball, but probably the man-of-the-match award as well. I took the textbook position with the ball still in hand as I made ready to unload it to Farr-Jones, and also give all the photographers and television cameramen plenty of time to get good shots.

Then it was like one of those surreal slow-mo scenes you see in the movies sometimes. I was about to at last give the ball to Farr-Jones when what do I see? I see a big hand appear, coming from between my legs, coming up at the ball, and then—*allez-ooooop!*—giving the ball the most gentle of slaps. I was entirely powerless to stop it, and was obliged to watch the ball sail back over my shoulder, perfectly into the hands of the Auckland halfback who sent his own backs away for a try.

That proved to be the highlight of my game against Haden, as after that it was all downhill. The worse part was having my own scalp bounce against his knobbly knees as he walked off at the end of the game.

Whatever lack of personal warmth there might have been between Jones and myself at this point, to his eternal credit the new Wallaby coach still believed in my potential as a player.

WALLABY SELECTION

So it was that at western Sydney's Concord Oval one cold and blustery afternoon in mid-May 1984, the New South Wales side had taken on Queensland in the afternoon, got thrashed in the at times bitter clash, and the survivors of both sides were huddled in the tent to find out who would be on the forthcoming Wallaby tour to Fiji.

The crowd caroused and drank as they waited for Alan Jones and the two other Australian selectors to appear. When they finally did so the tent went into a sudden hush, as tents are wont to do on such occasions, and Alan Jones stepped to the microphone. It was right away a break with precedent, and significant of what was to follow in the Jones era. The usual form on such occasions is for the manager of the Wallaby side, in this instance Charles 'Chilla' Wilson, to make such announcements. But Jones would have none of that. He at least observed however, the tradition of preceding the reading of the list with a few preliminary comments bearing the usual sentiments about the difficulty of selecting a touring squad of only thirty players when there were so many wonderful players available, blah, blah, blah. But the *list*, Alan. Get to the list. Ahem.

'Black, James,' he began . . .

Right away a ripple of surprise moved through the crowd. As his first official announcement as national coach Jones had named as a new Wallaby a close friend who had not even been a regular of the Sydney Firsts side. Black's playing ability would quickly justify his selection, but at the time Jones laid himself wide open to accusations of bias. Yet, as was to be a hallmark of his era, Jones for the most part was a dominant enough personality that he got the team he wanted.

But back to the list.

Coolican, John.

Farr-Jones, Nick.

FitzSimons, Peter.

We were off! Firm friends for the past five years, Farr-Jones and myself had now both been selected for the Wallabies. As we picked up our kit to head for the gate and our cars out in the street, I noticed something more than passing strange . . . What on earth could be wrong with Farr-Jones? Not only was he not doing cartwheels, not singing, not doing anything much at all, but he actually seemed rather subdued.

Hello? Hello? *Helloooo*? Nick, is it not a marvellous, marvellous thing that we have just been named in the Wallaby side together?

'Yes, but we still lost to Queensland,' replied Farr-Jones, which struck me at the time, and does still now, as something of the mark of the man. No matter that he had just fulfilled one of his greatest ambitions in becoming a Wallaby, he couldn't get over the recent disappointment of having lost a game where he could have played better.

So this was Fiji. Hot. Humid. Friendly black faces. An undercurrent of widespread religious belief which nevertheless seemed to have little restraining effect on the men and women who populated the late-night bars. An enthusiasm for rugby bordering on the fanatical.

And these were the 1984 Wallabies. A group of young Australian males imbued with a sense of privilege in wearing the green and gold; a sense of history in being but the latest generation of a tribe of Wallabies with a long and glorious past; and, of course, a sense of fun and adventure.

And this was Alan Jones, as Wallaby coach. Everywhere. Always. The constant centre of attention. Telling stories at the dinner table. Consulting his senior players. Nurturing confidence in his younger players. Exhorting all to have a 'commitment to excellence'. Talking. Talking. All the time talking. Introducing a kind of 'Jones-speak' which would become synonymous with his era.

An odd sort of bloke, Jones, right from the beginning of his tenure with the Wallabies. Jones around young people was like a master builder walking along a shabby street, who with every step could see a hundred different ways to make improvements. The difference was that while the builder would have asked for money to do it, Jones did it simply for the satisfaction. Indeed, much of his adult life seemed to revolve around getting young men to fulfil their potential in a variety of ways, be they academic, sporting or even social.

At the King's School in Parramatta where Jones had worked in his twenties as a teacher, he had quickly formed a coterie of eager young students and with them achieved extraordinary success. Mediocre students suddenly started performing well, and previously so-so sportsmen were seen forcing their way into the First XV and First XI. Along the way he also caused a great ruckus in the school, as it was divided between those who swore by him and those who swore behind him. He had the sort of personality which seemed to arouse either great loyalty or fierce antipathy.

So whatever the principles are of making young men achieve to their full potential, Jones had great experience in applying them well before he took over the Wallabies. A lot of it was simply hard work. In those first training sessions in Fiji, many senior Wallabies were heard to complain that they had never worked so hard, and while that was also true of the younger players, they kept their mouths firmly shut. Farr-Jones, who'd always loved to push himself anyway, was probably the one who minded the least how hard Jones worked them.

Australia won the Test against Fiji on the Saturday by 16–3, with Farr-Jones sitting safely in the stands as a reserve while Phillip Cox did the deed out on the field. The Jones-led Wallaby side had begun 1984 in a solid if not spectacular fashion. The Wallabies celebrated that night in the bars around Suva, and then drifted back to Nick's and my room at the hotel for a late-night party.

In the final wash-up to the tour, the players checked out of the hotel on the following morning and were just about to leave for the airport when Alan Jones got on the bus, and pointing to Nick and myself said, 'I want to see you and you'.

Feeling just a little like two boys who had been called before the headmaster, we left the bus to be confronted by an almost apoplectic Jones, who proceeded to berate us in front of the entire watching busload.

'Hear me, and hear me well,' Jones began, 'the room you two have been living in is a pigsty, a shambles, a shocker, a *disgrace*. It might be good enough when you're living at Wesley or Andrew's College at Sydney University, but it's NOT GOOD ENOUGH WHEN YOU'RE REPRESENTING AUSTRALIA!'

These proved to be just his opening remarks.

The Jones tirade continued for at least another three minutes and the upshot of it was that if we wanted to be considered to play for Australia again then we had better 'lift our game', as he for one was quite prepared to leave us behind rather than take us on future tours.

After the obligatory replies of 'yes sir no, sir, three bags full of sorry, sir', we two eventually got back on the bus and settled down quietly in the vain hope that our ears might eventually stop ringing.

The letter

Another letter from Alan. Explaining why I'd missed out on the 1984 tour of Great Britain, despite what was a fairly solid promise to me in Fiji that I would in fact be on the plane.

23 August 1984

Dear Peter,

Just a brief note, Fitzie, to thank you for your efforts last week, under some difficulty, in helping me to prepare the Test side.

I know that things haven't been easy for you in recent weeks, and I very much appreciated your presence in what was a vital period for the Australian team.

You would expect me to say also that I do understand the disappointment that you must feel in not having been chosen for the British Isles. However you would also know that one has to seek, wherever possible, to pick the best people and, to be fair, you do not fit into that category at the moment. If I might just offer a mild criticism it is that when I spoke to you in Fiji in the hotel room I thought I outlined to you the reasons for your omission from the Test side. I regret that since then in spite of an undertaking you gave me then you have not worked on your game as you should have . . .

You are not as strong as you might be and yet you have the ability to be the strongest second-rower in the country. Simply, your jumping skills have to be worked at and you must do a progressive programme of speed and strength work . . .

I shall see you soon. With best wishes.

Yours sincerely,
Alan Jones

I hate to say it, but the man was right. What he'd actually said to me in the Fijian hotel room was, 'I have no doubt you will make the touring side to Britain, if you embark on a serious weights program and work to improve your jumping,' and truth be told, I had done neither.

Farr-Jones, on the other hand, was clearly too good to leave behind. He played his first Test, against England, in 1984. The Australians won, and then went on to beat Ireland and Wales. The last Test was against Scotland.

GRAND SLAM

There was, understandably, a lot of pressure on the Wallabies leading up to the Scotland Test. After the final game at Murrayfield, they would either be known as the Grand Slam Wallabies or 'the side that did really well in Britain, winning three out of four Tests'.

Jones ran the players very hard—so hard it was inevitable that there would be a blow-up somewhere. Now with three Test selections under his belt, Farr-Jones felt much surer of his ground—less the shy new boy and more his old self: the one with a short fuse if the occasion warranted it, and sometimes when it didn't; the one who was rarely inclined to back down whatever the circumstances.

After a long bus trip, the Wallabies arrived late in the day at Southport to be greeted with the news that Jones wanted them to complete a brief training session, 'just to get some cobwebs out of our system'.

That is how it started, but long after the cobwebs had been brushed away the Wallabies were still at it, driving hard and continuing well after sundown. Jones, for some reason, was in a particularly foul mood that afternoon and lived on the whistle, constantly exhorting the players to new agonies in the name of being ready for the Scots in a fortnight's time. Farr-Jones took it all on board quietly enough, although 'hating every moment'. At last the blessed whistle to signal the end of training sounded, but Jonesy had one more announcement.

'OK, these people will do some extra work: Farr-Jones, Grigg, Reynolds . . .'

Surely, Farr-Jones thought, the coach couldn't be serious. OK, so Jones had a policy that if you hadn't played in the past three or four days you had to do extra work to maintain your fitness, but this, in Farr-Jones's mind, was ridiculous—he was totally exhausted.

He intended to invoke the only let-out clause he could think of. Jones had often said to them: 'Common sense prevails. So if you feel that your body is a little tight and you'll be risking injury by doing extra work, let me know.' Somehow, though, Nick's words came out wrong. Instead of saying, 'Excuse me, Alan, would you mind terribly if . . .' what came out, in a voice tinged with insolence, was, 'Alan, I'm *not* going to do this'.

Very quietly Jones turned to the other six players he had named and said, 'OK, you blokes go off and start some 50-metre sprints,' and then turned himself fully towards Farr-Jones, who remembers the blast like this . . .

'How DARE you talk to me like that! *I'll* be the judge of what work you can and can't do! I am the coach and my function is to decide such things, otherwise the whole structure of our team endeavour would fall to the ground. DON'T YOU EVER speak to me like that and . . .'

And so on. In a similar situation, 999 times out of a thousand, the castigated player, in the face of an angry coach who held all power over selections and his future rugby career, would have backed off, apologised and gone off to do his sprints with added vigour, albeit head bowed. But this time something inside Farr-Jones reacted angrily and he decided to take Jones on. With his blood boiling, the new Test halfback burst forth with what he now refers to as a 'non-intellectual response'—he swore viciously at Jones, likening him to a defining part of the female anatomy, and stormed off.

And still Farr-Jones wasn't done. After slamming the door behind him as he charged into the changing room he proceeded to amaze Michael Hawker, Chris Roche and Andrew Slack, among others, by kicking bags around and slamming his fist into the wall as he publicly vented his spleen. Slack and all were watching this display in stunned silence. But Farr-Jones was past caring, almost—until the focus of their gaze shifted from him to a point over his left shoulder, and he realised that someone else had come into the changing room.

It was the man himself—Alan Jones. Even then Farr-Jones refused to be cowed into submission, and continued to mutter under his breath, even as he threw his things into his bag and *harrumphed* his way onto the bus.

By now the entire squad knew what was afoot, and the busload of Wallabies went very quietly back to the hotel with the two focal points of their attention both still furious: a darkly thunderous Alan Jones up the front of the bus, and a carpet-biting mad Nick Farr-Jones down the back.

It was a confrontation which Farr-Jones could never win, and by the time the bus arrived back at the hotel he'd begun to reflect on the probable consequences of his actions. He'd be lucky to escape with just missing out on selection for the Scottish Test, and a listing of NTA (Never to Tour Again) seemed at least a possibility. Maybe his Wallaby career had finished before it had properly begun.

It was a slightly calmer, more rational Nick, then, whom Wallaby manager 'Chilla' Wilson collared in the hotel foyer upon arrival. Chilla told him he wanted to see him for a 'discipline meeting' in his room. As always with the affable Chilla, this involved a bit of a drink of whisky, a bit of a chat, a bit of discussion on how to get out of trouble. Basically, Chilla told Nick he had to apologise.

Half an hour later, genuinely remorseful, Nick was at Jones's door. He knocked twice, but no answer. Farr-Jones knew Jones was in there because he had heard the sound of running water, but he could hardly barge in or yell out, 'I know you're in there, Alan, and I'm coming in to apologise ready or not'.

There was nothing for it but to write a letter of apology and slip it under his door.

It worked, after a fashion. Farr-Jones again went to see Jones after dinner and again the coach let him have it, but this time with none of those annoying interruptions from the recipient. The gist of it was that never in Jones's life had anyone ever spoken to him like that, never would he have believed that Farr-Jones, of all people, would be so insolent, and if Farr-Jones were playing at Manly he would find himself playing fifth grade next week.

Sorry. Sorry. Sorry.

They left it at that, with Jones having firmly re-established his supremacy over the recalcitrant player and Farr-Jones still not at all sure he would be named in the final Test side to play Scotland that weekend.

The air was drizzly, the ground wet, and the Murrayfield stands packed with 65 000 rugby aficionados. While the Wallabies were playing for the Grand Slam, the Scots were playing for the huge honour of being the nation to deny them.

Nick had been chosen for the Test after all, and after he had fed the ball into the first Australian scrum the Scots were treated to the rare sight of the usually impeccable five-eighth, Mark Ella, dropping a ball coming straight to him, but it proved to be only a slight aberration in what was to be a masterly game. Not only did Ella throw a cut-out pass fifteen minutes into the game which led to a try by winger David Campese, but in the second half he was the linchpin of a move which went: Farr-Jones to Ella, inside to fullback Roger Gould, back to Ella and over for Ella's fourth try in as many Tests, his personal grand slam.

Australia ran out winners by 37–12 and the Grand Slam was theirs. In the wild scenes in the dressing room afterwards, the primary emotions were jubilation and relief. Relief that they hadn't blown it, relief that they wouldn't have to face the wrath of Jones, relief that they wouldn't spend the rest of their lives ruing the lost opportunity.

While upon their return to Australia, Jones prospered, using his success as Wallaby coach as the platform from which to launch himself into a radio broadcasting career, one of his key players in Mark Ella signed off without further ado. Many years later, I looked back upon his life and times.

MARK ELLA

It was a footie game and it was played daily right on Tasman Street, La Perouse, in the late 1960s and early 1970s. As many as thirty Aboriginal kids, drawn from the local mission and such bountiful houses as the Ellas'—which boasted no fewer than twelve siblings—would tear into it until the sun went down, and marginally beyond.

Can you see them there now? Amid squeals, laughter and grunts of sheer physical effort, the two opposing mobs are constantly colliding, rebounding, then coming together again, searching for a way through the densely massed opposition.

The peculiarity of this game is that while it is played to the rules of 'touch' on the road, the kids are doing full-blown tackles on the grassy verges. The way of the players is to finesse it if you can, belt it through if you have to, but play the game whatever.

And there in the middle of it all is young Mark Ella. With his twin brother, Glen, and young brother Gary never too far away, he is the one already notable for the bewildering speed with which his hands can make the ball whistle to his will, and the uncanny sense he displays of not only knowing where the ball will go next, but where it *should* go to get through.

'They were great days,' Ella says now with a laugh, 'a lot of fun. And we all learnt from it a way of playing which was basic to getting the ball through such thickly packed opposition—stand close, quick, short passes, run around in support, flat in attack, and go again. We loved it.

'The main thing, though, was not to let the ball die. Do whatever you had to, but keep it moving without dropping it or losing it. We hated it when the ball stopped, because that was boring. So we kept it moving.'

Not that football was anywhere near the focal point of young Mark's existence.

'It was just a part of being out of the house,' he says. 'Like on Saturdays, Mum would say, "Here's your breakfast, and I'll see you at dinner time". We'd wander around, maybe get a couple of bucks for caddying at NSW Golf Club, go diving for the twenty-cent pieces the tourists would throw us young Aboriginal kids at the Bear Island wharf—we were like circus animals performing for them, I guess, but we didn't care—and then in the afternoon we'd play footie in the street again. During the week we'd play pretty much every afternoon. Lots and lots of footie.'

In such a fashion did Mark Ella's childhood pass, as he almost unconsciously acquired the skills that were going to propel him to enormous fame. At the age of eleven, he went to Matraville High School (with Glen and Gary) and was exposed to a game called rugby union for the first time.

'We liked it,' Mark recalls, 'and we played it pretty much exactly the same way that we had played the game in Tasman Street. Trying to keep the ball alive whatever happened.'

Their coach at Matraville came to like that way of playing, too, as he couldn't help but notice that with the Ella boys in his side, opposition teams were being sent home weighed down with as many as 100 Ella points in their kitbag. Of course such extravagant talent needed some precise tutelage to make it grow strong and true. Enter, stage right, the famous Wallaby and Randwick centre of the 1930s, Cyril Towers, and the Matraville High First XV coach, Geoff Mould.

'Cyril used to walk from Clovelly, I think, to watch us train and play,' Mark recalls, 'and afterwards would get out the twenty-cent pieces on the grass to show us his theories.'

And did Towers's theories make sense?

'God yes, and we listened. In attack it was all about keeping it straight, short passes, draw, loop, go again, bang! break through, always a looping pattern of play, always attacking on the outside. It worked.'

Ditto what Geoff Mould told them, himself already a believer in Towers's theories. None of it was radically different from what the Ellas had already learnt naturally, and their skills were sharpened through constant execution. (Not least the footballing execution of opposing sides.)

'Everything we'd learnt on the street also worked, with a bit of refinement, out on the field,' Ella recalls. And the rest is history. The Matraville High side, which boasted many other Aboriginal graduates of Tasman Street footie, as well as one ring-in red-headed winger—it was said they were not so much a backline, as 'a black line with a red tip'—ripped apart all opposition. In 1976 and 1977, Matraville won back-to-back Waratah Shields, the competition to determine the best school sides in the state. When Mould became Australian Schoolboys coach at the end of 1977 he picked all three Ellas to go on the tour of Britain.

'That was a terrific tour,' Ella enthuses at the memory. 'We were happy, we were playing good football, seeing the world, and . . .'

And whipping them witless on the football field. As always, run straight, short pass, loop, and go again. And again and again. Under the guidance of Ella at five-eighth, with a bloke by the name of Wally Lewis as his first reserve, the 1977 Schoolboys were unbeaten through sixteen games. On their return, the coach of the Randwick first grade, Bob Dwyer, convinced the three brothers they were good enough to go straight to grade. By the fourth game of the season, the moustachioed one had selected them all in the Firsts. So how did they go?

'We were cutting them a mile apart,' Mark Ella says, 'because no-one knew how to play the game.'

Prima facie, one might accuse Ella of outrageous arrogance in saying such a thing, but when you consider that in that first grade debut of the Ellas, Randwick beat the previously un-defeated Norths side 63–0, you'd have to reckon he has a point.

True Ella-fever had begun, with Mark receiving at least his fair share of the rapturous plaudits. In fact, so overwhelmingly did Ella dominate from the five-eighth position, the theory would grow he was very much a 'natural genius', and that not even he knew how exactly he played the game—that it all just happened.

Not true. Bob Dwyer recalled in his book, *The Winning Way*, that Mark always had a very clear and calculated approach to the game. In 1979, Dwyer arranged for Randwick five-eighths of the lower grades to gather around the young star, and hear the football word according to Mark.

'Mark was only nineteen years old,' Dwyer recalled, 'yet he spoke with precision about how he played the position himself. He described things such as his angle of support, the timing of the pass, the angle of his run, and so on, in detail. This was a skilled operator talking, not some kind of free-spirited genius . . .'

By the end of 1979 Ella was in the Australian team touring Argentina, and the following year was a fully fledged Test player. When Dwyer became Wallaby coach in 1982, it wasn't long before he made Mark the Wallaby captain—the first Aborigine to captain an Australian team of any stripe.

'I took it as an extremely great honour,' Ella recalls, 'and was very motivated to do well.'

Not that everything went perfectly in his rugby career for all that.

There came, for example, the final moment of the Manly–Randwick grand final in 1983. Manly was hanging on to a skinny two-point lead when the ball came to Mark, perhaps 40 metres out from the goalposts. He snapped off a field-goal attempt and watched with everyone else in the ground as the twirling piece of leather seemed to slowly curl towards victory . . . before just as lazily drifting away to defeat.

Manly won. Randwick lost.

'There have been Test matches I've lost,' Ella says now, 'where it didn't really bother me too much because I knew that at least we had done our best. But after that match I couldn't sleep for weeks. Not for weeks.'

Whatever, it wasn't long before Jones was going after the Wallaby coaching job at the expense of Dwyer.

Alarmed, Ella spoke out.

'I was a fan of Dwyer's and so I actively campaigned against Jonesy. I believed there wasn't a need for a change, so I told players, officials, and anybody who would listen to me that Bob was still the way to go.'

Jones won through regardless, and before long the man himself was at Mark's left shoulder just moments before the first Jones-led Wallaby side was to be announced, in May of 1984.

'I'm sorry to have to tell you this, Mark,' said the new coach, 'but the selectors have decided not to make you captain.'

Ella waxes a certain indifference about the decision now, but acknowledges that at the time he was not too happy.

'I guess what got me most,' he says, 'is that I never really got an explanation for why I had to lose the captaincy.'

Could it have been that you simply weren't a good one?

'Well I thought I was pretty good,' he returns, and even at this distance of time there is no doubt that he sincerely means it, all mock self-flattery aside.

Whatever, under the captaincy of Andrew Slack and the coaching of Jones, a new era had begun. By any measure it was the most successful period Australian rugby had known to that point, with achievements on the field led most notably, by one . . . Mark Ella.

The boy from Tasman Street knocked 'em dead in Britain on the Grand Slam tour, ever and always managing to manoeuvre the ball through thick traffic in confined spaces, the same as he always had. Incredibly, he also managed to score a try himself in each of the four Tests. To the disbelief of all, at the end of the Grand Slam tour, Ella announced his retirement. He was twenty-five, and had played 25 Tests.

The eulogies on his departure were poignant.

The great English writer Frank Keating, for example, came up with this: 'If some destructive process were to eliminate all we know about rugby, only Ella surviving, we could reconstruct from him, from his way of playing and loving rugby and from the man himself, every outline of the game, every essential character and flavour which have contributed to rugby, the form of it and its soul, and its power to inspire.'

While the Wallabies had departed on their Grand Slam tour, I had gone to play rugby in Rovigo, Italy, an eye-opening experience that I think marked my approach to the game thereafter, as it was my first real taste of how very much more the game had to offer beyond scrums and lineouts. You could live in the hub of Europe for freebies, learn a new language and culture, all in exchange for your rugby skills! If this was foreign rugby, give me more of it.

For what it's worth, the following article will always have a special place in my heart, as it was the first piece I ever had published—the top of the back page of the Herald, *word for word as I wrote it, God bless their socks.*

PLAYING ITALIAN RUGBY

Plunging through mist late in the second half on a frozen field in Rovigo, Italy, it suddenly hit me that there really isn't much in common between the game played in Italy and the one played in Australia.

Perhaps of all the sports played internationally, rugby is the one that bears most distinctively in substance and style of play the national characteristics of each country. Played worldwide with exactly the same rules and regulations, it is a hybrid plant that grows differently in each country according to the ground in which it is nurtured.

With the arrival of the Italian rugby team in this country and the forthcoming Test match at Ballymore, the Australian rugby public will get a rare chance to see rugby as it has grown in Italy. Having played one very enjoyable season in Italian rugby, I believe I can give some description of the way in which their game and style of play has arisen.

Despite the relative lack of recognition internationally, the Italian game is flourishing in its natural habitat and has a loyal following from town to town, particularly in the north. The most distinctive feature of the game there is the emotionally charged atmosphere in which each match is played.

Whereas in the Sydney championship there are ten first division teams training and playing in the same city, in Italy each of the major towns has its own team and the championship is truly national from Sicily to Venice (where you can play only at low tide).

When I was there it was not unlike seeing modern-day warriors doing battle each Sunday afternoon for the honour of the town. In the Churchillian speeches that preceded every match we were continually exhorted to new heights against the heathen mob that awaited us and a loss, particularly on home turf, was catastrophic.

Our team, like most in the championship, was three times the side when we were playing at home in front of friends and family. I first became aware of the depth of this emotion fairly early in the season when we scored a narrow win over an invading team regarded as a traditional rival. At the final whistle, instead of the round of handshakes and 'thanks for the game' I was used to, I was suddenly awash in my team-mates' hugs, tears and kisses. Being true blue, I was *shocked*. But upon considering the 'when in Rome' adage I changed my mind and quickly got right into it. A similar theme was being played out between the 4000–5000 spectators in the stands and I remember reflecting at the time that it was a long, long way from sunny Manly Oval on a Saturday afternoon.

The weather also seemed a little bizarre to this Australian boy. Playing and practising on the snow in below-zero temperatures became normal and there evolved, of course, a series of tactics and strategies to be used when it was snowing. More interesting, though, was the game when it was played in heavy mist.

My host town, Rovigo (just south of Venice), was genuinely the mist capital of southern Europe, being situated between two rivers and the Adriatic.

On several occasions the mist was so heavy that opposing

five-eighths could not even see each other. But no matches were ever stopped because of the mist, and visibility—or the lack thereof—became part of the strategy.

In that situation of thick swirling mist the strategy was for us forwards to secure the ball the best we could and give it to our five-eighth, Stefano Betarello, who is also the Italian five-eighth. He, not unlike John Bertrand coming down the final stretch of the America's Cup course looking for a hopeful patch of wind, would direct play towards the thickest part of the mist.

When the opposition had the ball those of us cover-defending would have to head out into the wilderness on a search-and-destroy mission for the ball-carrier and just keep in touch with each other the best we could. And the spectators? What spectators, officer?

Needless to say, none of the experience gained by the Italians playing in these kinds of conditions will be of use to them at Ballymore. Nevertheless, I do believe the Italians have the potential to do a lot better than they have been given credit for in the lead-up games to this Test. Realistically, the Italians cannot hope to win, but if the ball bounces their way it could be an interesting spectacle.

Their forwards may be characterised, to borrow from Banjo Paterson, as having 'mighty little science but a mighty lot of dash', while the backs have their fair share of whatever that mysterious wellspring is that makes Latin sporting teams so unpredictable, creative and sometimes brilliant.

Although much has been made of the relative difference in size between the formidable Australian pack and the diminutive Italians, there will also be a problem, I think, because of shortcomings in technique. For example, in contrast to the seemingly endless discussions we have here about scrums concerning feet positions, synchronisation, wrist tightening etc, there we were lucky if we ever *saw* the scrum machine let alone talked about technique. The result was that scrums were usually a cross between a rugby league scrum and the fall of Saigon and I would expect the weakest point of the Italian forwards' game in fact to be the scrum.

In the lineouts the Italians should again be dominated, but

for the rest their dash should hold them in good stead and they should get at least some supply of ball for the backs. As to the latter, on their day they can be breathtakingly innovative and creative.

I suppose the most likely scenario is that this creativeness, and sometimes brilliance, will be firmly crushed by the troops sent up by General Jones, but if the Italian backs fire early it could be difficult for the Australians to keep up to the point-a-minute task set by the good general.

After Italy, I went to live in France for four years, playing rugby and writing. It took some time in France to get the hang of the lifestyle.

OODLES OF POODLES

The white-coats have all gone home now. Finally, by the cold light of a wan French moon, I relate my story. I pray fervently that this manuscript, written with a thumbnail dipped in tar, will someday reach the outside world.

People, my people, it's about the froggy doggies. Poodles. There's beaucoup of them. There's *très* beaucoup of them. Oodles and oodles of poodles. Everywhere. Always. In the fields. On the boulevards. In the restaurants. At the rugby matches. In the cafes. Sitting up like Jacky on the front seats of passing cars. Just everywhere.

I am not neurotic. Nor did I have an unhappy childhood. As a matter of fact I used to like dogs. But imagine living for four long years among a strange people who, essentially, possessed only one breed of dog. One, just *one*, God help me.

And then, imagine that this one breed of dog, the poodle, was always following you, *watching* you. That no matter where you turned, what you did, where you went, there was always one more member of the poodle network.

Staring at you. Wagging its stupid little tail. Yapping at you. Insolently. Incessantly.

Imagine all that and you'll start to understand. It was more than true blue flesh and blood could stand.

The first inkling I had of the seriousness of the situation was when the rugby club I play for here had a family picnic day to welcome me aboard. Needless to say, 'family' also meant dogs. The president and vice-president both had poodles. The treasurer and coach both had poodles. Of the fifteen players in first grade, no fewer than seven had poodles. Right in the middle of the president's welcoming speech his poodle piddled on my leg.

'*Please* don't kick your poodle to death *Monsieur le Président,*' I was about to plead. 'Allow me.'

Only just in time, I noticed he hadn't missed a beat of his speech. Odd. Very odd. But things were to get even more bizarre.

I went out with a French girl, Michelle. Surprise, surprise, she had a poodle. 'Love me, love my dog,' she said. God knows I tried. But did she have to spend 500 francs a month on taking it to poodle beauty salons, amongst other things?

Did it have to sleep on the end of her bed at night in designer dog-pyjamas? And worst of all did Michelle have to keep *three* photos of the dog on her bedside table? I am NOT making this up.

Enough already.

I'd turn on the television. Ads for pet medical insurance, featuring prominently a poodle. 'Doesn't your little doggy deserve the very best medical care? Take out this insurance now . . .'

I'd open a magazine. More poodle pictures. A story on this great new business that's just opened in Cagnes-sur-Mer. Basically a lonely hearts matchmaking service for poodles. I'd go for a walk in town. Promenading poodles leaving omnipresent poodle-poo.

So it went. My rugby team-mate Christian Dalla Riva, whom I'd seriously admired as the toughest man on earth, turned out to have had his poodle *baptised*. True, I swear it.

I'd go to a very classy restaurant. Froggy doggies everywhere. In the *restaurant*, I mean. At the goddamn *table*, I mean. Truly. Sitting up on their owners' laps as they ate. Over time I began to break down. I started seeing poodles everywhere I looked. That wasn't necessarily a problem though. It was when I started to turn into a poodle myself that I knew I was in trouble.

First, I started to grow fur on the palms of my hands. Then my feet began to turn into paws and my nose seemed to always be wet. I'd find myself rolling over on my back and begging people to tickle my tummy.

Finally, they had to come and get me. Two enormous poodles in white coats, driving an ambulance.

They took me back to this enormous white kennel and that's where I am at the moment. If this manuscript ever gets out at least you, my countrymen, will know that it's not *me*, but this whole nation that is just crazy about poodles.

All up I adored my period in France, though it did take some time to completely understand the French rugby culture. It helped, a little, when I wrote down the Golden Rules, or Commandments, as I gleaned them, and then put them together in an article I had published, of all places in the Australian Financial Review.

FRENCH RUGBY'S ELEVEN COMMANDMENTS

1 *People with titles and authority are accorded automatic respect.*
Put the tag of president or *dirigeant* (director) on anyone, and in the eyes of the French they grow a good foot taller. Even in the small rugby clubs it is not unusual for the president to be addressed by his minions as '*Monsieur le Président*'.

2 *Politics is everywhere.*
My club has about 50 *dirigeants*. Each of these knows to the nearest centimetre where the others are situated along the left–right political spectrum and so does *La Mairie* (the town council), which contributes heavily to the annual budget of the club.

3 *Proximity to one's town means power.*
When my team can hear in the near distance our own beloved church bells, we play like men possessed. In the four seasons I have played here we have never once lost a competition game at home. When we play away from home, the other team plays like men possessed and we, comparatively, play like 'puddy tats'.

4 *The spirit of a rule is everything and its precise meaning nothing.*
The rule that 'you must be back 10 metres', for example, doesn't mean 'that distance between 9 and 11 metres'. It means 'back a bit'. Equally, if a knock-on is just a very little one the standard procedure is to play on.

5 *Anything goes in a fight.*

If you take the *Manual of Standard Procedure for Regular Australian Guys*, and look up 'Fighting' it says, 'Fight with your fists and nothing else—only girls kick, scratch and bite.' (Hey, Germaine, I didn't write it.) In France, absolutely anything goes. Incidentally, the four most outstanding facial scars I bear all come from playing against rugby clubs that ring the Mediterranean. The further south you go, the more violent the fights become.

6 *Meal times are sacred. Repeat sacred.*

In those long bus trips that are so much a part of French rugby it doesn't matter how tired we may be, how many white-line kilometres remain between us and home, two hours after dusk the bus stops and we eat. But it is none of this just-a-quick-snack-and-we'll-keep-moving nonsense. *Quelle horreur*! Rather, it is invariably a three- or four-course meal with cheese and lingering coffees after-wards. An hour and a bitty later, sated, we move on. Liberal lashings of red wine are quite normal at the team's meal *before* the game.

7 *Handshaking and kissing are* de rigueur.

In a normal day over there I estimate that I shake hands about one hundred times and hand out perhaps twenty or thirty *bises* (kisses). Correct comportment when meeting any man you know is to formally shake his hand and say *ça va?* If your friend or acquaintance is with people you don't know, no matter—it's still handshakes all round. For women friends, one kisses both cheeks, perhaps twice if she is particularly close. With really close men friends a little cheek-kissing is also not out of order. At first I thought the formality of all this handshaking and kissing was the most unheard of thing I'd ever heard of—now I kinda like it.

8 *Age equals respect, almost.*

My team treats with obsequious respect anybody that has even a hint of grey hair. Everybody except referees, that is, whom we delight in insulting, particularly when the scores are close.

9 *Punctuality is just not on.*

'Training starts at seven o'clock' means training starts whenever you happen to get there, and 'the bus leaves at nine o'clock' invariably means about half past nine.

10 *Dress and presentation are particularly important.*
To be well dressed is to be normally dressed. All of my team-mates are capable of carrying on long and animated discussions about the pros and cons of this or that brand of clothing and can spot fake Lacoste T-shirts at 50 metres.

11 *There is no sense of personal space.*
If you take ten Australian rugby players and put them on a 10-metre bench, they will instinctively arrange themselves so that each player has exactly one metre of space and no-one will be touching anyone else. Take ten French players, though, and sit them on a 10-metre bench and they will invariably be draped over each other at random, sitting precisely as they landed. A hand resting on another's thigh raises no cry of 'poofta!' from the stalls.

GETTING OUR TEETH INTO THE TOULONNAIS

Brive-en-Limousin: Down here in this lost corner of France where the passion of the people runs to rugby union, there has been of late a new sound in the night air, mingling with the barking of dogs, the crowing of roosters and the haunting cry of a lost and lonely freight train whistling away in the distance. '*Krr-kr kr kr, krr-kr kr kr, krr-kr kr kr . . .*' It is at first hard to distinguish as it wafts back and forth with the breeze, but gradually . . . gradually . . . it becomes clearer and, yes, it is, astoundingly, the sound of 50 000 pairs of teeth gnashing away in rhythmic harmony.

The cause of this eerie phenomenon? None other than the prospect of the mighty Toulon rugby team, champion of all France, arriving by plane to play a game against my own team of Club Athlétique Briviste. The gnashing is in aggressive ecstasy at the thought of what we local lads are going to do to the uppity Toulonnais. Though this event is ostensibly a game, a fairer description probably would be a mini-war . . . from the Toulon side of things, at least.

My team-mates and I are above that. We will be on nothing less than a crusade. A crusade for the honour of our whole region, which has been held in a blind trust down in Toulon since the last time we played them. *Krr-kr.* On that dim December day . . . *Krr-kr . . .*

Black Sunday it's known as . . . *Krr-kr*, they won . . . ahem . . . *Krr-kr*, 62–0. (Truth be told, we were lucky to get to nil on the day.)

Impossible to exaggerate the seriousness with which our defeat was viewed by the good burghers of Brive. It was not merely that we were sportsmen of the town's best-known club and that we had gone down in a more than ignominious defeat against the hated big-city boys of Toulon. It was that we were the town's chosen warriors, with all the glories and comforts that this privileged position warrants, and we had disgraced Brive and the Brivistes by not even lifting our swords to defend ourselves.

On our return to Brive the next day, I remember reflecting that never had the sporting-hero business looked so gloomy. But that's all behind us now. This time things are going to be different. They may have won in crushing style last time by rattling up a good half-century (and the rest), but this time, by God, it is our turn to bat.

How can we even presume the possibility of winning after suffering such a hideous defeat? Because this time the Toulonnais are going to be playing on *our* turf and, as this is France, that makes all the difference. At three o'clock, when we Brivistes first pour out of the trenches to get into the hand-to-hand stuff with the Toulonnais, we will do so supremely confident of one thing.

That is that while our supply lines of emotional will-to-win are absolutely secure, coming to us as a palpable force from our own 12 000 supporters surrounding the battlefield, our opponents will be operating no less than 700 kilometres from their own base, drawing sustenance only from a bare scattering of supporters.

In such a hothouse emotional atmosphere, my team-mates and I, so timid at Toulon, will consider it a positive privilege to throw our bodies onto the ball in front of the whirling maelstrom of Toulonnais boots, a positive pleasure to tackle ourselves to exhaustion and beyond, and positive ecstasy to run all over anything that moves in a red jersey.

While the Toulonnais will hesitate that barest moment wondering if the effort is all worth it so far from home, we will storm ashore and swarm all over them before they know what has happened. That's why we'll win. That's why we'll moider da bums. That's why we are going to beat a team that only two-and-a-bit months ago atomised us by 62 points.

And that's why we are a very, very funny bunch of people, we French, now that I come to think of it.

And we did win. Nailed the brutes 4–3 for my single most memorable game in France.

THE DISCOVERY

A couple of seasons ago, my French club of Brive had a bye on the Sunday. To pass the time, a couple of us went to see a lowly second division game of rugby between the nearby small towns of Souillac and Cahors. It would have been an entirely Mickey Mouse affair except for one thing. In the middle of this rugby rabble stood one outstanding player . . . a young second-rower from Cahors whom I'd never seen or heard of before. I really don't want to lay this on too thick, but as we watched in growing wonder this guy all but single-handedly destroyed the Souillac team with an athleticism, aggression and technique that is as rare as Moroccan rugby players in France.

Funnily enough, that's what he was. A Moroccan, by the name of Abdelatif Bennazi, who'd played rugby at school in Morocco, then lobbed at a cousin's house in Cahors, joined the club and gone on from there.

At the time of witnessing this revelation, I was ranked the No 1 second-rower in France (even if I do say so myself), and while I might have strutted into the stadium, an awful lot of swagger had gone out of my step by the time I slunk out, feeling quite wretched as I recall.

In short, I knew I'd be hearing a whole lot more from him, however anonymous he was in his present circumstances.

Bennazi would of course go on to be perhaps the most impressive Test rugby forward for France during the 1990s, and would even successfully captain them. At the time of going to press, he is a likely starter for the 1999 World Cup after coming back from injury.

While I was otherwise engaged playing rugby in France, Australian and New Zealand rugby was constantly struggling with the question of whether or not to send an officially sanctioned tour to South Africa. I felt very strongly that they should not, and said as much in this piece which appeared in the National Times *in 1986—the third article I ever had published. It did little to invigorate my relationship with Alan Jones, who was, at least initially, a staunch advocate of touring, but that was life in the big city.*

WHY THE ARU MUST SAY NO TO SOUTH AFRICA

The Australian Rugby Union will decide on Friday night whether to sanction an official tour of South Africa or to reject it and thereby risk a rebel tour.

It may seem incredible that after a boycott of fifteen years, we would now seriously contemplate sending a team. Nevertheless, it is by no means certain that the ARU will vote to reject the invitation.

Australian rugby is currently controlled by the relatively new firm on the block of Jones, Jones, Jones and Turnbull (the last of whom is the heavyweight of the NSWRU). The 'senior partner' of the firm, Alan Jones, is not only the successful coach of the Wallabies but also the media's most vociferous advocate of closer ties with South Africa.

At the risk of lighting the great man's fuse, I would like to get in a word or two before the decision is taken.

The case against going to South Africa is straightforward. Over decades, the white minority has systematically brutalised the black majority. The most important sport for the whites is rugby.

We Australians cannot send in the marines, but we can effectively register our protest by refusing to associate with the ruling South Africans in that which is most dear to them. In the end, is it not the very least we can do?

Against this most basic supposition a whole range of counter-arguments has been brought.

- *That sport and politics shouldn't mix.* Stock currency. Its effectiveness relies on the impression that our problem with South Africa is only the relatively small and cerebral difference of ideology. Twenty rent protesters shot dead in Soweto three weeks ago is not cerebral and it does not deserve to come under the gentle sobriquet of 'politics'.

- *Apartheid is nearly dead anyway.* Citing the repeal of the mixed marriage laws and the hated pass laws, this line of argument seeks to assert, in rugby parlance, that the white South Africans have already 'lifted their game' and are now set to rejoin the world.

It totally ignores the news that manages to get out from the muzzled press of the shootings, the disappearances, the re-education camps for children, the suspension of habeas corpus and so on.

And it ignores the fact that the very essence of apartheid, the complete denial of political power to black people, has not changed one iota.

- *The Gleneagles Agreement is invalid.* In a long treatise published in the *Rugby News*, Jones took the agreement apart bit by bit and tried to illustrate in a legalistic fashion that Australian rugby wasn't covered by it. Whether he is right or wrong in this, who cares? The Gleneagles Agreement is but one expression of the international collective will that South Africa should be isolated from sporting contact.
- *Refusing the invitation will have no effect,* No, the Botha regime will not stand or fall on the decision of the ARU. Nevertheless, I know from my own experience in South Africa that for the average white, the most visible manifestation of the world's disapproval is the sporting boycott.
- *The moral selectivity argument,* Why sporting sanctions and not also trade sanctions, why rugby sanctions and not tennis and golf sanctions, etc? In essence, why us? Why not them? It is argued that it is manifestly unfair for sportsmen to carry the 'burden' while business seems to find a way to carry on trading.

Come now, 'burden?' Gimme a break. Since the beginning of the Jones tenure three seasons ago, the Wallabies have played twenty Test matches against ten countries. Early next year teams from fifteen countries will come to Australia and the Wallabies will be able to show their wares in front of a world TV audience. How much of a 'burden' can it really be to forgo playing another three Test matches against one more country?

Why not tennis and golf? For this reason: there's a big difference between playing with 'Australia' on your back and playing with 'Pat Cash' on your back. If Pat Cash were to play in the South African Open, that's uniquely his affair. But when playing for your country you answer to your countrymen and a duty is owed to the sensibilities and opinions of your country as a whole.

After much to-ing and fro-ing, and many tears before bedtime, the happy fact is that neither the Wallabies, nor a rebel team made up of them, ever did go to South Africa.

For three years, after taking over the helm of the Wallabies in 1984, Alan Jones proved to be an extremely successful coach, using much the same methods he had first unveiled at the Manly Rugby Club in 1983. Alas, in the fourth year of his reign, it all started to come apart as the team tired of his level of intensity. The following is an edited chapter from my biography of Nick Farr-Jones, which was published in 1993.

THE DECLINE AND FALL OF ALAN JONES

In many ways I regret I ever had anything to do with Australian rugby. In many ways, I regret that I was foolish enough to put my name forward for the coaching job.

Alan Jones, 1992

It should have been Alan Jones's finest hour, in the greatest year of Australian rugby history. If the Wallabies won the inaugural World Cup, being held over four weeks in May and June in New Zealand and Australia, they would become official World Champions, surpassing by far the feats of 1984 and 1986.

And why wouldn't they win? In the three years since Jones had taken over, the Wallabies had played twenty Tests, won sixteen and lost only four, of which two had been by a single point. The coach was feeling so confident that in an interview with journalist Terry Smith, he mooted the possibility that Australia could play Tests against both the All Blacks and Fiji on the one day.

'I'd like to think we could do that,' he said. 'It's like Cassius Clay wanting to pull all the heavyweight challengers into the ring on the one night.'

If not quite so confident as that, Nick Farr-Jones was also looking forward to a good year. Since he'd taken over the Test halfback role sixteen Tests earlier, he'd been a part of no fewer than fourteen winning sides and had every confidence that this would continue. First, however, there was a lot of work to be done. From early February, Jones began taking the Sydney-based Wallabies for private training sessions at Sydney University Oval. Jones was as relentless as ever in driving them hard, but the Wallabies were nevertheless enthusiastic—it was part of the Jones equation. Coach Jones = Hard Work = Winning = Ultimate Respect for the Jones Way.

The man himself, though, seemed to have changed. The glory of the previous year's Bledisloe Cup victory, when the Wallabies had ripped the All Blacks 2–1 in the three-Test series, had increased his public profile even more, which had brought its own pressures. While previously he had been unstintingly generous of his time for any members of his team who called him up, by early 1987 a certain *What-is-it?* had started to creep into his voice over the phone and in person.

Simply, Jones was an extraordinarily busy man. Outside his rugby coaching, he was a highly regarded after-dinner speaker, involved in the organisation of countless charity fundraising affairs, on the board of several companies and, most particularly, a very successful morning broadcaster on 2UE. It all demanded a great deal of his time, even if his energy for the Wallaby cause remained seemingly boundless.

The real problems with Jones's media commitments were only to show up during the actual World Cup.

They came from all five continents—sixteen countries gathered in Australia and New Zealand to see which nation possessed the strongest rugby team on Earth. The inaugural World Cup was the culmination of four years work by the International Rugby Board to give rugby its answer to the Olympics.

As usual, the Wallabies gathered in the Camperdown Travelodge, which was to be their headquarters for the next four weeks, with only a brief foray to Brisbane. This time, though, there was something different. And it wasn't just that it was a World Cup and the Wallabies were going to try to beat fifteen nations instead of just one. Instead of training in the mornings, as they were used to, beginning the day with hard work, they would only be training in the afternoons. The reason, Alan Jones said, was because he had an 'unbreakable commitment' to keep broadcasting on Radio 2UE, which meant his working on the morning shift.

Whatever. All through the World Cup, Jones continued to do his morning broadcasts from Radio 2UE and would then get back to Camperdown for training usually only in the early afternoon. Though the starting time of the afternoon training session was variable it still meant that the players were now free to sleep till noon, which in turn meant that they could afford to go out till the wee hours.

It was, of course, against the rules laid down by Jones for them to do that, but things weren't what they used to be in terms of discipline. The cat was away. This lack of adherence to the rules was exacerbated by the fact that the other man who might have been expected to impose them, new manager Ken Grayling, was already weakened by cancer, which would take his life less than four months later.

The problem with Jones's media commitments didn't finish with the timing of the training. There was also the matter of their greater intensity. When the Wallabies did train, there was enormous interest from Jones's media colleagues on how the 'Jones Wallabies' were going—which led to muttering among the team that Jones was playing up to it, driving the Wallabies longer and harder than necessary because it all looked so good on television.

These sessions were unbelievably physical, Jones having apparently become convinced for this World Cup that the best way to prepare for the tough games ahead was to have high-impact full-contest practices now, pitting the Wallabies against each other on the training field. Finally there was the problem, most particularly for the Sydney-based Wallabies, that their focus was inevitably fractured by the proximity of both their families and their jobs.

Normally when on tour and well away from the commitments that go with being at home, it was far easier for players to concentrate on the job at hand. But as Sydneysiders in Sydney Town, a dissipation of attention was inevitable. Just as every morning Simon Poidevin would go to work for as many as five hours with his firm of stockbrokers and Stephen Cutler would sneak home, so too Farr-Jones would steal away to work in the very early morning, and at night to see Angela, his girlfriend, or his family.

'Maybe we might have been less inclined if Alan had been dropping everything for the World Cup,' says Nick, 'but it was obvious to us he wasn't.'

Farr-Jones was in trouble with the coach on this issue early in the World Cup campaign, when he picked up the telephone in his office at 7.30 a.m. to be greeted with the angry words: 'Right, I'll see you in my room when I get back. I've told you I don't want you at the office.'

Farr-Jones still wonders why he didn't say, 'Hang on, Alan, where the hell are *you* calling me from?'

'It was just the way it was back then,' he says now, 'you didn't challenge him if you could at all avoid it.'

Right from the beginning of the World Cup the fact that things were not quite right in the Wallabies was apparent on-field, as they struggled and played sloppily against England, before finally beating them 19–6, and then appeared anything but all-powerful in beating the very weak United States team 47–12.

Then there was Japan. Under normal circumstances, predicting the score of a Wallabies–Japan match would require more knowledge of mathematics than of rugby, but amazingly, with five minutes to go in the game the Japanese had managed to score 23 points and the Wallabies were only seven points ahead. That they scored two late tries to take the score to 42–23 did little to alleviate the impression that the Wallabies were in singularly ordinary form, and at one stage they were playing so badly that they were booed by their fellow Australians in the stands.

In the quarter-final against Ireland it looked as if Australia had at last come good, when for the first forty minutes of the game they played as well as any Australian side had in living memory. Despite losing Farr-Jones to an injured shoulder in the first sixty seconds after he had taken a very heavy tackle by Irish flanker Phil Matthews, the Australians were well on top of their game and at half-time led the stunned Irish by the score of 24–0. Unfortunately for the Wallabies, the Irish came back hard in the second half to score fifteen points to eight, to make the final score the far more modest 33–15.

At least it was a good win, though, and the Wallabies were

definitely in the mood to celebrate. Unfortunately, Jones decided there would be no alcohol consumed at the happy hour, as the team had to apply itself totally to concentrating on the upcoming semi-final against France, a week away. For the Wallabies this was an unprecedented move, as traditionally the happy hour is exclusively the province of the players to run as they see fit, the one hour of the week when the power balance between coach and players is redressed, and the players did not take kindly to this imposition. Still, it was a measure of the hold Jones had over the players that, of the twenty-eight players in the squad, only one of them spoke up and said what the rest of them wanted to: 'Sorry, Alan, I'm having a beer.'

Roger Gould, the legendary Australian fullback, was a man apart within the team, particularly when it came to his relationship with Jones. Already regarded as one of the game's greats well before Jones came on the scene, he owed Jones nothing. Jones hadn't plucked him from obscurity, hadn't retrieved him from the rugby scrapheap, hadn't got him a job, made him captain—hadn't done anything at all for him other than pick him, which any coach would, such was his ability.

'Sorry, Alan, I'm having a beer,' said Gould, promptly opening one with a smile. 'I'm a problem. So drop me.'

As Gould was injured, and would be for the rest of the Cup, Jones couldn't drop him even if he'd wanted to. Besides which, Gould retained such a stature within the game, and was being such a great help to the team in the almost quasi-managerial role he'd assumed since Grayling's illness had worsened, there was nothing to be done but put up with it. Roger had his beer while the others tried to celebrate with lemonade and Coke the best they could.

The only good news to come out of the evening was Jones's announcing there would be no training on the morrow and that instead he had organised a harbour cruise to refresh them. Though he wouldn't be able to join them initially as he had another commitment, he would get to them later in the day if he could.

With the sun on their faces, the wind in their hair, good food in their bellies and at last a drink in their hands as the alcohol ban was forgotten in Jones's absence, the cruise proved to be a wonderful break from the rugby. And a victory of sorts, because they had finally succeeded in getting the youngest member of the side and the reserve halfback, Brian Smith, 'on the turps'— having a drink, in Wallaby parlance. This was a particular pleasure, because to this point it had been difficult to get Smith away from Jones's side and introduce him to more of the Wallaby ways.

Jones had selected Smith from the Queensland reserves bench the previous year and promoted him to the Wallabies ahead of both Peter Slattery, the halfback who had been the reserve to Farr-Jones in 1985, and Brad Burke, Nick's understudy at New South Wales level. Like Black, Smith would go on to prove that he genuinely had the qualities of a very fine footballer but there is no doubt Jones believed in Smith from the first. So much so that he was to be quoted in the *Age* that very week as saying, 'This young man is one of the most gifted players in the world. Every so often you find diamonds and you have to polish them up.'

On the boat, though, Jones was not around, and Smith would no sooner finish his drink than one or other of the Wallabies would fill it up for him with the instruction to 'get this into yer'.

Jones finally joined them in the early afternoon when the boat pulled into a ferry wharf to pick him up and he was immediately shocked to see the players drinking. The reserve centre, Anthony Herbert, was the first to receive the full force of the Jones blast as he happened to be holding a beer at the top of the gangplank when Jones arrived.

'What the hell are you doing drinking?' Herbert remembers Jones demanding. Herbert blustered the best he could, but in pique, if not outright anger, Jones announced that he'd changed his mind about giving them the day off and wanted all the reserves back at the hotel for a sprint session at four o'clock. He expected Farr-Jones too, as he had barely played the last game at all.

Not welcome news to a bunch of players who thought they had the day off and already had a lot of beer in their bellies, but most of them reluctantly tried to sober up. Only Roger Gould refused, telling them they should do no such thing. He stayed behind at The Rocks as the others went back.

If there was one thing Farr-Jones had no feeling for, with grog in his belly and clutching one arm tightly across his chest to protect his shoulder which he'd injured in the previous games, it was doing sprints to Jones's command. Somehow he managed, though, and finished the session at 4.30 p.m., leaving Brian Smith behind to do what he often did—extra work after training.

Farr-Jones, too, was just starting to feel more or less alright by the Thursday before the Saturday semi-final against France. The shoulder was beginning to come good and he felt that by Saturday he would be strong enough to play without painkillers. Which he might have been, but for some reason—and over physio Greg Craig's protestations—Jones insisted that Farr-Jones do a full-contact training session with tackles and all, and if Farr-Jones had to get a painkilling injection just to get through it, well, it was just as well to know how the shoulder would hold up now.

Farr-Jones did get through it, even though it hurt like the hammers of hell as he did so.

'I didn't understand why Jones made me do that, and I still don't,' Farr-Jones says now. 'My feeling at the time was that it probably put the recovery of my shoulder back by about three or four days, and I again had to have a lot of painkillers in my shoulder before playing against France in the semi-finals.'

It was a contest that would often afterwards be described by rugby aficionados as 'the game of the century'. (More often in France than Australia, to be sure.)

The halfback got the first inkling of what was to come in the game when at the first scrum he fed the ball into an Australian scrum that was just marginally giving way. When the camera flashed briefly on Jones in the stand he looked every bit as worried as he should be. If there is one sign that a coach looks for early on in a game to foresee the end result it is how the scrum is going. If it is going backwards, as it was in this case, then the omen is very bad indeed. It means one of three things: the opposition pack has greater strength, better technique, or more hunger.

Even though Australia was ahead by 9–6 at half-time, still the omens were not good. The French somehow refused to fall away, as was their usual international form in away games, and if anything seemed to be coming at the Wallabies more strongly. What particularly raised their morale going into the break was a try scored by their second-rower, Alain Lorieux. From a lineout close to the Australian line, the Australian second-rower Troy Coker had won the ball, only to have it ripped off him by Lorieux in the ensuing maul. It was to prove a costly mistake.

After a seesawing effort that went on for the entire game, the score was deadlocked with a minute to go when, after an amazing passage of play involving no fewer than thirteen Frenchmen, the ball finally came into the hands of perhaps the greatest fullback of the modern era, Serge Blanco, on the burst.

When Blanco got to two metres from the tryline, just on the edge of the sideline, Farr-Jones was still fifteen metres away and knew he couldn't catch him. All he could do was watch in despair as hooker Tommy Lawton made a last desperate lunge for him . . . and just barely missed. Blanco scored the try and the game was gone.

The dressing room was in a predictably wretched mood at the end of the game, and for the first time Nick could remember, Alan Jones simply could not speak. Only nine months earlier in New Zealand Jones had been able to turn the team around in the space of only two weeks; here there was no recourse. The Wallabies were out of the final and the chance to win the World Cup was gone. There was little to do that night for most of the Wallabies except return to the Travelodge and sit around in small disconsolate groups at the bar and try to cheer each other up.

'The depression was absolute,' Nick says. 'We knew we had blown it, that there was absolutely nothing to be done.'

When highly fancied teams have very public losses, it is not unusual to see an immediate division appear between players and coach as each tries to blame the other for the loss. In just such a predicament it was hardly surprising that as the evening wore on and more and more alcohol was imbibed there was talk that maybe Jones had come to the end of his natural term as Wallaby coach.

From there, it all began to unravel quickly. On the Monday the team gathered in the Camperdown Travelodge foyer in the early afternoon as always to go to training. They might have lost the semi but they were still obliged to go to New Zealand to play the consolation final against Wales at the end of the week to see which team would finish third and fourth.

But where was Alan?

After waiting for some twenty minutes, Gould and reserve back-rower David Codey ventured up to Jones's room and found him, in Gould's words, 'still only half-dressed for training, an obviously shattered man'.

'We've lost it, we've lost it all,' Gould remembers Jones saying. It was as if the enormity of the consequences of losing to France was hitting him anew.

'Listen,' Codey said to the coach, 'the whole team is down there every bit as disappointed as you, and they've fronted up, they're ready to train and you've got to too.'

Eventually Jones was persuaded to get himself together and come on down. And right away, he showed that he had recovered somewhat when in his opening remarks at that training session he managed to apportion some of the blame for the loss. In Jones's eyes the three main players to blame for the Wallabies' defeat were Farr-Jones, Campese and Coker. They would simply have to take a good look at themselves if they wanted to continue to be a part of this outfit.

By this time Gould for one had heard enough, and had had enough for that matter. After giving it some thought he walked back to the hotel, packed his bags, made a phone call and then walked back to St Johns Oval. It had only been a light training and the others had gone, but Jones was still there, putting Smith through his paces in another private training session.

'Mate, I've got to tell you something,' Gould said to Jones as they watched Smith run back and forth. 'This has been the most unhappy experience of my life. I'm going. I'm not going to New Zealand with you. I'm leaving for Brisbane in half an hour.'

Jones turned, momentarily disoriented as Gould recalls it.

'You can't do that, Roger. We need you. We need you to help us.'

'No, you don't, Alan. You'll find all the team money is in the safe, and all the tickets for New Zealand are in there too. I'm going. This team was very very happy in 1984 and now it is very unhappy because of you, and I just can't stand to be around it. I'm going home.'

'You can't go.'

'I am. See ya.'

And turned, and walked away.

'I knew that was the only way I could do it,' Gould says now. 'Jones is an extremely hard man to argue with. He's very good at arguing and I'm not. I knew if I stayed around, he'd probably be able to turn me around, just by force of persuasion, but I didn't want that. I wanted to go and I did.'

Yet for all his antipathy towards the Jones of 1987, Gould is typical of many Wallabies in naming Jones as 'easily the best coach I ever had'.

'The best organised, the most energetic, the best at analysing weaknesses in the opposition and exploiting them. But simply not someone you could spend a lot of time with, and after four years the team had just had jack of him.'

With Gould's departure the wheels of the Wallabies got wobblier by the minute. Another who was 'jack' of Jones at that time was Peter Grigg, the long-time Wallaby winger who had become extremely frustrated by his continued non-selection for the important games, even though at the beginning of the World Cup Jones had said to the press that he wanted to have 'a team full of Peter Griggs'. Now the last straw: he wasn't even to be selected for the consolation final. His position had been taken by Brian Smith.

It was only a few hours after Gould had left that Grigg went to see Jones in his room. The ensuing commotion brought the Wallabies from their rooms, and they soon gathered around the door, hardly daring to believe their ears.

Commotions coming from Jones's room were nothing new, but the amazing thing was that the person doing the shouting wasn't Jones. Up to now the times a Wallaby had been heard raising his voice to Jones could have been counted on the fingers of one finger—back in 1984 when Farr-Jones had 'spat the dummy' on the Grand Slam tour. But this exceeded even that.

The players around the door remember the thrust of Grigg's shouting thus: 'How DARE you put Brian Smith on the wing in my place when I'VE played for the WALLABIES there for years!

'You started the World Cup saying to the press that you wanted a team full of Peter Griggs, and now you haven't even got ONE Peter Grigg in the team!'

And Jones's reply? At first a great deal of shocked bluster, and then very little. The way Grigg would tell it to the Wallabies later, Jones was just standing there, dumbstruck at the extent of Grigg's fury. When it was over and Grigg stormed out of the room, he might have been surprised to see so many of his team-mates who happened to be suddenly passing the door, but he was too angry to pause.

Rotorua was just the sort of place for the Wallabies to be in their current mood. They had come to the end of the road and this felt and smelt like the end of the earth. The sulphurous geysers that the town is known for were surely the exhaust fans of hell, and the Wallabies settled into their hotel in a humour as foul as the wind.

The unravelling of the Wallabies continued. At the last training session before playing Wales, on the Wednesday morning, Jones simply didn't turn up. No show. No explanation. Assistant coach, Alec Evans, took the session and that was that.

Since Monday, when the news had got out, there had been much comment from aghast players about Jones's decision to drop Grigg as winger. On the Thursday morning before the game Nick was able to alleviate the controversy somewhat when he told the coach that because his injured shoulder still had not properly recovered he would be unable to play in the Test. This meant that Smith reverted to the more familiar halfback spot, Nick gained the relative comfort of the bench, and Grigg went back on the wing.

Four minutes into the game the Wallaby back-rower David Codey was sent off for over-vigorous rucking, and the Wallabies were down to fourteen men. On the bench, Farr-Jones had the same sense of foreboding as he'd had at the last game, when he'd seen the Wallaby pack go backwards in the first scrum.

It was to be a long afternoon, and all the longer because of the nasty atmosphere at the ground among the New Zealand spectators. Still smarting over the hostilities of the previous season, they were all barracking hard for the Welsh to win.

Then the worst happened . . . Peter Grigg waved his hand in the air in the internationally recognised signal for 'I'm stuffed and have to come off', which meant that Brian Smith went to

the wing position and Nick took over the halfback role. Jim
Webster would later note in his match report for the *Sydney
Morning Herald* that 'when Farr-Jones came on just after half-time
with his busted wing, he got the backs moving strongly'.

The Wallabies very nearly won it. But in a near-replay of the
game against France, Wales scored in the last minute of the game
and then slotted the conversion over to win the game 22–21.
That made two defeats in a row. It was a long bus trip back to
Auckland the following morning, Jones sitting up the front of
the bus, not talking at all. Behind him the players were subdued
to the point of silence. It didn't seem right. Like there was a
huge party, they'd got all dressed up to go and then been refused
admission at the door. On the Saturday afternoon in Auckland,
at Eden Park, France played New Zealand in the inaugural World
Cup final. Only six of the Wallabies attended, while the others
stayed in the comfort and sulky security of their hotel rooms.
While the All Blacks and the French were in the dressing room,
preparing to go out for the biggest match of their lives, Nick and
most of the Wallabies were playing cards, smoking and drinking
in their rooms. Although winning at poker, Nick definitely felt
none the better for it.

'I sort of felt like I was being a bad sport by not going to the
final, but really I just couldn't face it, and most of the guys felt
the same.' Whose deal?

The All Blacks won 29–9 in a fairly ordinary game, and back
at the Wallabies' hotel when the Australians finally flicked off
the TV, the mood was predictably black.

Despite the wretchedness of the season thus far, there was still
a chance that the Wallabies could salvage a great victory out of
the year. Thank providence that the new World Champions, the
All Blacks, were booked in to play Australia only five weeks after
their World Cup victory to contest another one-off Bledisloe Cup
game. If the Wallabies beat them, it wouldn't be the equal of
having the World Cup, but it would at least make Australia's failure
look like an aberration in a nevertheless very successful period.

It was another sign of the times for the Wallabies that despite
the published Jones opinion that there was nothing basically
wrong with the team, he nevertheless dropped both his captain
and vice-captain, Andrew Slack and Simon Poidevin.

Both players took it stoically enough, but Farr-Jones for one was shocked. Driving along Margaret Street, he heard the news of their sacking on the radio and turned it off straight afterwards so he could think.

'I just couldn't figure it out,' he says, 'how both the captain and vice-captain could be dropped and yet Jonesy insisted on telling us that there was nothing really wrong. I thought it very hard on both of them because whatever had been going wrong I was confident the replacing of Slack and Poidevin was hardly the way to turn around our fortunes.'

The new captain was even more of a surprise.

David Codey, the man who had been sent off in the last Test against Wales, was a popular figure in the team and an admittedly inspirational player when on the field, but in recent times Jones had selected Codey predominantly as a reserve. Now it was to be him leading the side.

Jones, though, had no doubts that Codey was just the man for the job. Quoted in the *Mirror*, the coach was glowing in his praise.

'Our new captain, David Codey, is a forceful, aggressive, uncompromising man,' he enthused. 'He is intelligent, leads well, and has the capacity to get the best out of people. He embodies the sort of spirit and commitment we need for this game.'

Sounds like just what the doctor ordered. Even then all was not as it seemed. Codey learnt of his elevation to the captaincy in a most unusual way.

For like Roger Gould and Peter Grigg, Codey had also 'had jack' of the whole Wallaby thing and decided well before the game against the All Blacks that he wanted no further part in it. And just like Gould, he didn't want to become involved in a long discussion with Jones on the subject, preferring simply to withdraw. So . . .

'I called John Bain [the chairman of selectors] to tell him that I was not available,' Codey says. 'There was this pause, and then Bain said to me, "Well, that makes things a bit difficult, David, because we were actually wanting to make you captain".'

'WHAT?'

Even then Codey, to his credit, did not immediately reverse his decision and only agreed to his inclusion on the condition that, as captain, he would be consulted on the running of the team, and things wouldn't be done the Jones Way exclusively. Codey defined his conditions to Bain as 'a complete back-off from Jones on his total control of the team'. For this game there would be no more mad-dog sessions where the players would be required to beat each other around. Codey said he wanted something of a return to the old days, where the players would train hard but not foolishly, and be disciplined in their approach but not to the exclusion of all enjoyment.

This was agreed to and Codey again made himself available.

The first Wednesday the team gathered at the Rushcutters Bay Travelodge (the team having refused to return to Camperdown by virtue of its ordinariness), beer was served to the players with their barbecue after training. It wasn't much but it was a beginning—not so much a need for alcohol as an acknowledgment that things were to be more relaxed.

And Jones was training them again in the mornings. Were they a happy side? Hell, yes they were a happy side. The day before the game, in a story in the *Mirror* headlined 'WE ARE A HAPPY SIDE', Jones came straight to the point: 'In spite of what some people might try to tell you, this is a very happy Australian side. Very committed and very ambitious. All the negative and divisive stuff comes from people who've never been to training, never spoken to a player and never spoken to me. This sort of nonsense fuels me up. It puts petrol in my tank. It puts me into overdrive.'

Overdrive?

'The whole *point* of why this was one of the happiest few days for the Wallabies all year,' says Farr-Jones, 'was that Alan had dropped back a gear or two. It was all a lot quieter somehow, a lot less frenetic. Jonesy seemed to have calmed down about everything and we really did do a lot of good preparation. Going into that game I was extremely confident that we could turn it all around.'

David Codey put his own imprint on the team by insisting that the Wallabies stand right up close to the *haka* as a sign they were not intimidated, and midway through the second half the Wallabies were winning by a slim margin.

That the All Blacks then shifted into overdrive themselves and went on to beat them 30–16 was the cause of some regret for the team but no disgrace. The All Blacks had rebuilt from the disappointments of the previous year and had put together a side that would be looked back on as unarguably the greatest in their history.

For Farr-Jones, it had been a long year, starting with the World Cup, the continued losses, the flip-flops over South Africa, and now the upcoming tour to Argentina beckoning on the horizon. It never seemed to stop, and for the first time since he had made the Wallabies four years earlier, Farr-Jones questioned whether he really wanted to go on this tour, and told his father, Max, so. He wanted to spend a lot more time with Angie, he wanted to spend a lot more time on his work, and most importantly . . .

'I just wasn't enjoying it any more, it was as simple as that. When I started playing in 1984 everything was so new and different and . . . glorious. It was like I just couldn't get enough of it. Now things were different and I remember telling Dad that I'd pretty much decided I didn't want to do it any more, or at least I just wanted to take a bit of time out and go back to living a normal life—not to go to Argentina.'

Max Farr-Jones thought that any such decision would be nothing short of crazy.

'The way I saw it,' he says, 'when you've got a position like Nick had, you shouldn't let it go for anything. OK, so he'd had a year when he hadn't been enjoying it that much, so what? It was something he'd enjoyed tremendously in the past, and I had every confidence that he would come to enjoy it again.'

Nick had little interest in being persuaded over the phone, so Max decided to head to Sydney University the following Saturday, where he knew Nick's Sydney University team would be playing Eastwood.

After the game was over he went straight into the Eastwood dressing room to talk to Brett Papworth, and asked him to help persuade Nick that going to Argentina was the right thing to do. Papworth, himself a little put out to find that Nick was thinking of not going, did talk to him soon afterwards and did in fact succeed in changing Farr-Jones's mind.

'I guess I just reminded him of the terrific times we'd had on previous tours,' Papworth recalls. 'And that this might prove even more terrific because it was all new territory.'

Indeed. New territory and new beginnings. Whether Alan Jones knew it or not, this was his last throw of the dice. Win or perish. With three straight losses behind him, not only were the dogs barking, but the wolves were also circling. Once again he looked for the grand gesture, something to signal that all had changed.

With neither Slack nor Codey available for this tour, he came up with Simon Poidevin as captain—the player he'd axed from the Test against the All Blacks. For the second time in succession a player who was not judged good enough to play in a Test found himself captain soon afterwards.

Further signalling that this was to be the beginning of a new era, Jones got the Wallabies up for 6 a.m. training runs twice in the five-day camp. Unheard of. Then, in a team meeting the night before they left, Jones read aloud a short story called 'Letter to Garcia', the gist of which was this: In a war, in ancient times, a general gives a messenger a letter with strict instructions to take this letter to Garcia. The messenger neither questions what is in the letter nor asks why he must take it to Garcia, and the rest of the story revolves around the messenger overcoming a series of ever more hideous obstacles to deliver the letter. In the end he does deliver it, albeit at great cost to himself, but it doesn't matter—he has carried out the general's instructions without question.

Such a beautiful place, such a painful injury. In the first game of the tour, against the San Isidrio Club on the outskirts of Buenos Aires, Farr-Jones hurt his knee when he tripped while gathering the ball at the base of the scrum and then happened to get caught under the wheels of the back-pedalling Australian pack.

That night, as the team went out to sample the wonderful Argentinian hospitality at a barbecue, Farr-Jones retreated to the hotel to ice his knee, and Alan Jones arranged for Ricky Stuart (who would go on to great fame as halfback for rugby league's Canberra Raiders and the Australian Kangaroos), to come over as Farr-Jones's replacement.

While waiting for Stuart to arrive, Brian Smith would have to play two games straight, but that was no problem. 'It won't worry him, because he is the outstanding athlete in this team,' Jones told the *Sun*, for the 12 October edition.

With Farr-Jones injured, the way seemed open for Smith to take over the Test halfback spot. The only thing that could forestall that happening would be if Smith himself got injured or if Farr-Jones recovered in time. At first this seemed unlikely, as the day after the game Nick could barely even walk on his injured leg, let alone run, but he and the Wallaby physiotherapist, Greg Craig, set about the recovery program anyway.

They attacked from two angles: 'Craigy' worked on the knee, moving and exercising the joint, keeping ice on it to reduce the swelling, while Nick made sure his fitness level stayed high, despite not being able to run.

While the rest of the Wallabies trained they would look over to see how Nick was going on the sidelines. The answer was always: constantly. At first he would just hop along on his good leg as far and as fast as he could until he could stand it no more, then he would hop back, then back and forth again and so on. Or else he would be doing sit-ups. Two hundred at a time. Then another two hundred. When all that was over he would go to the swimming pool, both to do laps and to exercise his trouble-some knee. In Greg Craig's estimation, 'he was pushing himself at least as hard as if he was training with the others'.

Jones was another interested observer of Farr-Jones's progress, as first Nick hopped and then jogged and finally ran. Watching, but never speaking directly to Nick. By his estimation, 'In two weeks, as little as a dozen words passed between myself and Alan. I think he was just like that. If, for whatever reason, you were no longer directly contributing to the success of his team, then Alan basically didn't have a lot of time for you. All of a sudden I was no longer on his table at dinner, no longer invited to go out with him . . . not even a "good morning" as we hopped on the bus to go to training. It was quite obvious there were more important people he now had to spend his time with.'

Farr-Jones and Craig kept working on the knee regardless.

In the meantime rumblings continued to come from home that Jones's position as coach was under threat with the Wallabies' dismal showing in the World Cup and later defeat at the hands of the All Blacks.

The increasingly well-regarded Parramatta coach, Paul Dalton, was now disillusioned with Jones, as he had heard that the national coach no longer supported him for the state coaching job that was coming up the following year. With that in mind he made his intentions the clearest of all: 'Give me Andrew Leeds and Nick Farr-Jones,' Dalton was quoted in the *Sydney Morning Herald*, 'and [Jones] can pick any Australian side he wants. I'll have second pick and beat him . . . flog him'.

The Wallabies of course heard about the Dalton challenge soon enough over the telephone and when they were preparing for the game against Mendoza, Jones gathered his team behind the goalposts after training and delivered a 40-minute lecture on the need for them to stay unified in the face of 'some people who are trying to divide us'. It is up to us, he said, to show that we are above all that, that we are not going to be affected by the dogs barking as the caravan passes.

The fact that Nick was named as part of the Dalton challenge did nothing to smooth relations between him and the coach, yet, according to Nick, 'there was no open hostility between myself and Jones, just maybe a consciousness that things had cooled further'.

Jones himself was clearly beginning to feel the pressure of it all. A few days later, when the Wallabies were losing to an Invitation XV back at Buenos Aires, the team was amazed to see that Jones had left his usual position with the reserves on the bench, and was up and shouting instructions at them from the sidelines. It would provoke a headline back in Australia the following day to the effect of 'VOCAL JONES LOSES HIS DIGNITY', but more importantly among the Wallabies it would promote the feeling, Nick says, that 'Jonesy was losing it'.

By this time Nick was back to running almost at full speed, and though he was as yet unable to 'step' with full confidence off both feet, he and Greg Craig felt that with continued work he would be right to play in only a few days, and definitely be right to play in the Test in ten days' time. On Friday, 23 October, Farr-Jones was confident enough on his knee to go in for the fitness test at the end of training, which consisted of four laps of the field. Maybe it was because he was still fairly fresh while the others were tired from the last two weeks of playing and training, or maybe it was because he just wanted to show Jones he was fit again, but Farr-Jones attacked the laps the way he did in the old days at the Sydney Cricket Ground. Top gear, full throttle, giving it everything he had. When it was over, Craig was satisfied enough to note in his diary that night that 'Nick won by a clear fifty metres'.

It seemed like all their hard work had paid off and he would be right to play in the Test the following week.

Which was why Craig was astonished when Jones took him aside the following day—onto a small balcony outside the room where the post-match dinner was being held—to inform him that as far as he was concerned Nick would be taking 'no further part in the tour'. Shocked that Jones should say this when surely his own eyes had told him that Nick was nearly right, Craig chose his next words carefully.

'Alan, that is your prerogative as coach. But on medical grounds I am telling you Nick will be OK to play in a couple of days. I'm declaring Nick medically fit.'

Craig didn't add, 'and I'll tell the press that if they ask', but it was implicit in his wording. Jones had been warned that if he wanted Nick out of the tour, then he would be getting no help from the physio. The following day, Jones announced Farr-Jones as part of the team to play in Tuesday's game against Paraguay.

The following night Farr-Jones felt good to be back playing with the team again. Running, passing, tackling. Showing the South Americans a couple of pointers on the game. His knee held up well. And so did he.

Peter Jenkins, reporting in the *Australian* on the comfortable Wallaby victory, wrote that, 'Farr-Jones, returning after more than a fortnight on the sideline with knee ligament damage, showed no ill effects of his enforced absence. His service was slick and he set many backline raids into action by darting through holes up the middle of the selection team's defence.'

Still barely a word had passed between coach and player at this stage, yet Farr-Jones felt every confidence that he would be included in the Test side for the coming Saturday. He was the incumbent and had proved to all that he was back from injury and back to his best.

But fie. On the Wednesday morning before the team was announced, Jones asked to see Nick in his room to announce to him that he had a new policy, and Farr-Jones remembers the conversation thus.

'Since the World Cup,' Jones said, 'I have decided that if you haven't done the work you cannot be picked to play. We learnt our lesson then, and we will stick by our new policy. I know you think your knee has healed, but the fact is you haven't really trained with the team over the last two weeks and so I'm not selecting you as halfback.'

The only thing Farr-Jones couldn't figure out was why, if to use Jones's words he was 'unavailable for selection' was he then listed as a reserve for the team? Ricky Stuart had arrived and been playing well, so why not put him on the bench? After all, whatever Jones said to Nick privately, the fact that he was on the bench made it look to the world as if Smithy had simply usurped him. Within the team Farr-Jones kept his chin up and, in the memory of Brett Papworth, 'acted very much as if it hadn't upset him much at all, that he quite understood the logic of him being out and Smith being in'.

In phone calls to Angie back in Australia, though, Nick could be a lot more honest, and although to her mind, 'it is a point of honour with him not to let disappointments get to him', she does remember him sounding 'the most down he's ever been when away on tour'.

The team itself was aghast.

'It was just madness,' says second-rower Damien Frawley, 'and we all knew it. Nobody could figure how Jonesy had possibly come to that decision.'

For the record, Jones's written memory of it, though faulty, is thus: 'The facts as opposed to the rumours were that Nick was injured early in the piece. He simply was not fit, had not played and had not trained in the lead-up to the first Test. I was certainly keen to have Brian Smith in the side because I regarded him as an outstanding player.'

Oddly enough, despite the sudden reversal of their roles, the incumbent becoming the understudy and vice versa, there was no apparent tension between Smith and Farr-Jones. Just as there had been no tension between Farr-Jones and Phillip Cox four years earlier. But this time it was for a different reason.

'Tension' connoted 'contact', and there was simply very little contact between them on that tour. Since his arrival in the Wallabies, Smith had stuck very closely to Jones's side, both socially and on the training field. Invariably the bus would be held up leaving training because Smith and Jones would have to finish doing extra work, and back at the hotel Smith was very much an early to bed, early to rise man.

Which was in contrast to the others. The rest of the players, including Farr-Jones, cite Argentina as possessing the greatest night-life of any country they'd ever toured, and they sampled it to the full. Part of the Wallaby folklore of this particular tour is that players would often go to bed with their dancing shoes on, with the sheets pulled up to their chin, and wait till Alan Jones had done the rounds to check that everyone was settled in for the night before getting up and tiptoeing to the lifts at an agreed time. Though this is probably overstated and it is hard to find any Wallaby who'll admit to such a nefarious duping of Jones, it is certain that a large part of the good times of the tour happened well after midnight. With the Argentinians all working on siesta time, most of the nightclubs never got going until 1a.m.

Often the return from the night spots would be accompanied by the sun rising, and on several occasions Jones was seen to be a little surprised at how well dressed some of the players were at breakfast. Smith was never a part of these midnight-to-dawn forays, and Farr-Jones, who often was, never really got to know him in a social context. Smith wanted Farr-Jones's spot and the latter didn't blame him for it, particularly.

It is another old tradition in the Wallabies and it is called 'deathriding'. A practice that dare not show its face publicly, it involves all those players on the tour who wish they were in the Test team, but aren't, secretly hoping that the Test team will lose and the players in their own position play badly so as to maximise the second-stringers' chances of getting in the next time.

As the first Test began in front of a crowd of 50 000 at Velez Sarsfield in Buenos Aires, with Farr-Jones on the sidelines and Brian Smith selected ahead of him, Nick at least admits to 'half-deathriding'.

'I wanted Smith to play badly and the Wallabies to win.'

The Wallabies could only manage a 19–19 draw, and Peter

Jenkins's report in the *Australian* on 2 November noted that in a lacklustre Australian performance, 'halfback Brian Smith had an unhappy day as well and failed to provide slick service to [the] backline', while the *Sydney Morning Herald* said, 'Queenslander Brian Smith played the blindside too often from the lineout when there was a space on offer out wide and his decisive passes to five-eighth Steven James were few and far between'. The wider issue was that for the fourth game in a row the Wallabies had failed to register a victory.

There was one game left before the second Test for Nick to impress upon Jones his worthiness to be re-included—the game against Rosario on the following Tuesday. Again Farr-Jones went well. Smith had reverted to fullback for this game and acquitted himself as well as could be expected of one not accustomed to the position and who had played another hard game only three days before. In the dressing room later Jones did him no favours at all by saying something that would be repeated endlessly for the rest of the tour, and often in coming years, becoming something of a running joke among the players: 'Brian Smith, many players have played as well for Australia at fullback as you did today, but none have played better.'

For Farr-Jones, though, still not a word.

The report of the match in the *Herald*, on 5 November 1987 tells the story the way Jones saw it: 'Jones said he was disappointed in the form of deposed Test half Nick Farr-Jones who seemed to do little wrong . . .

'Brian Smith, with whom Farr-Jones was vying for the second Test halfback spot, made some nice moves at fullback, but made a couple of handling errors under little pressure.

'Smith's performance drew great praise from Jones but Argentines will be amazed if Farr-Jones's game was not good enough to win back his Test spot.'

Not as amazed as the Wallabies would have been.

'It was just unbelievable,' says one of the senior Wallabies who prefers to remain nameless. 'It was bloody obvious to us all that Nick had to come straight back into it, and equally obvious that Jonesy was still pushing for Brian, come what may.'

That night after the happy hour, as Farr-Jones and a few of the players lazed by the pool of their hotel and listened to a recording of the Melbourne Cup that they'd just received, Nick was approached by two of the Australian journalists who'd interviewed Jones after the match, and was told in private some of Jones's comments, most particularly that he had been very disappointed in Farr-Jones's game and that he thought that Smith's game had been 'one of the best ever fullback performances'.

Farr-Jones: 'Basically, the journos knew that he was trying to talk me out of the team, so the guys would write in the paper "Farr-Jones not going well" and from a distance people would think Smith was justified for my job. I went to bed pretty certain I wasn't going to make it.'

Unbeknownst to Nick at the time, however, submissions had already been made to Jones on his behalf from powerful quarters. One was from Jones's great friend and supporter Ross Turnbull, who in a telephone call from Australia told Jones that Nick had been integral to the success of the Australian team in the past and they simply had to have him.

'I'm not sure what influence that had on Alan,' Turnbull says, 'but I definitely made the call.'

The other was from Michael Hawker, the most senior player on the tour, who took it upon himself to tell Jones what the clear will of the players was. The following morning Jones called Farr-Jones to his room in the Buenos Aires Hilton to tell him two things. First that he was back in the team (with Smith out and Michael Lynagh replacing the injured Simon Poidevin as captain), and secondly that while he might have told Nick last week that he wasn't going to pick anyone who hadn't done the work, the thing was . . . he was 'going to pick Troy for this one'.

'What I want from you,' Farr-Jones remembers Jones saying, 'is not to make a song and dance about it. I don't want you to go back to the other boys and say that I've gone back on my word and I suppose contradicted myself.'

'Of course I won't, Alan.'

Troy Coker was also a great friend of Jones and after being injured in the Paraguay game had hardly been able to train. But Jones had immense confidence in him, even picking him in the Test the previous week when it was obvious to all the players that he would have to drop out, so badly was he limping. This time Jones wanted him again, despite the continuing obvious seriousness of the injury. What footballers call a badly buggered knee was in this case a torn anterior cruciate ligament, and Jones had been advised by Greg Craig that Coker was only 30 per cent fit.

'That surely means, then,' Jones said, 'that he'll be right to play full bore for 27 minutes.'

'No,' Craig insisted, 'that means he's just as likely to break down completely in the first minute and will never be able to play at 100 per cent for this game.'

Eventually Jones gave in when Coker broke down in the first training of the Test team and had to again drop out of the side, but it was getting ever more bizarre by the minute. Brian Smith was clearly disappointed with his sacking in favour of Farr-Jones, and he was later to tell fellow Wallaby Ian Williams, when they were at Oxford University the following year, that Jones had told him the reason he had been dropped was 'not because Farr-Jones is better than you in himself, but because the other players at the moment play better when he is there'.

After all this, the worries and the turmoil, the end of a long year and with home beckoning, the Wallabies ended up being thumped in the second Test, almost predictably, by the score of 27–19. Though Australia was leading 13–3 at one stage in the first half, the great Puma five-eighth, Hugo Porta, chose that day of all days to play one of his greatest games, scoring 21 points for his team through no fewer than five penalty goals and two field goals on the run.

Jones was at least gracious in the dressing room afterwards, being quoted in the *Sun* as saying, 'It was a very important and proud day for Argentine rugby. It was very disappointing for us, but it must be good for the game here. We've had our share of wins in recent times, but this year we've had to become accustomed to defeat.'

Indeed. For the Wallabies it was now five games in a row without a win. On the morning after the second Test there was a breakfast in the Wallabies' Buenos Aires hotel, at which Jones spoke. In a way the meeting was to impart Jones's version of what is known in the Wallabies as the Tour Secrets Act—that what goes on tour stays on tour. Usually, the TSA is applied to amorous conquests while away, but in this instance Jones wanted the Wallabies to apply it to all of the tour itself.

'As I remember it,' Farr-Jones says, 'Alan's message was, "Let's not go home and break up and tell stories about each other—let's stick together. The people out there are the wolves—they're trying to get at us, they're trying to divide us, they're trying to be critical of us. Let's stay very much a tight-knit sort of team, hang in there together, and I know it's been hard but if we can do that we can come back bigger and better than ever next year."'

The irony of which was not lost on Farr-Jones. In his mind a lot of what had divided them in the first place, the schisms that had caused so many of their problems, was Jones's favouring of one group over another. Asking for unity was a bit much now. For followers of the fluctuating fortunes of Bob Dwyer and Alan Jones, the irony was exquisite. Back in 1984 Jones had been installed as the new Australian coach at the expense of Dwyer, after Dwyer had managed to guide the Wallabies to only a loss and a draw on tour in France. Now, four years later, almost exactly the same scenario was being played out in reverse—except that instead of failing in France the Wallabies were failing in Argentina.

Alan Jones, with the Wallabies, flew back to Australia to be greeted by the telling headline in the *Australian*—'JONES RETURNS TO FIND RIVALS' DAGGERS DRAWN.' The article by Bret Harris, opened: 'The Australian rugby union team has travelled down the Argentine and the daggers have been sharpened for Wallaby el supremo Alan Jones . . .'

Ne'er a truer word written. Despite the recent string of losses, for the last four years Jones had been incredibly successful in amassing an unheard of record with the Wallabies, of nineteen victories, one draw and only eight losses. But at cost. Being 'unapologetic in the pursuit of victory' had indeed earned Jones a lot of victories over the years, but it had also left an awful lot of people extremely angry that they hadn't been apologised to.

The result was that when he stumbled, as he had now, guiding the Wallabies through five Test matches without a single victory to show for it, there were too many people willing, as Harris put it, to 'stick the sharpened daggers into Jones'.

Chief among these, as was to be expected, was Bob Dwyer

himself. In the same article in the *Australian*, Dwyer succinctly set out the thrust of the attacks he would be making on Jones in the coming weeks.

There was the way the Wallabies had been playing: 'The indecision and lack of positive play in midfield is hampering the backrow's ability to maintain pressure at the breakdown.' Dwyer also raised the injustice of his own dumping from the Wallaby coaching job in the first place, with the implication that Jones had only capitalised on his own early good work: 'There was absolutely no reason to change coaches. If some genius had been on the horizon, it might have been different.

'When I was coaching Australia it was a perfect example of a team just starting to get into the swing of approaching the game the right way.'

And of course Dwyer also nagged at Jones's true point of vulnerability, the Wallabies' recent record: 'We've just gone five Tests without a win and I can't remember that happening before.

'Tempo [Bob Templeton] lost the job after losing three Tests in a row and I never even lost two in a row.'

Dwyer finished with the rather noble, but false, 'I don't care about the politics of the situation. I've got something to offer and if they don't want me, that's their decision.'

In fact, he would work just as hard lobbying as Jones had four years earlier. Phone calls, letters, the calling-in of old debts, talks with those Wallaby players who were most particularly in favour of his return, constant approaches to members of the media covering the story, trying to put his spin on their coverage.

He was helped in this, at least indirectly, by none other than Mark Ella, who came out against Jones on Sydney radio station 2KY just before Christmas. Ella had retired early in his career because he no longer wished to play under Jones, so this was hardly surprising, yet the tenor of his comments caused something of a stir at the time.

'I honestly feel the players will not allow him to coach them next year,' Ella said. 'I think Mr Jones is just too busy to coach the Australian side. He's got so many other interests . . . rugby has really suffered under his hands because of those commitments.'

Ella was also critical of Jones's selection policies on the recent tour to Argentina: 'Brian Smith and Troy Coker are certainly very good players but nowhere near the standard of, say, Nick Farr-Jones or Steve Cutler. Yet he pushes these guys to the forefront all the time.'

Such utterings strengthened Dwyer's challenge, but he was not the only one seeking the job. Paul Dalton also took the opportunity to throw his hat into the ring, as did former Australian coach Bob Templeton, though he withdrew just before the ballot. In the face of it all, Jones essayed to play with a straight bat, falling back on his overall record rather than his record of the last four months, being quoted in an article by Greg Growden to the effect that, 'We've lost eight Tests in thirty, and if that is the source of complaint then Australian rugby is hard to please.

'It is a fairly imposing international record we have amassed over the past four years and if I don't say that no-one else will. The best judges of all this are the players—and you should ask them.'

Two journalists, Peter Jenkins in Sydney and Jim Tucker in Brisbane, took Jones at his word and asked the players, every single one of them, so as to publish the results in the form of a player poll.

Farr-Jones got his call in early February.

Jenkins: 'Look, this is all off the record, and it will never come out what you say, but who do you support for the Australian coaching job, Alan Jones or Bob Dwyer?'

Farr-Jones: 'I think Jones has probably had a very good run and it might possibly be time for a bit of a change, but on the other hand . . .'

Jenkins: 'Who do you support. Jones or Dwyer?'

(*Pause.*)

Jenkins: 'Nick?'

Farr-Jones: 'Dwyer.'

It did not come easily to Farr-Jones, to do something that would help end the reign of Alan Jones, but he knew that it really was time for a change. Farr-Jones was to play no further part in the election process, refusing to talk to the press or to be drawn into the player factions as they jostled for position behind one coach or the other. Not that the faction behind Jones was particularly large. In the journalists' poll only nine of the thirty-one players contacted who had been a part of the World Cup campaign or the Argentinian tour said they would like Jones to return. One of the few players on Jones's side to stand up and be counted was Simon Poidevin, quoted in an article by David Lord in the *Sun* just before Christmas as saying, 'I'm in an invidious position, because Bob [Dwyer] is my club coach and does a great job and Alan [Jones] is my Wallaby coach and he too does a great job. [But] my loyalty is to Alan Jones.'

Too little, too late.

In the end the result was a foregone conclusion even before the vote was taken.

Jones went down.

While living and playing in France, I was still returning to Australia for three or four months every year, still hoping to crack the representative scene and force my way back into the Wallabies. I was mixed in my success in this endeavour.

NOTHING MATTERS, AS LONG AS WE 'MOIDER' AUCKLAND

I heard recently that Phil Scarr is back to eating solids again, which is great. If only I wasn't still haunted by the memory of what caused his many medical afflictions in the first place . . .

He was playing his first big representative game, on the wing for New South Wales against the mighty 1988 Auckland side at Eden Park. I was in the same side, and about midway through the first half we were taking such a drubbing from the swarming hordes of Aucklanders that I decided not only that something had to be done but also that I was just the man for the job.

Thus, entirely ignoring our halfback Nick Farr-Jones, who was screaming for the ball so it seemed his tonsils might very possibly fall out, I rolled from the back of the maul with every honest intention of heading upfield, taking the battle right into the teeth of those dastardly Aucklanders.

But . . . on second thoughts, maybe it would be better to head across-field instead. The Auckland forwards still looked a bit *willing*, and I thought there might be a break in the traffic a bit further out, where I could do even more damage to the brutes.

Nothing. No break. Just huge Aucklanders coming down hard from everywhere. I kept running across-field regardless, all the while dummying as if I might pass to one of my own backs—to confuse the defence, like.

Presently, though, there was only one of my backs left to whom I could possibly unload the ball, and that was Phil Scarr, out there on the wing, and . . . and . . . what was that? He was trying to signal something to me. What did he mean by shaking his head and waving his arms around in front of his body like that? Did he mean he *didn't* want me to pass the ball to him? Well, I never.

It was just about then that, out of the corner of my eye, I spied the extremely formidable figure of Scarr's opposing winger, Va'aiga 'Inga the Winger' Tuigamala, all 110 kilograms of him, flying flat-out straight for us and about to launch himself like an Exocet missile. His only momentary hesitation was in wondering whether I was going to keep or pass the ball . . .

Well, it was obvious, wasn't it? It was either the young 'un or me. I decided to give Phil the pass, even as Tuigamala tracked the ball and made his own commitment.

Even now I think if I hadn't got the ball into Scarr's hands in the absolute nick of time, the fearsome Auckland winger would surely have been sent off and spent a long time suspended, because, as it turned out, he was totally committed to the tackle even before the ball got to Phil. And I also think, in passing, that in the long and glorious rugby career of Tuigamala, it probably still stands as one of the most devastating tackles he ever made.

Whatever, somewhere between one-hundredth and two-hundredths of a second after I got the ball into Scarr's hands, Inga the Winger hit him like an exploding torpedo in the chest, with a force that rattled even *my* teeth and, when the smoke had cleared, all we could see was Scarr's left foot coming out at rather an odd angle from beneath Inga's body. The Aucklander then slowly got up, a little shaken with the force of his own tackle, and we all looked down aghast to see if there possibly could be any survivors from such a hit.

There were, but only just.

Sorry about that, Phil.

Anyway, as I said, he's now back on solids and is apparently doing quite well, so that's the main thing, what? Forgive and forget—that's what I always say. Admittedly it's not much to have on your rugby tombstone—'FitzSimons once delivered one of the great hospital passes of the modern age'—but there didn't seem like a lot else that I could do.

HONEST, Phil!

In one week in 1988 I twice played the All Blacks in sides that conceded a total of 126 points. It was a nightmare as black as the ensuing bruises on my thighs. The sports editor insisted I do a story on what it was like inside an All Black maul. 'Pretty bloody grim' was the short answer.

LIFE WITH AN ALL BLACK ON YOUR BACK

You know what I really hate? I really hate it when you're playing for New South Wales against the All Blacks, you dive on a loose ball, a maul forms over you and you have to watch helplessly as a couple of men dressed in black use their steel-studded leather boots to write their initials all over your lily-white legs—and your own guys can't quite get there to save you.

Geez, I hate that. I also hate it when you're invited to play for Victoria, your scrum collapses . . . but theirs doesn't and then you will swear, I mean you will positively *swear* that a giant black centipede has just danced a jig on your back.

Geez I hate that too.

Of all the varied sensations and impressions that one experiences on the inside of an All Black forward conglomeration, the most memorable are the All Black feet. Few players finish a game against them without lasting impressions on their backs and legs, and my games against them have been no exception.

In an upright position and pushing against the New Zealanders in the rucks and mauls, one sees their feet whirring around, spitting mud out behind them. Fall into that maelstrom and it feels like you are caught tying your shoelaces when the bulls of Pamplona pass through.

Sure, it is legal, most of it, but one is no less a sore little Vegemite at the end of it for all that. So much for the sight and feel of the inside of the All Black pack. Smell? I guess the All Blacks smell fairly normal in a rugby sort of way. Eau de mud, sweat and vaseline . . . that sort of thing. Though during my last game against them, my nose got so badly broken that I could not even thmell my own thocks let alone the inthide of the maul. I do seem to remember the usual pungent odour emanating from them just before it smashed. The sort of thing you might sprinkle on yourself if you were going on a date with a gorilla.

Sound? Groans and grunts of effort, exchanges of imprecations as the two front rows hit in the scrum, the sound of flesh hitting flesh at speed, the *ooooph* as a player fringing the ruck gets hit by an opposing player launched from ten metres out. If there is one difference to the usual sound score it is that there always seems to be a lot of chatter coming from the All Black side of the maul.

The All Black forwards might often be described as a 'machine', but there is always a lot of communication going on between them. Not only the fairly standard 'Drive it!' and 'Take it up!' but often the more specific calls of 'Here's the ball!', 'Rip his hands off it!', 'Roll it left!' and 'Get him!'. My own favourite All Black communiqué came from a particularly burly forward (even by All Black standards) towards the end of the Victorian game. I had rather mildly been trying to scratch my own initials into the leg of one of the All Blacks who had previously done it to me when their loose-head prop, Kevin Borovich, caught sight of me.

Looking my way with wonder, he demanded for all the world as if he really wanted to know: 'What the HELL do you think you are doing?' He looked so genuinely appalled it was all I could do to stop myself from apologising.

In retrospect I am glad I did not bother. In the next ruck I received some unsolicited souvenir autographs from the entire All Black pack that I will be able to admire for weeks.

Overall, a unique experience, if not altogether as pleasant as taking tea in the afternoon sun.

With plenty of milk in it.

At least by this time my international experience was expanding, if not yet at Test level. In June of 1989, I think it was, I had the pleasure of playing for the Australia B team against the Lions, the highly prestigious selection of the best players from England, Wales, Ireland and Scotland. It was quite something to cross swords with the best of British, as I recall.

PLAYING THE LIONS

'Aahhrrr, it's yoooo argenn, yer big oaf!!!' John Jeffrey, the Scottish breakaway, screamed at me as we clashed once more in the middle of a muddy maul. 'Coom orn then laddie, let's goo fer it!'

Which meant, I surmised, that he thought a bit of biffo might be the order of the day. I did too, but was rather nonplussed at his extension of a formal invitation. This is a far from usual procedure in international rugby matches. The All Blacks' signal for the fight to begin is usually a crashing blow from a big right hand. The French and Italians tend to send their fight invitations wrapped in a swinging boot. We Australians like to yell things such as, 'Oh *yeah!?!* Well cop this then!' before setting to.

But this was the British Lions. While calling them *gentlemen* would be an exaggeration, they seemed to be not a bad equivalent in rugby terms. Attempts at underhanded physical intimidation were not part of their repertoire—in this match at least. While they tackled hard and rucked ferociously, no other dastardly derring-do emerged. A fight could occur if the occasion warranted, but playing simple hard rugby seemed to be their main preoccupation.

Typically, just as Jeffrey and I were squaring off for the first round of our own bout, he happened to glimpse the ball in British hands upfield and, without a word, suddenly tore off in support. See what I mean? Any self-respecting All Black would have somehow made time in his busy schedule to give me a quick smack in the chops before leaving.

This *mentalité Britannique*, as the French refer to it (usually with a groan), also showed in other aspects of their game. Somewhere in their collective psyche it is obviously writ large in concrete that 'Thou shalt keep it simple, thou shalt keep it conventional'.

While the parameters of the conventional for the French stretch clear from one horizon to the other, for the Brits they go only about the width of the field. As long as the Falkland Islanders agreed to it, you could stake what remains of the British Empire on the Lions' fullback kicking for the line when in possession of the ball behind his own 22-metre line. No attempts to do the unexpected. No quick put-ins to the lineout. No tricky penalty moves. Overall, no razzamatazz. Safe. Simple. Conventional. Even such relatively standard fare as dummy passes, chip kicks and switch attacks seemed entirely absent from their play. So, as the game went on, we Australians learnt that the lines of the Lions' attack would come at us straight along the main highways, with no sorties out into the jungle, no tricky flanking movements, no snipers and no roving commando assaults. It was 'straight up the guts' as we say in the business. Not that it was boring, though. No sooner had we forwards set up satisfactory roadblocks to stop their highway advances, than the wretches would call in an air attack, invariably with bombers.

Once hard up against our immovable green barricade, captain Dean Richards would have the ball sent back to five-eighth Craig Chalmers, who would hoist it on high to come bombing down behind our main defensive lines. The retreat would then sound, and we forwards would have to hightail it back through the low country to form a new roadblock downfield, where the whole process would be repeated again.

But that wasn't the worst of it. The worst of it was their moral duplicity. Time and again, when we had finally managed to get the ball on our side of the maul we would discover a Lion, by now under the same muddy cloak as us, skulking around and trying to get the ball under the false pretences of being an Australian. Some of the guys were in favour of having the next Lion found doing this shot on the spot as a fifth columnist, but in the end calmer heads prevailed and we found a more moderate system.

For the last twenty minutes of the game no ball was passed in a maul unless the receiver could answer a question from the passer along the lines of 'How do you spell Vegemite?' and 'What are Bob Hawke's middle names?'. Any time we heard 'Vege-*what*?' or 'Bob *who*?' in reply, we smashed 'em. That put paid to their little caper. But the Lions' larger caper, of playing hard, risk-free rugby very well, should be a lot more difficult to stop in coming weeks as they become progressively more match-hardened. Stay tuned.

At last, the breakthrough I had long been waiting for. In 1989, after five years out of the Australian team, I was chosen by Bob Dwyer and his selectors to go on a Wallaby tour of Canada and France.

TOURING WITH THE TRIBE I—FRANCE

In a hotel courtyard in Lille, in far northern France, a sombre group of Australians is gathered around Bob Templeton, tribal elder of the Wallabies.

'They shall grow not old, as we that are left grow old/Age shall not weary them nor the years condemn . . .' recites Templeton amid the bowed heads, as curious curtains draw back all around.

It is 11 a.m. on 11 November 1989. Some fifty kilometres south is the Somme Valley, where lies the largest collection of Australian war graves outside of Gallipoli. In four hours time, half of this huddled group will go into battle against the French in the second Test.

Of course, this sporting skirmish will be trivial in comparison with the great massacres of the World Wars. And yet, without wishing to lay it on too thickly, there are parallels. Like the soldiers who left Sydney Harbour for France three-quarters of a century ago, the Wallabies have become comrades in arms nearing completion of what in many ways has been an almost military term of duty. Behind them lie six weeks of intense training, travelling and competing, wearing their country's colours across three continents. For six weeks, they have lived together, trained together, played together and fought together.

A collection of thirty individuals has been welded into the latest generation of a famous warrior tribe, with its own rituals, idiosyncrasies and exclusive warrior rules. To outsiders, some of these rites may appear anachronistic, shallow, even silly. Too bad. What the tribal elders have been doing is creating an insider ethos, making each player feel part of a team, and, more importantly, making them aware that they are inheritors of a long tradition.

It started far from France, on a Monday in early October when thirty of the best rugby players in the country, culled from

the offices and backblocks of eastern Australia, gathered in a
North Sydney hotel to be issued their kits and to put in three
days of hard training before flying to Canada. An old rugby hand
had said to me years before that, in his considered opinion, rugby
tours were 'the highest form of life on Earth'. Even allowing for
hyperbole, he wasn't far off the mark.

What? Sweaty men torturing themselves is meant to be a high
form of life? Damn right, but only because there's a lot more to
it than mere rugby.

'One, two, three, four, hit! Back. One, two, three, four, hit!' In a
little harbourside park at Cammeray, Wallaby coach Bob Dwyer
is putting the squad through its paces on the tackle bags, as one
after another, in military precision, we line up to punish these
infernal sacks of cotton. Of all the physical drills before departure,
the tackle-bag drill is by far the most exhausting. Not coincidentally, it is also the one we do most often.

'At least,' we console ourselves, 'they won't be able to take
these heavy tackle bags to Canada and France.' Error. Three days
later, we are appalled to see, while we are filing into the economy
section of the jumbo jet bound for Canada, the same wretched
tackle bags receiving first-class treatment from Dwyer, Templeton
and Andy Conway, the manager of the side.

We get the message: on this tour we are going to end up not
just physically fit, but mentally toughened.

'So guys, these are the two packs I want to compete against each
other in the lineouts.' Dwyer reads the names. 'Daly, Kearns,
McKenzie . . .' It is a painful moment. For the first time, instead
of being an integral thirty, we have been divided, halved into two
teams of fifteen. The selection process has begun. Suddenly
team-mates have become rivals. It is obvious to us that one line
of players is the provisional Test team; the other is likely to play
only the midweek games.

There are long faces in my pack. If the Test side were picked
tomorrow, we would be mere spectators. For the rest of the
training, there is just a little bit of venom in our tackles. Refusing
to acknowledge that we are in fact the B-Team, we call the other

provisional side the 'Bombers' just to spite them. Soon we have a name for ourselves: the 'Assassins' . . . the A-Team.

It is a piece of fun, but there is a serious side to it, too. Inexorably, the dotted line that is drawn down the middle of the squad when Dwyer reads the names becomes a little clearer and a little darker with each successive training session. Which is as it should be, from a rugby point of view. For it is precisely this internal competition which will give us the steel to face the French when the real Test comes.

In Fudpuckers Hamburger Grill in Edmonton, Canada, on the first leg of the tour, four Wallabies knock back hamburgers and discuss the opening match played the day before. Three of us have never played a Test, while one, the hooker Tom Lawton, is a veteran of no fewer than forty-one of them over the last six years. I mention how moved I had been the day before, when we fifteen Wallabies had stood arm in arm before the match and sung the Australian national anthem for the first time on a foreign field.

Tom snorts. To our looks of surprise, he narrows his eyes and replies: 'Mate, I'll tell you what "moving" is. Moving will be if you play a *Test* match in France . . . and they play the Australian national anthem and the fifteen of you can only just hear the tune from the band against the voices of the 70 000 Froggies who are screaming for your blood, but you all belt it out anyway . . . and you line up to receive the kick-off, and you can see this little sliver of white coming straight at you end over end like it's in slow motion and you take it, and get belted by four of them, but your mates close ranks to protect you and knock them backwards and you form the first scrum with your blood just trickling down your nose onto your lip and your eyebrow's swelling up and you can see the grass about three inches from your eyeballs and you feel this massive heave coming from behind you . . . and that . . . *that* is what "moving" is, mate.'

Throughout this whole magnificent speech (personally, I put it right up there with Lincoln's battlefield address at Gettysburg), and for perhaps ten seconds afterwards, we are totally silent. The unspoken thought is: 'Will we, too, know what all that is like?'

We're in a hotel in Toulouse. The day has been spent flying across Canada and the Atlantic. Most of the Wallabies are 'shot ducks' and retire to bed early. Three of the Wallabies, though, are having a quiet drink in the hotel bar when they decide to investigate music coming from a nearby ballroom. *Voilà!* A full-blown wedding. Almost instantly, the groom recognises one of the players as a particularly well-known Wallaby and immediately finds a place at his table for the three Australians. Into the wild night they go until 5 a.m., knocking back Bollinger and battling jet lag and eventually drowning in sheer rollicking adrenalin. Between the Wallabies and the wedding party there has been almost a total lack of linguistic comprehension, but to hear them tell it, no-one really noticed.

Tours are not just about tackle bags. It is about two o'clock in the morning. Nick, Tom and I are in a miserably dark and gloomy back alley, looking for a nightclub that is rumoured to be in these parts. It is slightly spooky. For the last three hours we have been loudly solving all the world's problems in a nearby bar. It has just shut and we are staggering . . . only very slightly. Suddenly, up ahead in the gloom we see three figures approaching. Enemy? Friend? Muggers? In this dark alley, in a foreign country, we close ranks marginally and keep moving forward, with muscles tensed, to meet our fate. 'Tom, *mon ami!*' a voice rings out. It proves to be Pierre Berbizier, the French rugby captain, with two of his friends. They, too, are looking for the nightclub. Berbizier knows Tom well from their recent World XV tour of South Africa and shakes his hand effusively. Me too. We have played against each other many times in the French domestic competition over the past four years and have had a few drunken soirees together.

   His reaction to Nick is interesting. Not only is Nick his opposing captain in the Test match due in a few weeks, but he will also be his most direct adversary of the match, as they both play halfback. After the most perfunctory of all possible handshakes, Berbizier somehow manages to place his body in such a position that Nick is excluded from the emerging circle, while he talks *dix-neuf* to the dozen to Tom and me. It is a direct snub, and doesn't he know it. In the dim light, I can just see the expression on Nick's face which says, sort of deathly calm-like, 'Pierre, for this slight you will be buried'.

Never a truer word unspoken.

'Here are the room lists,' says one of the 'duty boys' as the bus pulls into Clermont-Ferrand. 'Lawton and Crowley in room 105, FitzSimons and Williams in room 107, Junee and . . .' There is a groan from the front of the bus as Ian Williams, a relentlessly neat (read *ridiculously* neat) and tidy winger from the Eastwood club in Sydney, realises he will be rooming with me over the next few days. He makes his displeasure known to the whole bus.

'But Ian,' I later tell him, 'I'm different now, I've changed, I swear it!' He threatens to divide the room with yellow insulating tape into two clear halves, never giving me or mine permission to cross into his half. Foolishly, he eventually believes me, and by the next morning my dirty clothes have washed up on his shores, together with football boots, old socks, jockstraps and all sorts of filthy paraphernalia, as he sits marooned on the island that is his bed. 'Roomies' change at every stop and team management allocates the pairs based on some hidden psychological plan to form the unbreakable bonds that will forge a Test match victory.

'Here are the room lists . . . FitzSimons and McKenzie room 256 . . .' This time it is me who groans. Just before the team is to be announced for the first Test, I have been placed in a room with Ewen McKenzie. Not that I have anything personal against Ewen; it is just that he has been injured for the past week and cannot possibly play in the first Test. Once again it seems that I am a 'shot duck' because the tradition is that Test players always room together before the match to feed off each other's building adrenalin. For the next four hours my miserable room allocation is coursing through my mind until the actual moment the Test team is announced.

When my name is eventually called out to partner Rod McCall in the second row, the world shifts into slow motion. Each syllable of my name comes as a separate sentence. I remember little of the next twenty minutes other than handshakes, congratulations and the tune from the Swan Lager ad—'They said you'd never make it . . .' For all the joy felt by some of us, though, there is great disappointment in others and we head off to training as studies in opposite extremes of emotions.

'Australians all let us rejoice, for we are young and free.' Tim Gavin, the lock of the team, starts absolutely belting it out, as we fifteen Australians stand in an all-embracing circle, ready to do battle in the first Test against the best that the haughty, strutting Gauls can offer.

Something about Tim's passion for the anthem communicates itself to the rest of the Test team and from a merely enthusiastic rendition, we pass to a lung-bursting and slightly crazy rendition, which makes up in volume what it lacks in harmony.

The start of the Test itself was just like Tom said it would be . . . the anthem, the little sliver of white coming slowly end over end, the blood trickling down the nose onto the lip, the whole shebang. Tom was right. It really was moving.

But this is the beginning of Test rugby for me; the first time it feels really different from other important matches. We are not going to just win this one for 'junior' or for our club or state, for whoever or whatever, but rather this time, above all, we are playing for the very nation from which we have sprung.

Sure, it may sound like romanticised claptrap from the other side of the world, but for better or for worse that is definitely the feeling among us. We are resolved to either win or to go down with all guns blazing.

Whatever it is, there is no doubt that the fifteen Australians all have large lumps in their throats before kick-off. The whistle blows and it is on. Five-eighth Michael Lynagh puts the ball right on the money, and if we don't actually recover the ball from the kick-off, we at least deliver a telegram to the French front door, saying that if they want to win the game, they will have to bleed for it. Macho crap? Absolutely. But we deliver the telegram all the same.

At the end of the game, amazingly, we have won by the record-breaking score of 32–15. No foreign team has beaten the French in France by such a margin since 1905.

When the referee blows his whistle to signal the end (as I write this, the hairs on the back of my neck are standing up),

we jump, holler and hug. Five of us crab-walk together towards
the back-rower from Quirindi, Dave Carter, who is standing alone
and dazed with blood pouring from his brow. Then we were six.
If this is Test rugby, give me more of it.

Total uproar. It is the happy hour after the Test. The happy hour
is an institution after each Wallaby game. All the touring party
gather in a closed room to partake in secret rites and rituals
which it is totally forbidden for all non-Wallabies to know. (Sorry.)

The French have a phrase for it—*mettre à l'agonie*—and it means,
in the rugby context, putting so much pressure on your opponents that it is an agony for them . . . and scoring should
naturally follow. Sure enough, this is exactly what the French do
to us for fifteen minutes in the second half of the second Test.
We tackle them red raw, but they just keep coming.
   At half-time it had seemed so different. We had been leading
13–6 and had dreams of becoming the first team to whitewash
the French on their soil. Suddenly they awaken and play absolutely brilliant rugby, driving constantly forward in wave after
wave and never once making a mistake. It is, in fact, agony.
   Even now it is a mystery to me where they got the incredible
energy in those minutes . . . while we are tackling to exhaustion
. . . as well as the amazing concentration they needed to get it
right. Even allowing for the soil of Mother France beneath their
feet, which traditionally gives the French powers above and
beyond mortal men, it is an impressive display.
   By the time the storm is over, they are leading 25–13. A late
try for us brings it to 25–19, but it is too little too late. The
whistle blows.
   Having explored the outer frontiers of joy last week, this
time we've jumped back over the wall and patrol the edges of
darkness and disappointment. We are at least a little com-
forted by the knowledge that we haven't actually blown it so
much as lost to a side that played absolutely superbly at the
crucial time.

The final lunch of the final day of the tour we are in a restaurant
in Paris. It is the last gathering of the tribe before we go our

separate ways—some home to Australia, some to England and some to Italy to play in the off-season. After six weeks fighting countless battles with and against each other, we are nothing if not intimate. The final ritual is performed. The names of each of the tour party are put into a hat, and drawn out two at a time. On the clock, each of the two people whose names have been drawn out must talk about the other for no more than a minute. Amid shouts, cheers, jocular jeers and perhaps even the odd tear, the deed is done. The bus departs. The tribe disbands.

The following year, the Wallabies went on a full-blown three-Test tour of New Zealand.

TOURING WITH THE TRIBE II—NEW ZEALAND

Way back in 1975 when the British Lions team to New Zealand had completed their arduous six-week tour, the story goes that at the instant the jumbo left terra firma on the way back to the blessed home countries, there was an outbreak of spontaneous applause. New Zealand was behind them and falling further away all the time, God Save the Queen. Crank this kite up and let's get home.

Fifteen years on, that story was told to the 1990 Wallabies and raised not a single quizzical glance nor even a mildly surprised look. We understood perfectly. They just don't make tours tougher than this one.

In the array of possible rugby achievements for international teams, beating New Zealand in a Test series is right up there on the summit of Everest . . . and commensurate efforts are required. Sure, there'll be good times and bad times, as there are on every tour, but on no other tour are the hills so steep, the winds so cold, and the crevasses so potentially deep as they are on this one.

In early July, as a touring party of thirty-five players and officials, we set out for the distant mountain. Touchdown, Auckland airport. If ever there was a testament to the powers of modern technology, this is it. Flying blind, the pilots managed to bring the plane right from the sunny skies of the lower stratosphere down through the greatest rainstorm since Noah, right onto what we hope and pray is a runway.

This is not rain as in 'raining' or wind as in 'windy' . . . it is lash as in 'lashing' and scream as in 'screaming'. While starkly impressive to us at the time, by the end of the tour a storm like this would occasion little comment. Only, like Pavlov's dogs, we would start to look for our boots, because if there is wind and rain outside, it's a sure bet that training must be soon. Bewdy. Lemme at that mud. Welcome to New Zealand.

And so it's north to the town of Hamilton in the province of Waikato. Whatever else you may say about New Zealand, it surely has some of the most spectacular scenery on Earth, and even those small parts of it that have been developed have the 'Approved by Mother Nature' logo pressed upon them. The Waikato team are known locally as the 'Mooloos', presumably a reference to the importance of cows to the economy, and the traditional method for encouraging the team is to ring cowbells (without a word of a lie) throughout the game.

As the countdown to the kick-off moves into bare minutes, the packed crowd becomes increasingly restless with delicious expectation. Three minutes, two minutes, one minute and counting. With the whistle to start the game, the crowd lets out a collective, satisfied 'oomph!' and happily settles down to watch.

In New Zealand, where rugby is as much a part of the blood as white and red cells, the crowds don't simply watch games so much as *feed* off them. Ergo, the kind of half-starved look in the eyes of the Waikato crowd before the game starts fades at the end into a sort of glazed, well-fed look. They are happy, as their team has won and won well.

Our team has lost one that we probably should have won. Dammit.

We've lost Bobby. The news is disastrous. In the first half of the game against Auckland, Brendan 'Bobby' Nasser, the breakaway who comes to the Wallabies from a dentistry practice in Queensland, has fractured his cheekbone. Preliminary diagnosis is that the damage is such that he will have to immediately return to Brisbane for an operation. This news hits hard, partly because we have lost a good warrior for the coming crucial battles and partly because we are conscious that a good part of the Wallabies' collective soul resides in his gentle breast.

At a team meeting at the hotel, Bobby, back from the hospital and with an icepack on his cheek, manages to get out a few choked words wishing us well for the rest of the trip. If we were feeling lowly before, we feel positively wretched now. As I recall, no-one in the room actually sheds tears, but there is no doubt that if all those lumps in the throats were to be stacked end on end, there would have definitely been five out and out bawlers.

Scrum training. The wind and mud and rain. A godforsaken field on the west coast of the South Island. 'Fitzy, your back isn't straight, your feet are too far back and you're absolutely *ruining* our scrum,' forwards coach Bob Templeton is screaming at me through the gale. This piece of information comes as no surprise to me. There is something about some guys which makes them excellent captains . . . and about others which makes them destined to weave their way through opposing backlines. Unfortunately, there is something about yours truly which makes coaches love to pick on me whenever it comes to scrum training. Ever since, as a little boy, I first pulled on a pair of boots, it has been my lot to accept full blame for the scrum whenever anything goes wrong. That is my cross and I bear it with as much grace as I can under the circumstances. But it is hard.

On this occasion, Tempo has decided we need another good half-hour of scrum training in an attempt to get it (and most particularly me) right. The mud below, the grey above, the wind behind, my head strangled between two sets of incredibly muddy and gritty thighs . . . why, oh why couldn't I have been a cricketer? They never have to go through this hell.

The morning of the First Test breaks over the Australians gathered in the trenches. For those playing, there is mixed in with all other thoughts a very acute awareness of just how long it is until the battle commences. 'In just five hours and forty minutes, I'll be out there.' 'Eighty minutes of play, only eighty minutes. Make each one count.' '*Hit ! Hit ! Hit !*' 'Scrums: I gotta get my shoulder right on his hammer.' 'Aggression, aggression, aggression.'

'Whaddya mean you're feeling tense? This is absolute child's play compared to Gallipoli. Think of that and give it everything. Five hours, twenty-three minutes to go . . .'

Playing Test matches is a big deal. Playing Test matches against the All Blacks, to give them their due, is the biggest deal of all. Even when you feel you are holding three or four aces, it is still a big deal.

Of the game, I now remember perhaps only two minutes of the eighty. A first scrum where it felt as if an errant bulldozer had wandered into their pack . . . but our scrum holds. A kick-off where I am able to get a good hit on the All Black captain, Gary Whetton. A barely missed tackle from which they score immediately.

And Kieran Crowley, the All Black fullback, running after our captain Nick Farr-Jones, yelling: 'Mate! Mate! Mate! Pass me the ball, mate.' It's the old impersonate-an-Australian-on-the-field-by-yelling, 'Mate'-at-him-over-his-shoulder-and-hope-he'll-pass-you-the-ball trick. Nick was too smart by half. Ultimately, I remember defeat. You guessed it again: it tasted bitter.

Barely three minutes into the Wallabies' tour game against Auckland at Eden Park, the All Black centre Bernie McCahill got the ball and prepared to run a 'crash-ball' into the Wallaby backline. In reply Tim Horan crouched and steeled himself to make the tackle, when just to his right a flying black flash launched and exploded just in front of him. Over the next two years Horan would through force of habit get used to that happening, although this first time it gave him quite a turn. It was Willie Ofahengaue doing what Willie did best—tackling an opposition player so hard that other players swore they could hear the teeth rattle.

McCahill was sent flying backwards, losing the ball in the process. The World Cup campaign had found itself a back-rower and another piece fitted into the puzzle.

'Bubba' is running up the snowy mountain in three-metre 'moon hops', as on the deck Wallabies are collapsing in fits of laughter. We are at the ski resort at the top of Mount Hutt the day after the first Test, and just what is needed has occurred—something so hilarious that for seconds at a time the misery of defeat is forgotten.

Undeterred by our lack of skiing equipment, Bubba, aka Matt Ryan, our slightly rotund prop, puts a shovel over one shoulder, attaches the handle to the bunny ski rope gripped between his thighs and trundles off up the mountain. It is pure comic genius, reaching even greater heights when he eventually reappears, roaring down the mountain on his shovel and riding that nag until it drops. Definitely one of those 'you had to be there' stories, but it was something to see.

Dropped. For the second Test, myself and four others have been omitted from the line-up in an effort to come up with a solution to the growing All Black problem. Having given away three penalties in the second half of the first Test, which the All Black five-eighth Grant Fox promptly slotted for nine points, I'd disappeared from serious contention. The Wallabies had gone on to lose by only six points and there was suddenly a big opening in the jigsaw puzzle for a second-rower who didn't give away stupid penalties. We are all suitably devastated and stagger singly off to our rooms to stare at the walls for a while and, with pure black malice, call the wrath of the rugby gods upon those who have done us down.

'Hear me oh great Thor, for I beseech thee/May the mud of New Zealand swallow them whole/May the goalposts fall upon them/May they never be allowed to forget the venal sins they have visited upon me this day.' This sort of routine works well in solitude, but after half an hour or so we know we need to pool our venom to properly maintain the rage . . . it is time for the Tearing Down Ceremony.

The TDC is something of an institution on all international tours; those who have been dropped for Test matches get together in private (all of the so-called Test players are banned) and proceed to tear down anything and everything involved even remotely with their demise.

This particular TDC is a great success. It is cathartic—even as the rage builds, it is being released, and by the following morning you can almost bring yourself to choke out 'good morning' to one of the selectors. Almost, but not quite. The ingrates. Trouble is, we lose the Second Test. Gloom. Doom. Seemingly.

'Come quickly, you gotta see this!' Paul Carozza, the Wallaby winger (and my room-mate for the New Plymouth leg of the tour), has burst into the room to give me news from 'the front' at the hotel bar. For what is known locally as the 'Dance of the Desperates', the bar has been overtaken by the monthly meeting of the local mature-age singles club, and a small pocket of Wallabies in the corner is manfully resisting the continued assaults of all and sundry.

We send out for reinforcements and by close to midnight have managed to secure all the forward posts well enough to soak up the scene. With the jukebox blaring, the moosehead shaking on the wall, and the well-oiled singles dancing up a storm and bouncing from wall to wall it is a marvellous slice of life to have happened upon. We carouse till closing time, early training be damned.

In the game against Bay of Plenty, there is among us a strong body of opinion that we have indeed copped plenty and that, in so doing, our opposition has gone well beyond the allowable amount of assault and battery.

In what was to be the only real brawling and foul play of the tour, we lose Bubba Ryan with a deep gash in his head, and Bobby Nasser, who had unexpectedly rejoined us from Brisbane, again is forced to depart the field, this time with a long cut along his eyelid.

On a field of slush, in rain and wind, we have been ambushed, bushwhacked, hung down, brung down, strung down—and Bay of Plenty emerges unexpectedly victorious. Violence aside, Bay of Plenty is a superbly committed team and it is a salutary lesson to us that in New Zealand even anonymous teams are capable of knocking you over. But we are about to give a lesson of our own . . .

Going into the Third Test, the chips, as they say, are down. We have lost the first two Tests and if we lose the last we will be the first Australian team since 1972 to have been whitewashed by the Blacks. But we nailed them. When the final whistle blows, we have won by 21–9 and are the first team to beat the mighty All Blacks in the last four years. And unlike the French in Nantes in 1986, we have done it without resorting to untoward tactics of violence. It was fair and square, without even accusations against the referee, so thanks for coming.

The outpouring of joy on the field snowballs through the tunnel, gathering the non-Test players as it goes, bursts through the door and explodes in the confined space of the dressing room. War cries, champagne, the national anthem, the requisite pounding of backs and much hugging.

The victory is all the sweeter because, like all great victories, it was against the odds and unexpected by the outside world. We didn't scale the summit of Everest by winning the series, but nor did we fall into the deep crevasse so many had predicted.

The All Blacks, for their part, are gloomy and chastened, but sincere in their congratulations. This tour was marked by unusually cordial relations between the two teams and every cliché there ever was about the camaraderie of opponents after the battle is fulfilled that night at the Test dinner.

Later, *en masse*, the two teams hit the Arena nightclub in Wellington and party into the night. At dawn, our Queensland brothers must up stumps and catch a plane back to Brisbane. The tour is over. *Auld lang syne.*

GRUNT-MAN OUSTS PLAYMAKER IN LINE-BALL DECISION

For the hell of it, let's talk about words and phrases. Every year for the past few yonks, the various sports have come up with new ones. Some fade quickly, others endure. Still others receive the ultimate accolade: carried off on the shoulders of raiding business troops, they are taken back to offices all over the land where 'team players', 'line-ball decisions' and 'selling the dump' suddenly become all the go.

Between the sports themselves there is also no little amount of exchange (to wit, tennis's original 'unforced error' now has universal currency) though often something gets lost in the translation.

Rugby union players, for example, have long been under the impression that ice hockey players are always saying to each other, 'Let's get the puck outta here'. But I checked recently and that is not so. They say 'let's go' like everybody else.

The point of all this? There is no point particularly, other than it amuses me and helps pass the time while sitting in this rugby World Cup camp watching endless videos of England and Wales. (Actually I love it, really I do.) Often the words describe concepts and as the word gains currency, so too the concept. (Or maybe the chicken came before the egg . . . I don't know.) A few years back, the rugby league 'playmaker' suddenly emerged. This was the team's linchpin, around whom much of its attack would revolve. As soon as the word appeared, much of league analysis seemed to rely on it. Would Balmain beat Parramatta? Invariably, the expert opinion would be that a lot depended on how the two playmakers, Ben Elias and Peter Sterling, fared. There still are playmakers around, of course, but somehow we don't seem to hear as much of them.

This year, the guys who are getting all the press are the 'impact players'. If Johnny Bloggs is an impact player, it means he is sure to have an impact on the game if you throw him into the breach. In this sense, an impact usually means either a try or the creation thereof.

Scott Gourley, when he played union, was a classic impact player in that once or twice a game he could be counted on to do something extraordinary, which would frequently result in a try. Much as he now does in league. But he was not what the New Zealanders call a *grunt-man*. For them, the grunt-man is the guy who does all the selfless and anonymous work, like tackling, pushing, mauling, rucking. Actually, you know, the description sounds a lot like mysel . . . no, never mind.

Of course, without at least a few grunt-men the impact player cannot bloom, and in return the grunt-men need the impact players to turn their work into points. The concept of the grunt-man has not yet crossed the creek from New Zealand, but for what it's worth, it gets my vote as a really thuper thuper phrase.

In French, the vogue sports phrase of the moment in football is *le leaderrrr*. (Not actually spelt like that, but that's how they pronounce it.) They've taken the word of obvious English origin and turned it into a paramount concept.

Le leaderrrr is not necessarily the captain, and frequently isn't, but he's the guy who can be counted on to get the other guys' mustard up. By his tackles, his rampaging charges, his generally aggressive play, he is figuratively the guy who is first out of the trenches waving his arm in the classic 'follow me' fashion.

The French wisdom is that without *un leader* a football team may as well not turn out, no matter what skills they might have on board. And in the US, the big word of the moment, to judge from the wire services, is 'gamer'. A gamer is one who may not be the strongest player, the most skilled, or with the most flair, but, hell, he or she knows how to win a game of whatever it is. Their ability lies not in the way they hit the ball or make the tackle or throw the dart, but in the way they are able to choose how to play the game to win it.

A good example of a gamer is former French tennis Open winner Michael Chang who, the pundits say, is way higher in the rankings than his technical ability would place him. (Though, to be fair, that's maybe because he has God on his side.) So that's about it. The rugby videos are almost over now. England look great, Wales look terrible.

The year of the second World Cup in 1991 was indeed a time when every player within cooee of the representative scene was even more dead keen than usual to have himself noticed by the selectors. Some got it right in thrilling fashion.

Marty Roebuck

On the way back from Argentina, the New South Wales team stopped in New Zealand to play the North Harbour side. There was great interest in the game, not least because the 'Bring Back Buck' (as in Buck Shelford, the deposed All Black captain) campaign was gaining momentum and Shelford was captaining North Harbour that day. Sure enough, twenty minutes into the second half, Shelford, perhaps the most damaging man with the ball in his hands in world rugby, gouged the ball from a maul and set off upfield.

Three shoulder charges and one palm-off later, he was through. Almost. The only thing that remained between Shelford and the tryline was the slender New South Wales fullback, Roebuck.

Wha . . . wha . . . WHAM! In three precise movements, Roebuck drove his shoulder deep into Shelford's midriff, straightened his legs to lift him high above the field and then drove him straight into the turf. The mud splattered at Shelford's point of impact.

Around the ground, the momentary stunned silence gave way to an excited buzzing. On the field, Marty gazed down upon his still prone and dazed quarry with the truly appalled expression of one who didn't even know his gun was *loaded*, let alone pointing in such a dangerous direction . . . but by then it was too late. The damage was done.

The Bring Back Buck campaign was derailed and Marty . . . *toot, toot!* . . . was slowly shunting his engine the other way with a 'Roebuck for Test Fullback' banner on it. His engine would gain momentum as the season progressed.

For others, the face of fate did not beam so benignly.

TIM GAVIN

It was one of those days. Nothing you could put your finger on—there was just a bad feeling about, a sense of foreboding on this unseasonally humid, dog-day afternoon of August 1991. In the middle of the Easts v Wests rugby union game at Concord Oval, the players paused in their play as one screaming police car after another barrelled up Parramatta Road heading west, followed by at least a dozen ambulances with their sirens blaring. That had in turn died down when two helicopters buzzed overhead in the same direction.

Tim Gavin, the Wallaby No 8 playing in the same position for Easts that day, remembers wondering in the middle of the fray, 'What the hell is *that* all about?'

Well, no time to worry now. His side had to put a scrum down against Wests. Gavin took the ball from the base, according to the plan, passed to the winger and received it back, before heading upfield to glory.

Oddly enough, he heard it before he felt it. A crack like a distant rifle shot, then the agonising pain as the principal joint of his left leg was turned into so much sushi by a brutally efficient regulation tackle from the Wests' lock.

Gavin went down like a felled steer, clutching what had been his knee, and was taken from the field all but certain that the World Cup due to start in three weeks had dissolved for him. Which was true, and as it turned out close on the least tragic thing that happened in Sydney that day . . .

'It was in the dressing room that I heard that the Strathfield massacre had occurred,' Gavin recalls.

If his own woes were as nothing in comparison, the next three months were nevertheless difficult. The crutches that suddenly sprouted from beneath his armpits were not due to fall away for months and in that time, of course, it meant that he had to wave the Wallabies goodbye at the airport when they winged their way north to the World Cup, instead of going away with them as was his due.

'It felt like I'd paid my ticket to go all the way to Central and been made to get off at Wyong,' he said at the time.

After a long rehabilitation, Gavin would make his way into the Wallabies the following year, and again cover himself with distinction. He retired from the game at the conclusion of 1997 and is now a farmer in the country. Hi, Tim.

In late September 1991, the Wallabies flew away to Britain for the World Cup. I wrote many pieces for the British audience, this one being the first of what would become a weekly sports column for the London Daily Telegraph.

AUSSIES ARE LOADED WITH GOLDEN BULLETS

There we were, the boys and I, fighting out in the deep jungles of New Zealand when the news came through . . . I wasn't selected for the World Cup and they were. I was wounded, I'd taken a big mortar right in the guts and couldn't go on. I knew it, they knew it.

'Don't worry,' they said. 'We'll leave you here, propped up against a tree with a rifle, some supplies and ammo . . . plus one bullet just for you in case it gets too bad . . . and as soon as things sort themselves out we'll send back help.' I'm still waiting. From the constant 'boom-booms' I hear from our guns up at the battlefront I gather the battle is going well for us, but I'll be damned if anybody has actually come back to get me.

Actually (soft music here please, maestro), I miss the guys.

Like our fullback, Marty Roebuck. Few representative players have worked so hard yet been beset by so many misfortunes as Marty. Over the years, if it wasn't his ankle, it was his knee, if not his knee, then a rare bad game at the wrong time. But somehow, against all odds, Roebuck burst out and started dancing.

Then there's Bob Egerton, our flying winger. So often in rugby, as in life, someone's success is tied to someone else's failure. The really *nice* thing about Egerton's success is that it came about precisely because of Roebuck's. Egerton was originally called in as a late back-up fullback to Roebuck on the New South Wales tour to Argentina. Never played winger in his life. But with Roebuck playing so well, there was nowhere else for Bob to play than as a stop-gap winger and, joy of all joys, he made tries fall from the skies and has done so ever since. And David Campese . . . not a lot more to say really. He's a good 'un and undoubtedly the best attacking player in the world.

The guys working inside Campo, shovelling out the really hot ammo at just the right time are, of course, our centres, Jason Little and Tim Horan. They're live ones, those two. One time in France, the whole squad had been ambushed and shot up pretty bad by some French dive-bombers and it really looked as if we were going to have to bite the big one, when these two guys suddenly took over the show and started shellacking the French from all angles.

Given confidence, the rest of us suddenly tore out of the trenches too, and gave the French a good pounding ourselves. We eventually won a great victory in what was ever afterwards known as the Battle of Strasbourg. The almost intuitive under-standing that exists between Little and Horan is no fluke as they have been playing side by side since they were eleven years old in the backblocks of Queensland.

The not-so-secret weapon of the squad is Michael Lynagh, the 'One O'Clock Gun' as the Wallabies know him. When he fires, the whole team fires. His goal kicks may have gone awry this tournament, but the Gun is still firing accurately and long, destroying all before it. Watch out if he gets the goal kicking back too.

Then there is Nicko, son of Chico, father of Jaco, master of all he surveys—Nick Farr-Jones. If the Martians came down and said, 'We're going to play a rugby match against you next Saturday and if we beat you we're going to turn your planet to mush' then Nick would be my choice as captain and halfback of the Earth team.

Up in the foot-slogging infantry there are also a few useful performers. The ageless Simon Poidevin, for example. He was playing for Australia when Noah first threw away his gumboots, and will probably still be playing one hundred moons from now. A good man to have covering your back in the hand-to-hand stuff.

And Willie Ofahengaue. We found him in a raid on New Zealand, converted him to our cause and have been following him into battle ever since. Unless I miss my guess, Willie is currently featuring large in the nightmares of Test players from New Zealand, Wales, Western Samoa and Ireland. As they toss and turn in restless sleep, the same terrifying vision must come back to them: they have the ball, they are advancing upfield, the sun is on their faces, the wind is in their hair, all is right with the world, then, again, it's him! Willie O, coming at them, two-storeys high, fast as a runaway truck.

Wham! They are awash in pain and the ball has floated away to who knows where. After the final, my guess is this recurring nightmare will also be showing up all over England.

Now, what really gets me, as I sit under this tree, is my old buddy and second-row partner, Rod McCall. I mean, even as we speak, Rod is sleeping in my bed at the team hotel. Come on Rod, get up. The joke's over, you and Bob Dwyer have had your little laugh at my expense, making me think I was really going to miss out, but don't you think you're taking it a bit far now? I mean, the final is tomorrow. I've got a field-phone with me, I've got the passport, and I'm ready to go.

As for his partner, John Eales, why, only a short time ago he was dubbed a 'player of the future'. Hear that John? Future, F–U–T–U–R–E. Not now. How dare you get your tenses mixed up? And I don't care if you are able to leap tall buildings at a single bound. Get off the bus and come back here and get me.

Look, I almost can't go on. But quickly, hooker Phil Kearns is our modern answer to the Sherman tank, undoubtedly the prototype for the rugby player of the year 2000. You'll be hearing a lot more from him for years to come. And the props . . . On a wet Monday some two years ago, the then all-but-anonymous Tony Daly underwent an Australian Rugby Union test to see how much he could benchpress. If I remember correctly, Daly benched something like 170 kilograms and in three days was on his way to New Zealand to make his Test debut at Eden Park. If you're reading this Bob Dwyer, I might just mention in passing that only yesterday I benched 200 kilograms.

I'm almost as strong as Ewen McKenzie, the other prop. And if Ewen's not actually the strongest tight-head prop in the world he could probably fit into a phone booth with the guys ahead of him. He is also that rarest of the prop species who can not only spell 'cut-out pass!', he can also do one. Which leaves us with the coaches. The brutes.

Bob Dwyer stands a good chance of being hailed as the messiah of world rugby, in the same way that Alan Jones once was, if the Wallabies get up. He is ably supported by Bob Templeton, the assistant coach. The grand old man of Australian rugby, Tempo is also a very capable coach but his role is more than that. If the Wallabies were to develop a dance around a sacred totem pole, Tempo's face would loom large at its very top. He is the deeply respected elder of the Wallaby tribe. And finally Jake Howard, the assistant assistant coach. His place on the totem pole is just below that of Tempo.

So that's them. And that's me. Goodbye cruel world. Any calls for me? Where's that bullet . . .

LYNAGH: DOING HIS OWN THING

Blessed is the sportsman whose finest moment on the field coincides exactly with the instant when his country's need is greatest. For Michael Lynagh that time came around 4.24 p.m. on 20 October 1991—with just scant minutes to go in the Wallabies' World Cup quarter-final against Ireland.

Australia had been tenuously holding onto a 15–12 lead when the Irish breakaway Gordon Hamilton broke through a David Campese tackle and ran the length of the field to score in the corner. The situation, as General Custer once remarked, was looking rather grim. On the very edge of the abyss, against an Irish team just minutes from a historic victory in front of 40 000 of their own, the only way out for the Wallabies was to score again themselves.

In the injured Nick Farr-Jones's absence, Lynagh took command. Leading the team away from the scene of the tragedy—the spot where Hamilton had put the ball down—he gathered his thoughts.

'How long to go?' he asked the referee.

'Four minutes, after the conversion,' came the reply.

Easily long enough to work a miracle if the whole team kept together and stuck to it. In a calm voice, Lynagh then spoke to the Wallaby huddle in concise, clear terms.

'Be calm and controlled. There's still plenty of time left. From the kick-off we will kick the ball long and to the left. The forwards must secure clean possession and we'll go from there. If ever in doubt about what to do with the ball, just hold it tightly and head towards their line. We will win this game.'

Two minutes later, from a Wallaby scrum in Ireland's half, Lynagh called to his backs to execute a move called 'Cut Two Loop'.

Then, from halfback Peter Slattery's pass, the Wallaby pivot sent the ball out on its appointed course before doubling around in support. The ball found its way through the hands of Tim Horan, Marty Roebuck and Jason Little to David Campese on the wing. The last, though hit by two Irish defenders, managed to bounce back inside a Hail Mary pass to keep the ball alive. Hovering right there for just such a ball was Lynagh, who gathered and burrowed his way forward.

'It was only about three yards to the line, but it felt like three miles,' recounts Lynagh now, remembering the two Irish defenders who came along for the ride.

TRY!!!

They say you could hear the silence from three kilometres away, in the all but deserted streets of downtown Dublin. Such was the momentary stunned shock that a dog barking in the park beside Lansdowne Road was clearly audible. Australia had won the game and the empire was saved. Lynagh recounts the story now quite flatly, without embellishment.

'It just happened like that,' he says, with the slightest of shrugs.

Not quite. For if there has been one quality to stand out in Lynagh's rugby career it has been that of 'assemblage'—that rare quality of being able to learn something from each experience, and add it to an ever-growing reservoir of tested knowledge to guide future action.

Those brief minutes in an Irish afternoon, dissected, can tell much of Lynagh's story. Like his speech to the players under the goalposts.

One of the things his sports-psychologist father had emphasised to him over the years was the importance of being positive in thought, deed, and direction.

'Instead of saying to the players, "DON'T do something . . .", which is immediately negative,' Lynagh says, 'it's far better to lead along the lines of, "DO be sure to . . .", which is positive. And whatever you say in a situation like that has got to be simple and clear.'

He was that.

Then there was the particular move that led to the try. One of the more valued things that Lynagh says he learnt from his four years under the national coaching of Alan Jones (1984–1987) is the beauty of a structured attack framed specifically at exploiting opposition weaknesses until their noses bleed.

'Jonesy didn't invent the move we used,' Lynagh says with a laugh, 'but I think one of his tactics that I most appreciated was being ruthless in continuing to hammer a weakness once you'd found it. That afternoon we'd used that particular move lots of times with great success, so I thought that now we really needed it, that was the one to go with again.'

Even the specific action that led to Lynagh regathering the ball at the death, seemingly coming out of nowhere, had its origins in a lesson Lynagh had learnt long before—the importance of being 'lazy' in support.

That was something the great Wallaby five-eighth Mark Ella had taught him back on his first Australian tour, to France in 1983. Watching Lynagh in training one day early on the tour, Ella had noticed that when looping around in support, the young 'un was rushing everything in his eagerness to get his hands on the ball again.

Ambling over in his typically lackadaisical fashion, Ella had opined that 'Noddy' would find everything a lot easier if he dropped back about three gears and lazily held back, without busting a boiler. Wait for the right moment, and then go like the clappers.

'It worked immediately,' Lynagh recalls. 'I tried it out in the next game we played and was immediately successful with it. I guess the next few games after that I thought about being "lazy" in those situations, but after that I just did it without thinking.'

Lynagh's personal triumph that day against Ireland meant Australia survived to continue their World Cup campaign.

On 2 November 1991, the Wallabies took on the English side in the World Cup final, at Twickenham.

THE FINAL

The Final, played before 70 000 at Twickenham and hundreds of millions worldwide, went well for Australia from the beginning. They were slick in attack, robust in defence, and went out to an early lead after Wallaby prop Tony Daly barged over for a try.

Towards the end of the game though, the penalty kick by the English goal-kicker Jonathon Webb narrowed the margin to 12–6, Australia's way. It seemed to many as if the match must surely go to overtime, for the English forwards were winning so much ball an English try seemed a probability. All the Wallabies could do was tackle themselves red raw and wait for the storm to pass.

Now the tension around the ground was palpable, and perhaps the man who felt it most was Bob Dwyer, up in the stands and dying a thousand deaths every time the Wallabies got the ball and exposed themselves even to the slightest risk.

On one occasion when an isolated David Campese and Michael Lynagh tried to put on a move right in front of the mounting English defence, Dwyer could contain himself no longer and leapt to his feet.

'KICK IT TO THE SHITHOUSE!' he bellowed, with both hands cupped around his mouth so as to send the sound further. A woman dressed in red a few rows away didn't turn to look at Dwyer, but she was the only one. Then again, she was the Queen of England, so might very well have judged it politic to pretend she hadn't heard.

Out on the field the battle continued, while back in Australia Alan Jones listened to it all blow by blow on his car radio, as he drove back to Sydney from a speaking engagement in the country.

At last though, the final whistle of redemption. The Wallabies had won the World Cup.

'The melancholy of all things completed,' Nietzsche called it. It wasn't that there was no tremendous exuberance in the dressing room after the Wallabies had won the World Cup; there was. But not too far below the surface, in the breast of some players, there was also a sense of *so this is it?*

Few players will admit publicly to feeling a little sadness when they should be experiencing their greatest joy. Dwyer characterised it as 'a feeling almost of let-down and anticlimax', while Campese admits that he felt 'none of the elation you are supposed to feel on these occasions'.

And Nick Farr-Jones was another one.

'You're happy, of course you are, basically. But really mixed up in the middle of it all is maybe the sense that in conventional terms a lot of people would regard this as probably the pinnacle of your life—and now it's fifteen minutes behind you and getting further away all the time.'

After a few quick comments to the press and a few hugs here and there, it was all he could do to drag his body to the bath, there to quietly soak for half an hour. And it was also perhaps the measure of an extraordinary day that when through the steam he saw the British prime minister looking over at him, obviously wishing to speak, it didn't strike him as at all odd.

He wishes now he'd thought to drape himself in a towel. Undoubtedly there have been other times in history when someone has spent fifteen minutes chatting to a British prime minister while stark naked, but Farr-Jones is surely one of the few, if not the only one, to have been standing up at the time. The photos look odd to this day. John Major, wiping the glasses that kept getting fogged up with the steam, Farr-Jones, starkers, and happily chatting away regardless.

It had been an odd sort of day.

Every damn one of them was now internationally famous, none more so than the coach.

The passion of Bob Dwyer

The curious thing about Bob Dwyer's enormously passionate involvement in the game of rugby union is that it all came from such meagre beginnings. At school, he only played the game because it was compulsory for Waverley College students. Cricket was his real love, and rugby only fine as far as it went, which was not very far.

And even when given a chance to see rugby played at its highest level, in a Test match involving the Wallabies, he was left feeling at best 'indifferent' and at worst 'totally bored'.

'I remember going out to the Sydney Cricket Ground to see the Springboks play the Wallabies in a Test match when I was fifteen and thinking the whole thing was just totally deplorable,' Dwyer said. 'I just couldn't understand why both teams were kicking it all the time, why no-one seemed to have any interest in running the damn thing.'

In stark contrast to this were the times when his father, Ted, would occasionally take him to see Souths play rugby league.

'It was terrific. Souths didn't kick it, they *did* something with it,' he said. 'Dad used to play league himself, first grade for Canterbury-Bankstown, so he knew something about the caper and I suppose some of his enthusiasm for that game rubbed off on me too.'

But at school it was back to the humdrum of union. Bit by bit, though, he started to enjoy the game. Though never rising higher than the Fourth XV at Waverley, he at least had begun to take a minor interest in the structure of the game, starting to discern patterns of play in what had previously seemed like one big shemozzle.

And as an honours maths student, which involved trying to break everything down into its smallest parts till it became understandable, such an intellectual approach came naturally to Bobby.

'For me doing maths is like being a detective,' he said. 'You've got a logical progression of information, which gives you a clue, which then gives you more information and another clue, and you eventually get to a conclusion.

'When you really get into it like I was, doing Maths I and Maths II for my Leaving Certificate, I suppose you start looking at everything as information which will give you clues, which will give you more information and so on.'

Perhaps the first real seeds of the possibilities of coaching were laid just after he left school, when at eighteen he watched a training session of the British Lions at the Sydney Sportsground and was stunned to see how organised they were.

'It was like a revelation to me really,' Dwyer said. 'I just didn't know before that a training session could be like that, so organised, so disciplined, something that really had a bearing on the way to play the game, and not just a bit of a run-around like I was used to.'

It was a seed that would gestate in Dwyer's mind for some time.

In the meantime, he decided to pursue his playing career with Randwick, albeit primarily in the lower grades.

'I think I probably just wasn't blessed with an enormous amount of raw talent, which prevented me going higher, but that didn't matter in the end,' he said. 'The main thing was that I'd come around to just loving playing the game.'

He'd turn out to be one of Randwick's great lower-grade stalwarts, captaining many sides and turning out no fewer than 347 times for them. As a friendly, if argumentative type, he was into everything like pepper 'n' salt, on the committee, at training, at the bar after the game—very much around.

Bob Outterside, Randwick's first grade coach through the early 1970s, remembers Dwyer well as one who displayed a surprising astuteness.

'He was extremely intelligent in his conversation and revealed himself to have a lot of insights,' Outterside said. 'He was very thoughtful and analytical and I always thought in my discussions with him that he'd make a good coach. Mostly I guess, I was impressed that he was such a good listener, eager to expand his knowledge of the game.'

In 1975, Dwyer was Randwick's reserve grade captain, as he had been captain of many lower grades through the years. For the life of him he can't now remember who the coach was. But who needed a coach when you were already captain and had a head full of ideas? The constant background noise of Dwyer's life at this time was the voice of old club stalwart Cyril Towers—a great Randwick player and Wallaby of the 1930s—who kept bending his ear about the way his team should be playing the game.

'He was always going on at me, on and on and on, trying to explain to me his theories about the correct pattern of play, and his whole thing was that it wasn't enough to win; you had to play the game in a certain way, his way, or you'd missed the point entirely,' Dwyer said. 'I could never quite understand exactly why his way was the right way.

'After one game, he came straight up to me and said: "You don't know what you're doing, you've got no idea of the game," and I said: "Hang on Cyril, we've just scored six tries to nil."'

'You don't know what you're doing,' Cyril repeated. 'Come around to my place on Monday night and I'll try to explain to you how you should be playing.'

That Monday night, the same thing happened that always happened on such occasions: Cyril's family—his wife and four children—made themselves scarce. Having heard Towers *père* a thousand times already on the same subject, they had no desire to listen to it all again. The two were left alone at the dining-room table, Bob momentarily left to twiddle his thumbs as Cyril got out his ha'pennys and pennys to again show the young 'un what he was on about.

'Now, say this is my backline,' the old man growled, pointing out one row of pennies, 'and say this is yours . . .'

Dwyer, too, had heard the same theories from Cyril many times before and was wondering why he had bothered coming again, when like the first light of the sun coming up over the horizon, it suddenly started to dawn on him that Towers was right.

'"Cyril", I said. "We've wasted years by you not making me understand this before, why couldn't you have explained it better?"'

The essence of Towers's theory has been explained many times (often to a lot of us footballers who still don't get it), and it revolves around the backline standing in a flat alignment, the players running straight, and . . .

'And engineering the situation so you can maximise the natural advantage you have in attack to get overlaps, either by looping or by having blindside wingers and fullbacks coming into the line, and minimising the possibilities of the defence covering you . . .'

The next night at training, Dwyer gathered his troops and explained in his own terms the essence of Towers's theories, why he thought they were right, and how they were going to go about playing the game that Saturday. Using the system, tries started falling from the skies and Dwyer had achieved his first satisfaction from coaching, albeit informally.

Two years later, he was first grade coach at Randwick and the young Rebecca Dwyer, as a toddler, can remember a succession of men coming to her parents' house and sitting down at the dining-room table as her bespectacled father explained the intricacies of his backline theories . . .

'He would sparkle whenever he talked about it,' she said. 'He just loved it.'

So it went. Rebecca learnt to count by reading down the team list on the way to the game, and Randwick won five premierships in a row. From there, Dwyer was catapulted into the Australian coaching job, was thrown out just as suddenly by Alan Jones, fought his way back to the job in 1988, beat back no fewer than three serious coup attempts over the next three years, triumphed at the 1991 World Cup, blew 'em away in the 1992 season, wobbled a tad in 1993 but survived the usual coup attempt, and now here he is—on his way to the airport again, about to fly out to another rugby commitment, being interviewed in the passenger's seat as the journalist drives.

It's all very chummy, when suddenly the journalist remembers someone in the car was once unjustly dropped from Dwyer's Test team—and it wasn't Dwyer. So why not fire off a few quick curly questions before the terminal doors swallow him?

So yes Bob, you really have done well, and goodonya, but surely there comes a time when enough is enough. Surely after nearly a decade as national rugby coach, it might be time to move on?

'No. It's not,' he said. 'I don't understand that line of thinking. I mean it's not true in business, if you've got someone who's been braining them in business—or at least is the head of a company that's been braining them—nobody contemplates moving them on just because they've been there a while. Why should it apply in sport?'

Hmmm. What about the accusation that your actual business, in something called 'corporate hospitality event management', relies heavily on your position as Australian coach and the real reason you hang onto the job so determinedly is you'd drop a lot of money if you lost it?

'No again. My remuneration from my business life I cut in half so I can do the job of Australian coach properly. If I wasn't Australian coach, then I'd make a lot more money than I do. The time I put into coaching is a lot, but I do it because I love it, because I believe in what we're doing, not because it helps my business.'

One last torpedo to fire.

ARE YOU KIDDING WITH THAT MOUSTACHE OR WHAAATTTT, BOB?

But he's gone.

Byo rugby club

So you loved the World Cup. Finally you figured out what the rugga buggas have been on about all these years and now you'd like to start your own rugby club . . . Welcome aboard. You've got about six months before the next domestic season starts, which should be plenty of time. First, get yourself a *field*.

Don't be fooled by the fact that you will henceforth be known as being a part of 'grassroots rugby'. This is not because anyone actually expects to find any grass roots beneath their feet when they come to play you. Plain dirt is fine, though it probably should have at least a few token tufts of grass here and there.

Now you need a *coach*. This guy has got to really, absolutely, and I mean totally, love the game. Greater love of rugby hath no man than he will agree to coach—and it is a fair bet that his life will become absolute hell from the moment he accepts the position. To prepare him, make sure your coach announces pre-season training sometime around the middle of January. No-one will come, of course, which is the very point of the exercise. It's important your coach gets used to getting disappointed early, otherwise he'll never make it through the long season.

A *treasurer*. A good rule of thumb is that to make a decent treasurer, be it for a rugby club or the nation, you need to have one of the names of the twelve apostles. Look for a guy called John or James or Peter or something like that. He should be a fairly serious, sober, long-suffering sort of bloke and it would really help if, in his own life, he somehow managed to feed and clothe a family of four on the basic wage. Steer a mile wide of guys with nicknames like Flash Larry, Elvis or Lothario. They make good five-eighths but lousy treasurers.

Now for the *players*. The best way to get these is to start scouring the pubs in your area. We'll start from the bottom up, so let's presume your club is going to have three grades. The most essential ingredient for a good third grade is personalities. Really livewire sort of blokes who love the game, are not much good at it . . . but that doesn't matter because their main role is to be keepers of the club soul. They should have names like Louie, Jacko, Thommo, that sort of thing. At least two of them should be absolutely legendary for some late-night feat of the recent past.

This should be constantly referred to by others in the team, not necessarily explicitly, but along the lines of, 'What about the time Jacko . . . !?!?!' and the sayer should be unable to finish for all the other guys in the team falling around laughing, digging each other in the ribs and giving each other knowing looks. Whatever it was that Jacko did, it should get better and better with every passing month.

For the second grade, and more particularly the first grade side, you need slightly more serious types with a bit of ambition. Seriousness can be measured by smoking fewer than two packets a day, sobriety on the day of the game and, occasionally . . . just very occasionally, actually turning up to training.

Tight five. Look around where the motorbike blokes hang out. If you can find a couple of blokes called Igor, Nutcracker or something like that, then they're exactly the ones you're looking for. In fact, any guys with nicknames like these would fit well into your forward pack.

Backrow. Here you need all those forwards who are fond of thinking, and saying, that they really have the speed and ball-handling skills of backs. They don't, of course, but it helps if you humour them in this line of thought. Essentially they are 'no-where men', neither the truest of the true forwards—which is the tight five in front of them—nor more than temporary visitors to the ranks of the backs.

Which brings us, as a matter of fact, to the *backs*. What would be really terrific would be if they had last names like Campese, Farr-Jones or Lynagh, but you're probably setting your hopes a bit high there, so don't make that an absolute condition. Instead, look for smaller guys with discernible parts in their hair, shirts neatly tucked into their trousers and no known criminal records. These are the sort of guys who generally make the best backs.

Finally, you'll need some *barflys*. These shouldn't be too hard to find. A bare minimum of five or six of these should be sprinkled liberally around the bar where you drink and they should at all times have only the very slenderest of holds on sobriety.

Furthermore, and this is most crucial, they should constantly express at the top of their voices their opinions on all matters concerning the club. The subtext of everything they say must be, 'If only I was president/coach/captain then everything would be going about ten times better'.

There you go, that's more or less the basic ingredients. Add water . . . or beer, if you must, and enjoy.

Willie Ofahengaue had performed stunningly at the 1991 World Cup, and by 1992 was firmly installed as a great favourite of the Australian rugby community. This was not just for his play, but also for his shy, becoming manner. For those of us his team-mates though, he remained quite a hard man to get to know.

WILLIE O . . . A GLIMPSE OF A DIFFERENT SORT OF MAN

Willie O really didn't want to stay for this particular after-match function during our tour of New Zealand, and neither did I. So a quick 'LOOK!' to the left, as we ducked to the right, then through a door, out a window, down a fire-escape, and we were out into the drizzly Wellington night. And not a taxi to bless ourselves with.

There was nothing for it but to walk back to the hotel, half an hour away. Trudging, trudging, trudging along. So, who is this man beside me, anyway? What does anybody know about Willie Ofahengaue, other than that he's from Tonga, plays a football game straight out of hell, and is a very good and likable man? Willie doesn't give interviews and is excruciatingly embarrassed by his own fame.

If given a choice, he would walk four blocks out of his way to avoid a single question from a journalist. But this time I had him. We had to walk thirty blocks together, and as I was cleverly disguised as a fellow footballer, there was nothing for him to do but to answer a few questions.

Did he enjoy the World Cup?

'Yes.'

Did he love playing for the Wallabies?

'Yes.'

Did he want to go to rugby league?

'No.'

Did he come across any racism when he was recently in South Africa?

'No.'

Trudging, trudging, trudging along. No, it wasn't the stuff from which Pulitzer Prizes are made, but it was a start . . . and besides, that was at least four Willie quotes that, with his permission,

I could put in a story, which was a lot more than most Willie profiles could claim.

Trudging, trudging. Sometimes, surely, people must mistake Willie's reticence to speak for a lack of the smarts. It is not. As a small example, there are more than ten complex moves that can be made from the back of the scrum in the New South Wales team. The rest of us have been trying to get them securely in our heads for the past four months. Only one player has never joined our discussion of them. Willie had them from the first moment he heard them. Never asked a question, never made a mistake.

Although these planned moves go against the grain of the way he would prefer to operate, admitting once, in a rare moment of verbosity, that he would prefer to 'just play', it is enough that this is what New South Wales coach, Rod Macqueen, wants. No arguments from Willie.

And the rest of us, in the minute before going onto the field, do all manner of things to get ourselves into a suitably aggressive frame of mind. We jump, sit, wave our arms, punch our palms . . . *anything*. Willie prays. Not ostentatiously, so as you'd even notice—and it is not clear whether he prays for himself or the safety of his opposition—but that is what he does. And the rest of us sometimes get drunk, sometimes have smoked. Willie has done neither of these things . . . ever. His strong Christianity forbids it, and for him that is the end of the section. Yet he never has even the slightest forbidding air about him in the middle of our worst excesses. Let it be, each to his own.

And how is it that Willie can be the most feared forward in the international game, featuring large in the nightmares of players from Auckland to Tokyo to London, yet has never raised an unprovoked fist in anger, or even engaged in mildly untoward rucking? A different sort of man to be sure.

The hotel is up ahead. Whaddya say we go to the bar and get smashed, Willie?

'No, Fitzy.'

A small smile and a shake of the head. Suddenly, in the back window of a parked van in front of the hotel pops up a little boy's smiling face. Then another, then another. Uncle Willie is back. Out of the small van comes an impossibly large number of people, Tongans all.

In the middle of the throng, Willie turns and says: 'Family.
See ya.'

See ya Willie.

A different sort of man.

*On that same tour with the New South Wales team in New Zealand
in 1992, I was amazed to see in Wellington's* Dominion *newspaper a
diatribe from the former New Zealand prime minister, David Lange,
about what a boring, class-ridden game rugby was. I penned this reply
which the paper published the following day.*

IF YOU'RE DOWN ON YOUR RUCK . . .

Sorry to be churlish about this, but one cannot allow to pass
without comment David Lange's thesis of last Monday that
rugby union is a crashing bore. It almost put us players of the
New South Wales rugby union team, currently on tour in your
fair and muddy land, off our Weetbix.

And, simple oaf footballers that we are, it seems only fair that
we make an attempt to put Mr Lange off his Weeties in return.
Soooo, try these names on for size Mr Lange: Mike Moore, Jim
Bolger, Sir Robert Muldoon . . . Do I hear a cry of 'mercy'?

Mr Lange's first point is that no serious television news
program should ever begin with a rugby Test loss, as TVNZ did
recently.

With due respect to Mr Lange, the fact is that 99.99 per cent
of the population are not professional politicians and thus unfortunately retain the tendency of the great unwashed to be interested in all sorts of things that do not even remotely touch on
commercial interest rates, new legislation on bottle-caps, and
visiting heads of state. Things like the fortunes of the country's
most revered football team really interest them. Dreadful, isn't
it, how people are?

As one who has suffered no little damage at the hands of the
All Blacks, I might add that if given a choice, my news would
always be headed by the newsreader saying, 'More bad news from
the All Black camp today . . .' Next, Mr Lange says that while
rugby league is good and fast-moving on television, showing off
many skills, rugby union is none of the above.

Fast-moving, sir? Perhaps, but surely only in the manner of a windmill.

The fact is league is amazingly repetitive: player takes the ball up, gets belted, falls over, player takes the ball up, gets belted, falls over. Add water, repeat a thousand times till your nose bleeds and *voilà* your average league game.

As to the apparent difference in skill levels of the two codes, Mr Lange offers up for denigration the rugby union scrum. Sir, even rugby league's most ardent supporters admit that the league scrum is generally a cross between the fall of Saigon and a brothel at midnight. Of all parts of the two codes you could have chosen to make a comparison, this was not the one. But moving right along . . .

The All Blacks are 'now named, boorishly, after a beer', sniffs Mr Lange. True enough. Uh, but is it not also true that the league people over here are falling over themselves to become part of something called the Winfield Cup? Enough said? But onto the strangest claim of all in Mr Lange's article. 'In terms of international competition,' he writes, 'rugby doesn't rate.'

The world's second biggest football code, played in 126 countries, doesn't rate? Surely he means rugby league? Played only in scattered parts of Australia, New Zealand, Papua New Guinea, France and England, rugby league is little more than a parish pump game with pretensions to an international grandeur it will never possess. But forget all that for the moment.

Even as we speak, another Lange slander of union is coming down hard. According to the former PM, 'Union is a poor role model for young people because of its hypocrisy.'

The terrible 'hypocrisy' Mr Lange names is that 'while league is up front about offering young working men the chance to profit from their ability and commitment', some of the 'union players are driving around in late-model cars, with no visible means of support'.

Well, whip me hard with wet spaghetti! To think of the truly devastating effect the hypocrisy of all this must have had on young people as they contemplate life's cruel injustices; it is just too much. Can Mr Lange be serious that this is the reason rugby is not a good role model for young people?

Anyway, on he goes. The gist of the rest of it is that rugby is a game for 'snobs', a pillar of the establishment, 'administered by fuddy-duddies in London' and 'a bastion of conservatism' to boot. Scary stuff, indeed. And to think that such a fierce form of political repression has managed to masquerade as a simple, muddy football game for all these years.

Best of all, though, in the same vein, is this: 'If union ever does go fully professional', he writes, 'it would cast aside the mystique of the elite with which it is enshrined.'

Again, I cannot pass.

What mystique? What elite? I'm here to tell you, sir, the bottom of an All Black ruck is one of the most classless places on this earth. Lenin and Marx would have loved it.

See, never before, when Fitzpatrick and Co have near rucked me to death, have they first paused to determine my social background, how much I earn, or who I vote for. They just set to with a will and rucked the hell out of me all the same.

And, I dare say, if from some part of New Zealand were to suddenly arise a man, with legs like tree trunks and feet like rocks, who proved to be even more adept than the others at rucking me to a wet and sticky pulp, then whatever this man's social standing, religion, race or background, one of the All Blacks would eventually be obliged to stand aside for him so that he, too, could take his turn at me. The brute.

Does anyone doubt that this true classlessness of rugby is so? Can anyone name another fifteen in the country, working tightly together, who can boast such a wide social, racial and religious mix as the All Blacks? Though an outsider, I should be much surprised, but perhaps Mr Lange can set me straight. I'd be interested to hear. Apart from all that, I thought his was a good and well-informed article.

As a result of the article I was flown back to New Zealand a couple of weeks later to have a nationally televised debate with Lange. There were two problems.

Two days before the debate, I received a very bad gash over my right eye, resulting in stitching and bruising everywhere, making it difficult to argue what a truly great and sophisticated game rugby really was.

And in the make-up room before going on, Lange proved to be an extremely likable and interesting bloke, his article notwithstanding. It made it difficult to get any real venom up for the debate, but we somehow bumbled our way through.

TIME TO FACE THE ALL BLACK MUSIC

Ka mate! Ka mate!
Ka ora! Ka ora!
Tenei te tangata puhuruhuru
Nana nei i tiki mai
I whakawhite te ra!
Upane! Upane! Upane!
Ka upane! Whiti te ra!

The curious thing about facing the All Blacks in a *haka* before the game is that their eyes don't actually focus on anything. They're not staring at you, or through you, or even over your head to the homeland. Their eyes are just entirely glazed and unseeing, which is eerie.

Combine it with the fact that all the veins in their necks throb in unison as they yell at you at the top of their voices, while they're making all these ferocious hand movements besides, and it's almost overwhelming in effect. In reply, you almost want to yell '*Taxi!*' just to get the hell out of there. But there's nothing for it but to stand there and face the macabre music.

And it does not help even when, in a previous effort to demystify the *haka*, you happen to know a translation of it as roughly thus: It is death! It is death! It is life! It is life! This is the hairy person, who caused the sun to shine! Abreast! Keep abreast! The rank! Hold fast! Into the sun that shines!

The only part that really makes sense to me is the 'It is death! It is death!' part. Anyway, eventually the All Blacks stopped shouting, we stopped our knees from knocking together, and the game began. The South Australian XV, bolstered by six of us ring-ins from interstate, up against the might of New Zealand.

We had one, and only one, advantage. That is, that while it was a tremendous honour for us to be playing against the All Blacks, the New Zealanders had the dubious honour of playing against a side which previous All Blacks had pushed into the *Guinness Book of Records* by beating it 117–6.

So they took us lightly while we took them deadly seriously, and many of the South Australians played the game of their lives; which is surely why the match turned out as it did. Far from running riot against us, they managed only to cross our line five times in eighty minutes, for a final score of 48–18.

Not bad when you're up against a side that includes Steve McDowell, Ian Jones, Mike Brewer, Michael Jones, Zinzan Brooke, Vai'aiga Tuigamala, Terry Wright, John Kirwan and Grant Fox. And despite such pedigree, two of the All Black tries were simple runaways, relying naught on construction, and two others came after I had been sent from the field and South Australia were thus down to only fourteen defenders.

Further, the All Blacks' adaptation to the new rules was not terrific. They made no quick taps, took no quick throw-ins and tried nothing new under the new-rules sun. In the past in such games, it was not uncommon to sight the ball only after an All Black had placed it between the posts, after the whole pack had mauled it all the way downfield. But in this game, we were all surprised at how often we could get our hands on the ball and simply hold on for grim death until the referee, under the new rules, was obliged to award the scrum put-in to us.

Was this unexpected vulnerability of the All Blacks in this phase of play because they are caught betwixt and between as to the best sort of maul to pursue under the new rules? Maybe. Or maybe it was just a rare off-night for them. The latter is more likely, because they were also off their game in rucking. In past games against the All Blacks, my back has looked as if the brutes had been playing noughts and crosses on it with their boots. But after this game, there were just a few casual grazes.

Lineouts? Ian Jones was imperial in the middle as usual, but we managed to snaffle a lot of ball up the back from them, as well as a lot from two-man lineouts. All in all, not a great performance by the New Zealanders, though probably an aberration. As for my getting sent off, for fighting and obstruction, gimme a break.

Of *course* I did everything possible to disrupt the flow of the All Blacks' ball from the maul. What else are you going to do, playing with South Australia against the mighty All Blacks, when you don't want to trouble the *Guinness Book of Records* people one more time? And of course they belted me for my trouble, and of course I belted them back. No problems there from either side, and no hard feelings.

That this led to me being called out four times by the referee with four different All Blacks no doubt gave the impression that I spent the whole night brawling, whereas, in fact, I only spent a minor part doing that, and all for a good cause . . . defending South Australian soil from the incursions of notoriously voracious raiders.

As a matter of fact, the then coach Laurie Mains later wrote in his autobiography that 'FitzSimons declared a one-man war on the All Blacks'. Couldn't have written it better myself, except I would have added it was a 'holy war' . . .

INTO BATTLE WITH A BAND OF BROTHERS

An odd room. Spacious, fluorescently lit, carpeted, a couple of windows, a few scattered bare benches. Nothing peculiar in that. Rather, it is the people in it and the situation we face which gives it such an unreal quality.

Look over there . . . *pttt, pttt, pttt* . . . at the source of the only noise. It is Scottish fullback Gavin Hastings, passing a rugby ball back and forth to Martin Knoetze, the Springbok winger. The two do it with grim, single-minded intensity as around them everyone else is lacing his boots, getting a final rub-down or shaking hands in an equally odd sort of consolatory manner.

Though I know for a fact that everyone here has spent the last few nights singing loudly and rollicking around town together, we are now only ten minutes from a full-blown Test match. Against no less than the New Zealand All Blacks.

Though there has been a Barbarian atmosphere in the last few days—which is to say a free-wheeling rugby carnival feel in the air—the exigencies of playing the All Blacks allow no such lassitude as kick-off approaches. This is the third and final Test of the centenary series of 1992 and, with the score at 1–1, the New Zealanders are deadly serious. Not that we expected anything less.

Pttt, pttt, pttt.

Suddenly, a knock on the door and a loud voice: 'Can we have the skipper to make the toss, please?'

No fewer than four faces look up instinctively. Wallaby captain, Nick Farr-Jones; former All Black captain, Gary Whetton; the leader of the Scots, David Sole; and Western Samoa captain, Peter Fatialofa. If you have to go over the top of the trenches against the All Blacks, then these are good men to have beside you.

Farr-Jones is back from the toss and speaks for the first time. At moments like this, many captains are like steaming kettles of words, boiling over with random configurations of aggressive phrases, all of which are ultimately meaningless. The thrust of what they say is: 'Belt them, for they are vermin.' Farr-Jones is never like that. Now, as always, his instructions are as precise as his sentiments.

Each man must concentrate on fulfilling his task, he says, beating his opposite number, making things happen, and the scoreboard will take care of itself.

And do not forget the historic opportunity that beckons here—for there are perhaps twenty times more prime ministers and kings on this earth than people who can claim to have beaten the All Blacks in a rugby series. And win, he says, win for each other, if not for the 'World' we represent.

True enough. When Nick finishes speaking, there is a collective outlet of breath as everyone feels the immediate compulsion to get up and walk around. As the final seconds tick away, there is a lot of touching between the players, warm pats on the belly and back and yet more handshakes.

It is somehow an affirmation of unity before the coming battle. Then another knock on the door, and the players of the World XV file out, to sunlight, the crowd's roar, and the All Blacks.

I hate being a reserve. Though I would push a peanut up Main Street with my nose to be a reserve for this particular team, it is nevertheless incredibly frustrating. In fact, all there is to do is to do what all reserves do: wish an injury on your team-mates that will disable them long enough to get you on the field and into the game.

I concentrate most of my hexs, spells and malicious wishes on the knees and ankles of Wallaby Troy Coker, who is playing in my spot in the second row, but through some cosmic mix-up, it is Willie Ofahengaue who eventually succumbs. He has injured himself and must come off. So with ten minutes to go I am on against the All Blacks in a Test match.

But these can't be All Blacks. See. All Blacks are not born, they are quarried; they don't have faces, they have canvasses of skin on which scars, squashed noses and cauliflower ears are randomly attached. And these guys don't look like that. Most of them look young and fresh-faced. They don't look intimidating at all. The recent All Black purges seem to have all but wiped out cauliflower ears and broken noses.

But the new guys, like Blair Larsen, still run and hit and ruck pretty much like All Blacks for all that. The game is incredibly fast and physical. When, on one occasion, I fall into the whirling maelstrom of an All Black ruck, I know for sure that I'm in a real All Black Test match.

The game is over and we have lost. Damn, damn, double damn. The particularly galling thing is that we have lost to a team which though good, does not have the aura of invincibility of its predecessors. It may get that aura in time, but for the moment it is no more than a very good rugby team.

It is rising midnight at the reception after the game, and perhaps ten of us are standing around singing the Scottish national anthem, 'Flower of Scotland', led by Gavin Hastings and coach Ian McGeechan. We are giving it our all, for no other reason than that we loved it.

Having retired myself from all levels of rugby at the conclusion of 1992—not coincidentally the same year my dad died—by the beginning of the 1993 season, I found it grand to suddenly be able to play the 'old man' and give advice to youngsters on the way up.

WELCOME TO FIRST GRADE, LADS!

Even as we speak, there are perhaps twenty-five or so of them out there. Young blokes picked to play in their debut first grade rugby union game tomorrow. First grade! They've made it. So congratulations.

For what it's worth, here are a few tips about how to get along.

- Be on the quiet side of things for at least your first few weeks in the team. For new chums, a certain silent resilience is generally regarded as the appropriate air to affect within the team, as is respect for your older team-mates and the opportunity that has been given you in equal measure. Things will loosen up in short order, but that should come from them, initially, not you.
- Come the day, expect to be as nervous as a hedgehog trespassing in a balloon factory. Particularly if you're a forward, outright fear about the coming battle is a rite of passage. And rightly so. In the middle of the game it'll happen like this: you'll be minding your own business, fringing on the side of a ruck, when some mean mongrel dog who's played for years will have lined you up from twenty metres out, and will hit you so hard with his shoulder he'll send you cartwheeling backwards over and over. Your head will hit the ground every time as you turn, and the thought may very well occur to you that 'if this is first grade, let me out!'.

   Don't worry. It's just his way of saying 'welcome to first grade' and it's nothing serious. Besides, it gets better. While the top grade is a big step up from Colts or schoolboys or second grade or wherever it is you've come from, it doesn't take long to adapt.
- At the end of the game, always be sure to go up and shake the referee's hand and look him in the eye as you say something to the effect of 'thank you very much sir, good game'. Say this even if the ref hasn't had a good game, because he'll appreciate more than ever a friendly word and . . .

   And here's the rub. Ten minutes later, when this same ref sits down to award best and fairest points, he'll very possibly remember you with affection. No kidding. Even when you've played like a dog, it's still possible to squeeze a point or two out of him and you'll show up better than expected when the end-of-season tally is announced.
- After the game, if perchance you find yourself talking to a rugby journalist, avoid at all costs mouthing empty banalities about how you thought rugby was the winner on the day or it was the bounce of the ball that decided it. Say something, *anything*, but don't be boring. If you want to get your name

in the paper, and let's face it, you do, saying something interesting helps.

- Enjoy it. Sure it's first grade and sure it's serious, but don't become so serious about it all that you don't have time to lie around on the tackle bags after training is over and talk about the events of the day. Just as you should always stay back after the game to have a drink with the other team.

Through it all, never doubt that you're part of something magnificent. If you get to tackle Farr-Jones on Saturday, don't forget that in the past he's tackled Jeremy Guscott who's tackled Serge Blanco who's tackled Paul McClean who's tackled John Hipwell who's tackled Ken Catchpole . . . and so on. BOOM! One tackle on Farr-Jones and you're connected—worldwide and right back through the ages.

And whether or not you go on to representative honours it doesn't really matter. The pleasures of grade rugby are plentiful. Maybe ten years from now you'll be drinking tea on your front porch on an autumn afternoon, and you'll see some guy walk past who you used to play football against for years and years—a really nippy five-eighth, for example, who you always dreamed of creaming, but you could never get close enough to the brute to do it.

But no matter, you'll talk for a little while about old games you played and other players and what they're up to these days, and presently he'll go back to walking his dog, but as you return to your tea you'll reflect that all over Sydney town there are guys who you've played with and against, and you'll be glad you played the game.

Love it as much as we do, the downside of rugby has always been the possibility of serious injury, none more so than spinal injury. Though mostly these injuries occur in the front row, the backs aren't safe either.

ONCE MORE WITH FEELING: A WINGER'S PRAYER

It is an odd sort of happy story. The misery gauge only shifted from 'total tragedy' to 'grave misfortune', but everyone seems delighted all the same. With four minutes to go in the first half of the New South Wales v Waikato game at Concord on Saturday, Waratah winger Chris Saunders received the ball, swivelled, and at the precise moment he passed the ball was hit from behind in a legal tackle.

And he could still hear them, all the yelling of the players and the yahooing of the crowd as the game went on around him . . . but he was powerless to move. He lay numbly, lying on the ground with his face to the skies. He tried to move his legs . . . tried, tried and tried again, but still they wouldn't move.

Then, as the game continued to move back and forth and the players had moved on from over the top of him, he was able to wave his right arm. He weakly tried to make himself heard: 'Stop the game, stop the game.'

The game moved on, oblivious, and still he was left there, trying to turn his head to an angle where he could see his legs. But that, too, was useless and he began to think 'about the paraplegic bloke next door, and how I might be . . .'

The obvious.

The way Saunders tells it, though, he was not hit with the sort of blind panic you might expect. Almost as if the numbness of his neck and legs had spread to his emotions, he was noting what was going on without feeling that he was a part of it all. Now Waratah physiotherapist, Ian Collier, was bending over him. Now the other players were gathering around. Now team doctor, Miles Coolican, was pinching his legs and asking him questions. Now they were waving to the stands for someone to bring a stretcher. It all seemed a little unreal.

Up in the stands his mother, Anne Taylor, was in no such state of suspended reality. From the first moment her son had gone down her eyes had stayed on him, and while the rest of the crowd followed the ball, she *willed* him to get up and dust himself off. But he wouldn't move.

'I was thinking wheelchairs,' she said. 'I was sure he would be spending the rest of his life in a wheelchair, and had to restrain myself from running out onto the field immediately.'

She arrived at the players' exit tunnel with her husband and other son just the barest moment after the winger was carried from the field, and followed the crowd up to the New South Wales dressing-room door where, bizarrely, they were stopped by a security guard. Inside the dressing room, the first glimmer of hope came for Saunders as they took the strapping from his ankle and he could faintly feel the adhesive pulling a few hairs out.

'Not a lot, but I could feel it just enough to know that it wasn't totally dead down there,' he recalled.

Bit by bit over the next few minutes a little feeling started to come back to his feet, though still no movement. Saunders could hear the doctors for the first time start to make positive noises amid all the worry . . . things like 'spinal cord may be only bruised' and 'air ambulance not necessary'.

Over in the Spinal Care Unit at Royal North Shore Hospital that evening, at about 6.10 p.m., he moved one foot for the first time, then moved it again, and it was almost like his parents wanted to break out champagne, such was the palpable relief. By yesterday, Saunders had been discharged from the hospital to rest at home for the next two weeks.

Although he will have to wear a neck brace for a while and still has a strong feeling of pins and needles, it is expected he will regain full movement in all his limbs. He is, however, under strict medical instructions never to play rugby again—in fact, never even play so much as touch football—for fear of damaging what will forever be a weak point in his spinal column, but he appears relatively untroubled by it.

This is in part because he remembers a small incident from the early hours of Sunday morning in the hospital. Saunders was awake in his room, next to a fellow in the other bed, an 'incomplete' quadriplegic who had been in a bad surfing accident about thirteen weeks ago.

'He had a respirator and had great difficulty speaking,' Saunders recalled. 'But he saw I was awake and asked how I was. I said, "Look, I can move my foot," and he looked and said very softly, so I could just hear him, "Lucky bastard". That's pretty much what I think I am.'

An odd sort of happy story.

THE RISE AND RISE OF PHIL KEARNS

Where was Phil Kearns? Our agreed time and place to meet was six o'clock, Thursday night, in the foyer of the

Wallabies' plush Sydney hotel, and yet there was neither sight nor sound nor echo nor whiff of the newly anointed Australian captain.

No answer from his room. None of the other Wallabies had seen him. Where could he be?

Taking a punt that in this time of tension in the build-up to the Western Samoan Test he would surely gravitate to his natural habitat, I checked in the hotel gym . . . and sure enough.

Second cycling machine from the left, against the back wall, straining away like he was coming down the Champs Elysées after a burn around France with a yellow jersey on his back.

So what the hell is it with you and gyms anyway, Phil? You don't think it's a bit weird to spend half your waking hours in gyms do you?

'No I don't. I like doing gym work.'

And he really does. What else can you think of someone who after being part of the team that won the World Cup on a Saturday in November 1991 was back in his favourite Mosman gym the following Thursday—straining away, lifting weights and pushing what-nots endeavouring to recapture some of the strength that had dissipated over the time of the World Cup.

But we are ahead of ourselves. The rise of Kearns from an all-but-unknown rugby player in 1988, to Test player in 1989, to arguably the world's best hooker in 1991, to alternate Australian captain from late 1992 onwards, to being on the verge of equalling Peter Johnson's record of 42 Tests as a Wallaby hooker when he plays the All Blacks a week from tomorrow is . . . (phew) a long one.

And it starts, of course, well before that. There he is, the rotund crew-cut seven year old playing his first game of rugby for the Blakehurst Blues under-8s, taking the ball from the back of what he was told was a maul, and charging forward with the ball in hand. Try! 'And then all the other guys were crowding around me, patting me on the back, congratulating me,' Kearns recalls, 'and I thought, yeah, I like this.' As did his parents Keith and Nereda. Not in any over-the-top fashion, for they're simply not the type, but to Kearns's mind, 'they've pretty much always been there, encouraging me from the sidelines without ever pressuring me'.

BUMMER. Dropped from the Newington First XV. Damn nigh the most prestigious position possible for a student at that school is to be a member of the rugby Firsts, and the previous week Kearns had been delighted when in front of the whole school he had been handed his special Firsts jersey by the headmaster in honour of his selection for the first game of the season against Riverview.

In that game, young Phil thought he had acquitted himself rather well, and so did his dad as a matter of fact, but now the Firsts' coach had decided that perhaps the other lad, Tim Smythe, would be the better man for the job. Would Phil mind finding Tim and giving him the jersey?

No . . . not at all.

It was, frankly, enough to put a fellow off serious rugby for keeps, and at the beginning of 1985, having begun an arts degree majoring in commerce at New South Wales University, he reluctantly decided to give the game away and concentrate on his studies.

Herb Barker, a teacher at Newington and father of one of Kearns's closest schoolfriends, had other ideas. 'Why don't you go down to Randwick and try out with them?' he said. 'I'll give Jeff Sayle a call.'

Kearns did just that, without any pretensions to glory, and was as surprised as everyone else when at the beginning of the season, after playing his first trial game at Eastwood in 40 degree heat, he found that he was graded in Randwick Colts Firsts, ahead of the previous year's Australian Schoolboys hooker.

Rrrrrrrrrracing now. Off and running in the Firsts (Colts) at Randwick.

It was four years later, and Kearns had now graduated from the Colts side and a stint with the Australian under-21 team, to playing for the Randwick seconds behind the Galloping Greens' estimable first-choice hooker, Eddie Jones.

One afternoon in early August, he was just minding his own business labouring on a Bondi Junction construction site, when the foreman told him he had a phone call.

It was Bob Fordham, the executive director of the Australian Rugby Union.

'Phil,' he said, 'are you sitting down? You've been selected to play for the Wallabies against the All Blacks at Eden Park on Saturday.'

!!!!!!

Elated, sure, but also nervous as a mouse at a cat convention.

It was a shocking, windy and wet day at Eden Park. First scrum. Arms up and around his fellow debutant, Tony Daly, on his left, and the vastly experienced Andy McIntyre on his right. Facing them were arguably the All Blacks' finest ever front row of Richard Loe, Sean Fitzpatrick and Steve McDowell.

Grip. Crouch. HIT!

In the middle of the massive strain, the wrestling of shoulders as they waited for the ball to come in, Kearns was suddenly aware that the mouth of Sean Fitzpatrick had curled around to his ear, and his opposite number was speaking to him. 'What are you doing here, Kearns? You're just a little boy, you don't belong here. I'm the best in the world and you're a little kid. Go home to mummy. You should be back home watching this on TV . . .'

And so on. The way Kearns remembers it, that line of patter went on for pretty much the whole game, from first to last. Kearns's reply? Nothing. Hole in the doughnut.

'I just didn't want to say anything. I was concentrating on getting my job right in the scrum and in the lineouts and didn't want to be distracted by Fitzpatrick, which is of course why he was saying it.'

The Wallabies eventually lost the game, but Kearns amply vindicated his selection. He particularly remembers one moment in the second half when, being fed off the back of a maul from Nick Farr-Jones, he was able to take the ball up a full ten metres into the teeth of the All Black defence, and thought, yeah . . . I *do* like this.

There was to be no handing the jersey back this time.

Almost exactly a year later, and now a hardened Test player, Kearns was in the Wallaby side that was playing out of its collective tree in the third Test against the All Blacks at Wellington.

This time Fitzpatrick did not presume to so speak to Kearns, perhaps marshalling his own resources to counter what was a particularly devastating Australian scrumming performance that day. Then, from Kearns, the final squaring of accounts . . .

Three minutes into the second half the Wallaby hooker re-gathered a bouncing ball on the All Blacks' side of a lineout with only one defender between him and the tryline.

Sean Fitzpatrick.

Shoulder down, torso tensed, legs churning forwards, Kearns exoceted his way straight over the All Black for a try. In a moment that has since secured a very forward position in rugby folklore, Kearns immediately leapt to his feet, gave Fitzpatrick a two-fingered salute and leant over him, the better to scream an anatomically impossible suggestion at him.

All square on the card.

These days Kearns says that he has a 'healthy respect' for Fitzpatrick, which he thinks the New Zealander returns, and although they're unlikely to ever be best buddies, 'I quite like him'.

Even after such a wonderful Wallaby win in that third Test there was no letting up in the coming off-season from Kearns's particularly gruelling training regime.

For it was around this time that Kearns began to come most heavily under the influence of Bob Dwyer's 'techno rugby' program—an intricately organised daily regimen of running, weights, swimming and exercises combined with an equally pre-cise diet. All set out on page after page of dense data.

There were no few of us in the Wallaby squad at that time who glanced at Dwyer's massive missives only in the time it took to walk from the letterbox to the rubbish bin—and most of us were at the airport to see the others off when they flew out to the World Cup the following year.

Kearns, needless to say, followed it rigorously.

'Basically, because,' he says, 'once I got in the Australian team, I always wanted to stay there and I was conscious that a lot of guys would be coming at me for my spot. I figured the only way I could be sure of my spot was to get better, and to get better the best way was to follow that sort of program. Plus, I really enjoyed doing it all, and still do.' (Weird, I know, but that's the way our Phil is.)

At that time, and still now, Kearns's off-season training regi-men included a seven-kilometre run, two swimming stints and as many as six or seven sessions in the gym. And that's just Monday.

I'm kidding. That's the week. But the point remains: for whatever success Kearns has had, he has worked extremely hard for it.

Not that such an intense career for one so young has been without its costs.

His heels, ankles, knees and shoulders have all broken down at one time or another, and at the grand old age of twenty-seven, Kearns has 'arthritis in my right shoulder'.

'It doesn't worry me particularly, as I have a lot of faith in medical science. It will advance and maybe I can have artificial shoulders,' he says with a laugh. 'So long as I can swing a golf club I'll be right.'

And where were we? Ah yes, back in the here and now, and Kearns is lying on his bed after the gym session, relaxing a moment before going downstairs to join his Wallaby team-mates for a round-table session he will lead on the coming game against Western Samoa, which, as it turned out, must have been excep-tional. (Australia had gone on to a massive 73–3 win against them.)

And what was it that you were saying, Phil?

'And sometimes you think, My God, am I really here? Am I really Australian captain? You don't know how it all happens, it just does.'

How it happened, precisely, is that when Michael Lynagh broke down on the Wallabies' tour of Ireland and Wales at the end of 1992, Kearns took over the job and has filled the role when Lynagh has been unavailable. Very frequently, as it's turned out, as Kearns has captained Australia eight times since, against Lynagh's seven—as the latter has been hampered by injury after injury.

Kearns cites as his captaining influences those who have captained him with greatest effect: 'Nick Farr-Jones because he always wanted everything to be done with urgency, and his commitment to getting everything done right every time was absolute. Noddy [Lynagh] because he would only speak if he had something to say, and it was always very well thought out before he said it. And perhaps Simon Poidevin, because of the way he would lead by example, being the first to take the ball up aggressively and make the tackles that needed to be made.

'You've got to be your own style of captain,' says Kearns, 'but I'd like to think I could incorporate some or all of their best points.'

And as a matter of fact, Kearns has been an effective captain, with the Wallabies having recorded only two defeats under his stewardship.

But enough of this sycophantic pap. What about some harder questions? Over the years, amid all the positive publicity, there have been two basic themes of criticism directed at Kearns.

First, that his lineout throwing has not been up to the international mark, occasioning his friendly nickname among the players of 'Lightning'—because he never hits the same place twice. What about that then Phil? Aces high, jacks low, your call.

'At first, there's no doubt that every criticism I got about my throwing was deserved. But I think if you look at the lineout statistics over the last years you'll see we're on the right side of most of them. The jumpers usually get all the credit for that, and that's fair enough, but I think the thrower's got to have something to do with it, too.'

The second line of criticism has been, precisely, that when any criticism is offered he does not react well to it.

'There may be something in that, but only when it's not constructive criticism. I actually think I get a lot more upset when my fellow players are criticised, more than just me. Particularly by people who don't know what they're talking about. A prime example of that was just last year in one of the French Tests when Peter Slattery got blamed by a few commentators for missing a tackle on the French halfback from a scrum, which ended up in a try.

'Anybody who knows anything about rugby would know that that wasn't Slats's tackle to make because he was on the other side of the scrum. He would have had to have been superhuman to jump across the scrum to make the tackle. That sort of criticism I don't like.'

Whatever the truth or otherwise of the criticism, he's done

well, very well. And should in all probability continue to do so. In between working as something called Sales Development Manager for a brewing company, his extraordinary commitment to training continues apace. Every day, most nights, on and on.

At least there is some respite. In February Kearns will marry Julie Marden . . . whom he met in a gym.

Five years later, and Phil Kearns is still in the Wallaby squad, and though he lost the captaincy after an extended bout with injury, his career has been as remarkable for its longevity as for his talent on the field.

Kearns's principal opponent through all those years for the title of 'best rugby hooker in the world', was of course Sean Fitzpatrick.

AS BLACK AS THEY COME

Here he is again.

Sean Fitzpatrick, captain of the All Blacks. Come across the creek to personally lead the charge against the best Australia can throw at them tomorrow night at the Sydney Football Stadium. Just as he has done now on some seventeen occasions over the past nine years.

While having a drink with him at the bar of the All Blacks' Sydney hotel last Saturday night, there can be only one question for Fitzpatrick that counts . . . and you all know the one I mean.

How's your *ear*, Sean?

The All Black captain takes some time before replying, instinctively putting his hand up to the ear that only three weeks ago was famously bitten hard enough to draw blood by the South African prop Johan le Roux in the middle of the second Test of the series between the Boks and the Blacks.

At last, Fitzpatrick takes his hand down from his ear, is about to speak, and then suddenly puts his hand back up to it.

(Yes, Sean, your ear's still there. Promise. Speak to us . . .)

'It's fine, it was no big deal.'

Informally invoking the international rugby clause which says what happens on the field stays on the field—so long as it's not one of your body parts—Fitzpatrick demurs from any further comment, at least while the tape-recorder is on.

All he will say for the record is, 'He's a strange guy. If he'd smacked me in the mouth, fine. But I just don't understand the whole [biting thing].'

If it's not the strangest thing that's happened in Fitzpatrick's career, it's certainly right up there. And it's a career, as a matter of fact, that goes back quite a long way . . .

It was mid-1986 and it was a rather traumatic time for the young fellow, himself the son of a 1950s All Black. Fitzpatrick had only three games for Auckland under his belt when all hell broke loose in New Zealand rugby.

The rebel tour of All Blacks to South Africa, under the name 'Cavaliers', had returned to New Zealand shores, only to have all members promptly suspended by the NZRU. It meant the national selectors had to suddenly find a whole new slew of All Blacks—the so-called 'Baby Blacks'—to face the Alan Jones Wallabies in the first of a three-Test series. It meant, after Andy Dalton and Hika Reid dropped out, the new All Black hooker was Sean Fitzpatrick.

'I was nervous, of course I was nervous,' he said.

Not just because anyone is nervous when playing their first Test, but also because he would be making his debut against the man then considered the best hooker in the world, Tommy Lawton. First scrum. Tommy's shoulders seemed to go right across the whole front row the way Fitzpatrick recalls it.

'You know what Tommy's like, a gorilla,' he says. 'I was 22 years old, and Tommy was like . . . like . . .'

(*Tommy looked big.*)

As the two front rows came together with that odd sound of six pairs of shoulders meeting with massive force behind them, Fitzpatrick became aware that Lawton's mouth had curled suddenly around to his ear and was speaking to him . . . even as both front rows wrestled their shoulders around each other in the search for supremacy. Tommy's voice, coming in loud and clear, the way it would for the whole game.

'*What are you doing here, Fitzpatrick? You're just a little boy. You're not a real All Black, you're a mistake. Why don't you go home to mummy?*'

And so on. Did Fitzpatrick reply in kind? Not on your nelly.

'I just kept pushing and was way too busy to speak.'

Brrr, brrr, brrr, brrr.

And that'll be my shoe-phone now. It rings at the damndest times. But what the hey? It's Tommy Lawton himself. Is that true, Tommy? Did you speak to Fitzpatrick like that?

'Not that I specifically recall, at least not those exact words. I really thought he wasn't up to it, even if I was definitely proved wrong. And I told him . . .'

So? So fair enough.

Four years later Fitzpatrick would reply in kind when a young man named Phillip Kearns replaced Lawton from out of the blue, for the one-off Test against the All Blacks at Eden Park in 1989.

Fitzpatrick was shocked the great Tommy could have been dropped for this whippersnapper and decided to baptise Kearns in similar fashion to the way he had been by Lawton. The mouth curling around to the ear, the insults, the lot.

'Sure, I let him have it. I just couldn't understand why they'd dropped Tommy, and I told him so.'

Six years on, though, he would never presume to so speak to the Australian hooker.

'Listen, I do respect him totally as a player. I think he's a fantastic player. I sometimes wonder if he understands that. I mean, I'm so competitive, and he's so competitive that you can occasionally have clashes on the field, but there has never been any question that I greatly respect his abilities.'

Now in his ninth year as an All Black, Fitzpatrick has won 61 Test caps, established himself in the front row of international front-rowers, and generally been a very effective thorn in the side of many, many Australian teams.

In 1992, though, came the pinnacle of any All Black's aspirations, when he became captain.

How? Fitzpatrick's interpretation is that it was 'because there was no-one else. When Mike Brewer injured himself in the trials, I guess I was the last one left who was in a position to do the job, so they asked me. I never aspired to the position, never sought it, it just happened. I remember thinking, Oh, our centenary year and I'm captain . . .'

Tell them, Sean, of the pressures involved: 'It's often asked in New Zealand, "Would you rather be the prime minister or the All Black captain?", it's that sort of job. The prime minister himself recently said that when the All Blacks are winning he'd rather be All Black captain, and when they're not he'd rather be prime minister . . .'

Fitzpatrick knows how he feels, more or less. It's not that the All Blacks have lost more games than they've won since he's taken over, or anything so desperate as that, but things have been difficult.

A series loss against the Wallabies in 1992 was followed last year by a shock loss to England at Twickenham, and then this year began with two straight losses to the French. While Fitzpatrick's personal form has remained outstanding throughout, it cannot have been easy for him. Most particularly with the example before him of his two immediate predecessors as captain, Wayne Shelford and Gary Whetton, having both been sacked in action, straight from the captaincy to rugby oblivion. One might have thought, in such circumstances, that every phone call Fitzpatrick got these days, every tap on the shoulder, would be enough to make him jump from the chair in fright. Your thoughts, Sean?

'Yesss, it means you get to sit in what we call the ejector seat on the bus,' he says with a laugh. 'It's not easy, but still very satisfying.

'When I took over in 1992 I was particularly concerned that the All Blacks change our whole approach—not fall into the same traps that we maybe did in 1991, where the team perhaps had two distinct groups of older players and younger players, and where, too, our whole attitude to the rest of the world might have been off-course.'

Too arrogant? Too self-absorbed to the detriment of the team's relationship with the wider rugby community?

'Not exactly, but maybe a bit along those lines. One of my great satisfactions was at the end of the 1992 series against the Wallabies, when Nick Farr-Jones said this particular All Black team was changed from the previous ones in our approach to things, and I think we really have.'

This particular Test against the Wallabies falls at a difficult time for the All Blacks, as Fitzpatrick acknowledges. Though they won the series against the South Africans with two wins and a draw, the public was far from satisfied.

'When we didn't beat the Springboks in that third Test it was crazy,' Fitzpatrick says. 'It's been like the whole country has gone into national mourning or something. I think they're pretty keen that we win this one . . .'

One would have thought so. Part of the upshot is that All Blacks' coach, Laurie Mains, is under pressure as never before to hold his position. And while part of a captain's job is to automatically support his coach, Fitzpatrick sounds genuinely sincere when leaping to Mains's defence.

'Mate, he really is a good coach. Very good on preparation, on tactics, on taking care of everything that needs to be taken care of before a Test, but there's nothing he can do once the whistle blows to begin the game.

'That is our responsibility as players, and it's up to us to get it right. He's done everything he can, but ultimately it's got to be up to us.'

And the way Fitzpatrick tells it, the All Blacks definitely know what they're up against tomorrow night, no mistake about that.

'When we were at the final dinner with the Springboks at Eden Park, we were all watching the Wallabies versus Western Samoa game on the television, and when the Wallabies scored that first try after only a few minutes we thought, Mmmmm, this might be interesting.

'Then they kept going and going and when we had to leave to go back to the hotel I think there were twenty minutes to go and it was 50–3 or something, and then 73–3 by the time we got back to the hotel to watch the last few minutes. It was amazing.'

The feeling among the All Blacks at witnessing such total destruction of a team that has troubled them little in recent times was clear.

'Well, I think you could say we all felt it was a good idea to have an early night,' he says with a laugh. 'It put a bit of a dampener on things.'

Win lose or draw this game against the Wallabies, Fitzpatrick can already see the end of his own career coming over the horizon, not that far away.

Now married with a two-year-old daughter, and a demanding job in public relations with Coca-Cola New Zealand to boot, it's not that he's at all tired of playing for the All Blacks, but 'everybody has to know the right time to get out, and you've just got to be able to judge it right'.

The bottom line then?

'I'd like to play the World Cup next year, and that'll probably be it. Not definitely, because you never know, but that's the way I'm feeling at the moment.'

Which means tomorrow night may well be the last time we'll see him in these parts. Are there any thoughts he'd like to leave the Australian rugby public with, a few pearls of wisdom or farewell or something?

'Not particularly, but I guess generally I would like to be remembered as a good All Black.'

He is that.

But the All Blacks lost the Test anyway, 20–16, in a thriller. The result would have been different if George Gregan hadn't pulled off THE tackle, to bring down All Black winger, Jeff Wilson, just inches from the line with two minutes to go on the clock.

DAVID CAMPESE

It was *the* joke going around the Wallabies in mid-1991. 'Have you read Campo's autobiography?' they would ask anyone who would listen. 'Wait till you hear the opening paragraph!'

Then they would begin to read, in suitably pompous tones: 'In that short, abbreviated hour between the fading of the winter's afternoon sun and the onset of that bitter night cold which persuades me I could never live in the British Isles, I turned over in bed at a Surrey hotel where I was staying to take a telephone call which was to offer me the chance to change my life forever . . .'

The Wallabies' translation of what Campese had probably told his ghost-writer was slightly more succinct: 'Shit, it was cold, and then the bloody telephone rang.'

Haw, haw, haw. How far from the true Campese style of address could the writer get? But if the biography wasn't of the type to give a true picture of the man, none of the Wallabies doubted that Campese's stature was such that he deserved that sort of attention. These days, as the Greatest Rugby Player Ever, Campese seems to get through life in aeroplanes, landing occasionally to play a match somewhere or other in the world—Australia, South Africa, Italy, Hong Kong, the British Isles et al—but it wasn't ever thus.

The first time I heard of him was in May 1982, just before the New South Wales under-21 team took the field against the Australian Capital Territory under-21s, when the New South Wales coach told us: 'Now watch out for this bloke Campese, I've heard he's dangerous.'

'Camp-*who*?' we said. Campese. We did go on to beat the ACT, but not before damn nigh every last one of us had made a fool of ourselves trying to bring this insolent fullback to ground.

Campese was soon selected for the senior Wallaby team to tour New Zealand under the coaching of Bob Dwyer.

'Are you nervous about facing Stu Wilson tomorrow?' the New Zealand journalists asked Campese before his debut in the first Test against the All Blacks.

'Who is Stu Wilson?' Campese asked. For the New Zealand journalists it was a moment of breathtaking arrogance, or stupidity, or *something*—but it defied belief that this young pup could not know the name of the greatest winger New Zealand had produced, and the same one who would surely be burying him on the morrow.

With his first touch of the ball the following day, Campese stood Wilson up, and ran around him for a marvellous burst. He scored a try later in the game, also at the expense of Wilson, and has since scored some sixty Test tries, played in another 85 Tests, enthralled crowds whenever he has played and constantly picked gaps others didn't even see. The most famous of these gaps was surely the one that led to his try during the 1991 World Cup semi-final against New Zealand.

How Campese determined it was possible to score such a try has been the subject of endless analysis.

The irony and wonder of it is best seen in the context of Dwyer's coaching philosophy. The first commandment since he first took over the Wallabies has been 'Run Straight!'.

Yet, on this occasion, Campese broke every rule in the proverbial, running at an almost 45-degree angle across the field, right under the guns of the momentarily mesmerised All Black defence. It seemed as if none of them could make out what on earth Campese was up to, perhaps each expecting the other to tackle him and, at the death, Campese was able to slice neatly inside the All Black winger John Kirwan for a try that would take Australia to a crucial 4–0 lead.

'How did he do that?' the rugby pundits wanted to know. *Why* did he do it like that?

Nick Farr-Jones, the Australian scrum-half, says: 'How does anybody even begin to try to analyse what Campese does? It always amuses me when people try to work out why Campese did this or that on a rugby field, when I'm sure not even David himself knows why he does it.

'It's an instinctive thing and David has been blessed because his instinct is one that is not only adventurous but it also usually seems to send him in the right direction at the right time. It's something you can't try to work out, you've just got to enjoy it.'

Which people do, of course, revelling in his offensive capabilities, and forgiving him his frequent defensive lapses. Come what may, they want to watch him play.

When at the end of the 1991 World Cup, Campese suggested he was thinking of retiring, the Australian television network Channel Ten, which had just signed to broadcast rugby for three years, rightly saw that a lot of interest in Australian rugby would fall away with his departure and made him an offer he couldn't refuse.

If he continued to play for Australia for the next three years, they would employ him as a part-time rugby commentator at an annual salary of over $100 000. Put together with the prodigious sums he now earns in Italy and the profits from the sports store he owns in Sydney, and Campese has some claim to not only being the best rugby player, but also the best paid. Which is only fair.

Such is Campese's stature in the game now, he is the subject of articles and word-portraits in numerous publications, and most of these portray him as a generous, giving sort who has a charmingly frank way about him that can occasionally border on the acerbic, but only so as to add delightful spice to his character.

Hmmm. Strictly speaking, this is not quite the way he is. Within the Wallabies, Campese is well respected for his abilities and admired for his totally professional attitude to training . . . but not particularly cherished as the man closest to the warm beating heart of the team. One with Campese's extravagant talents is always going to be a man apart within any side, but his apartness has been exacerbated by what Dwyer has described as 'a wire loose between his brain and his mouth'.

The reason, for example, I didn't actually get the man himself on the blower to write this piece is because we're not on warm terms any more. The cause was nothing too earth-shattering, just that I took exception to a few vicious things he once publicly and piously expressed about a Test brawl in which I was involved. As a matter of fact, it was in the same wretched biography I mentioned earlier.

Knowing Campese, I very much doubt if there was so much malice aforethought as a sudden acidic bubble coming to the surface at the wrong moment—as has happened many times before, and will no doubt happen again.

Many players over the years have been similarly burnt and share more or less my attitude: he is as marvellous an offensive rugby player as ever drew breath; he has in his career done rugby extremely proud and left it immeasurably richer for his passing; and he's as hard a worker for his success as ever we've met.

That he doesn't in the bargain also happen to be an engaging personality and loyal friend is regrettable. But what the hell. In the end, we're fairly glad he played the game.

WHAT EVERY PARENT SHOULD REMEMBER
ABOUT SPORT

There is madness in the air. On one field, schoolboys are going at each other like drunken sailors in a Marseilles dockyard brawl; on another, parents and spectators are beating to a bloody pulp a linesman with whom they disagree; on thousands of scattered fields, lesser atrocities are happening all the time.

Clearly, somewhere or other, we've lost the plot, or the plot's lost us, or some damn thing, but the times are out of joint when the whole sense of 'the game for the game's sake' has died like a dog in a ditch.

With that in mind, I re-offer here a Code for Children's Sport I came across long ago, which was developed in New Zealand by the Wellington Rugby Union to provide compass points to prevent officials, parents and kids becoming lost in the youthful sporting jungle. It has been so successful in changing the culture in which the game is played there that it has since been translated and duplicated around the world in adapted forms.

Having taken the liberty of rejigging it for all sports, it looks like this.

PARENTS' CODE

1. Do not force an unwilling child to participate in sport.
2. Remember, children are involved in sport for their enjoyment, not yours.
3. Encourage your child always to play by the rules.
4. Teach your child that honest effort is as important as victory, so that the result of each game is accepted without undue disappointment. Never ridicule or yell at your child for making a mistake and losing a game.
5. Applaud good play by your team and by members of the opposing team. Do not publicly question the referee or umpire's judgment and NEVER his/her honesty.
6. Support all efforts to remove verbal and physical abuse from children's sport.
7. Recognise the value and importance of volunteer coaches. They give up their time and resources to provide recreational activities for your child.

So far so good? My guess is that if you haven't been involved in children's sport, you're finding it a bit trite—whereas if you have, you already have a particular parent in mind whose nose you'd like to jam it up. Actually, make that whose pocket you'd like to slip it into.

COACHES' CODE

1. Be reasonable in your demands on the players' time, energy and enthusiasm. Remember they have other interests.

2. Teach your players that the rules of the game are mutual agreements which no-one should evade or break.
3. Avoid over-playing the talented players. The 'just average' players need and deserve equal time.
4. Remember children play for fun and enjoyment and that winning is only part of it. Never ridicule or yell at the children for making mistakes or losing a game.
5. The scheduling and length of practice times and games should take into consideration the maturity level of the children.
6. Develop team respect for the ability of the opponents, as well as for the judgment of referees and opposing coaches.
7. Always follow the advice of a doctor in determining when an injured player is ready to play again.

All you demons got that?

Now to the players. A first bit of advice has to be: forget all the really serious stuff you often see on TV—there'll be plenty of time for that when you get older. The following code may not be the way we adults always behave, but it's at least the way most of us started out.

PLAYERS' CODE

1. Play for the fun of it, not just to please your parents or coach.
2. Play by the rules, and never argue with the referee's decisions. Let your captain or coach ask any necessary questions.
3. Control your temper. No mouthing off.
4. Treat all players as you would like to be treated. Don't interfere with, bully, or take unfair advantage of any players.
5. Remember that the goals of the game are to have fun, improve your skills and feel good. Don't be a show-off or always try to get the most points.
6. Co-operate with your coach, team-mates and opponents, for without them you don't have a game.

All up, cherish childhood and teenage sport for what it is—fun. No more, no less. If they're telling you any different, the problem is theirs, not yours.

And stop belting other kids. I know it seems like a good idea at the time, but it looks very ordinary on the evening news.

Trust me, I know.

HOW INVENTING TRADITION GOT THE BOKS
OVER THE HUMP

This is about the tiny town of Kuttabul, in the hinterland of North Queensland, about half an hour from Mackay. About a rugby club which was formed there only three years ago called the Kuttabul Camelboks and the story of how they've fared.

Brilliantly well is the short answer, but there's a longer one.

The club was conceived by three local farmers—Bill Needham, Colin Coles and Scot Allman—in late 1991. To begin, they put some five hundred fliers into the local letter boxes saying that a rugby club was being formed which was in desperate need of players, and in return received . . . one reply.

That was from a local bloke, Shane Maloney, who said he hadn't played rugby for the past fifteen years or so, but he'd be buggered if he didn't have half a mind to give it another burl. So that made four.

From there they went door-knocking, telephoning, tackling and collaring, until at last, after some months, they'd mustered some dozen likely local lads for the first training run on a sallow patch of sloping ground beside the Kuttabul pub.

They trained by the lights of their utes and tractors, which they'd parked in a circle around the ground, and kept going. Over the ensuing weeks, former soccer players were taught the basic mechanics of cut-out passes, and broken-down rugby league second-rowers learned the facts of life in scrums where you actually *pushed*.

With the club now formed and readying for the 1992 season, they instituted three basic rules, as a few odds and sods continued to join.

1. No kicking. The joy of rugby, to their mind, was running the ball and if you wanted to play for the Camelboks you had to understand that was the only way to proceed.
2. No train, no play, no excuses. Training would be only once a week, but if you didn't make it, for whatever reason, you simply missed out.
3. Absolutely no kicking (see Rule 1).

Things proceeded steadily, but still all was not quite right. Needham and his cohorts realised early on that the really fair dinkum clubs had long and glorious traditions, which were not only wonderful for their image, but more crucially gave the clubs enough historical ballast to hold their course even through the inevitable difficult times.

To rectify this shortcoming, they invited a lot of the older local farmers to be members of a team they invented—'the famous Kuttabul Camelboks '63 side'—which according to their creative legend had won the local premiership back then.

They even got these gentlemen to come to the Kuttabul pub to pose in period costume for a nice grainy black-and-white photo. The farmers themselves became enthused and have since been an integral part of the burgeoning local rugby community.

With the '63 side such a triumph, it was decided after the first year had been successfully completed that it would give added incentive for everyone to stay on board if the club held its centenary in 1994.

And so it went on. The results in 1993 were even better, an under-19 team was added to the club, and this year the jerseys did indeed proudly display the '100 YEARS' emblem on the right breast.

The left breast was of course reserved for the famous and historical Kuttabul emblem, a camel jumping over a football— amazingly similar to the Springbok emblem, as a matter of fact.

(There is some feeling among the Camelboks that the Springboks probably stole the idea for their emblem from the Kuttabul boys in the early part of the century, but in the true spirit of the game they have been big-hearted enough to forgive and forget.)

But to the best part. In this, their centenary year, the Camelboks won their local competition, beating Proserpine 15–0. With such a stunning result, the Camelboks made the usual extravagant plans for the traditional end-of-season dinner, and flew a former Wallaby and his wife up from Sydney.

Typically, instead of simply driving them to the pub on Saturday evening—which would have been boring—they took them the 'scenic route', which involved a three-hour trip by boat, truck, horse 'n' buggy, train, tractor, horseback and finally a grand entrance on camelback.

It was a good night. The captain of the famous '63 side himself was there, together with most of his team-mates from the era, and he regaled the club with some wonderful tales of that unforgettable grand final of three decades earlier, when the fearless boys of Kuttabul had taken on the Fairleigh Arrows and beaten them at the death, 17–16. And so on . . .

The point of all this? Like rugby itself, there is none, particularly. But when it's done in the right spirit it can be more fun than a mud fight. The Camelboks think so anyway.

If rugby was thriving down there at the grassroots level—with many happy little Vegemites for whom the lack of pay-for-play was of absolutely no concern whatsoever—the same could not be said of the elite level of the game. In previous years there had been increased agitation from representative players for remuneration for their efforts, and in 1995 it all came to a head. On 1 April that year, Rupert Murdoch's News Corporation launched an attempted takeover of rugby league, called 'Super League', which ultimately meant that the sort of money on offer for footballers of all stripes—including rugby union players—was now three or four times what it had been previously.

Clearly, the only way for the elite level of rugby union not to be decimated by league was to come up with money, fast, to pay the players—and with that in mind there were quick declarations by Australia's provincial unions that rugby was no longer amateur.

Ironically, the establishment soon realised that the only entity which could come up with the money needed was News Corporation, which they duly set out to woo. In the meantime, three other men—Ross Turnbull, Geoff Levy and Michael Hill—with the backing of Kerry Packer, set up their own entity, the grandiosely named World Rugby Corporation. Their intention was to create an international rugby competition wholly outside the establishment, by contracting the players themselves. The stage was set for one of rugby's most tumultuous battles.

SUPER LEAGUE FALLOUT: NOW RUGBY UNION GOES PRO

What was the significance of yesterday's announcement by the New South Wales and Queensland Rugby Unions? Simply this: for the first time in the history of rugby union, official bodies of its administration have broken ranks and declared that the first article of faith on which it was built worldwide—amateurism—is no longer valid in the world of modern sport.

They have formalised what has been previously an informal understanding, brought out into the open what has previously been under cover, saluted what previously has only been nodded at. While many players had expressed the opinion that the game should go professional, a sentiment echoed occasionally by a few officials, yesterday's historic announcement will surely be looked back on as the day the dam broke.

It can only be a matter of time before the Australian Rugby Football Union follows suit, as there is equally no doubt that the announcements of the New South Wales and Queensland Rugby Unions were orchestrated by the ARFU. And from there, after a requisite amount of screaming, we will surely see other nations fall to the professional way echoing the domino effect apparent over the past twelve days with clubs in the Super League.

New Zealand, the other nation where the union code is most at risk from the incursions of rugby league, will likely be the first to follow suit. As recently as last week, the All Blacks' coach, Mr Laurie Mains, made a plaintive cry that rugby had to go professional or risk losing everything to the Auckland Warriors and the like. In South Africa, although rugby league is not a significant threat, the ethos of strict amateurism was long ago dropped as just so much ballast and it is an open secret that players have been paid, or handsomely remunerated, at a provincial level for many years.

Ditto the situation in at least the first three of the countries in the Five Nations competition—France, England, Wales, Ireland and Scotland. Wales, particularly, has lost many players to rugby league over the years and would surely welcome an opportunity to stem the flow, and perhaps even turn it, by going openly professional.

While England and France have not had such a problem with rugby league, the former is likely to soon, with the arrival of Mr Murdoch's Super League, and the latter has long been an agitator for a looser definition of the word 'amateur'.

In short, in declaring for professionalism, the New South

Wales and Queensland Rugby Unions have put themselves at the forefront of a revolutionary change in rugby union that was always going to come. One of the most pressing aims of yesterday's announcement though has surely already been accomplished—to send a cogent message to the code's elite players. That message runs like this: 'DON'T GO!' Maintain the faith, don't go to Super League and you'll be taken care of financially. You'll stay with the game and the people you know, and you'll get rich.'

The downside of it all? That the unique culture of the game will change forever. That the Wallabies, and perhaps even club players of 2010, will shake their heads with wonder that the players of yesteryear could ever have busted their butts for naught but the joy of the game.

That's not the way it is now, strictly speaking, but it's the way it was—and we will not see those times again.

Late conversion makes it an All Black day for union

Dammit, John, what did you have to go and do that for? The news that John Kirwan, perhaps the most famous and accomplished All Black of the past two decades, has signed a two-year contract with the Auckland Warriors league team is troubling for those of us who hold the union game dear.

If Kirwan, who was more of an international rugby union icon than merely a great player, can go over to league, just who can be judged as definite to stay? If the Rock of Gibraltar can suddenly turn to dust, what landmark of the union world is truly solid?

The equivalent of Kirwan's defection on this side of the Tasman would be Nick Farr-Jones coming out of retirement to sign on with, say, South Sydney. (Unlikely, just quietly . . . but moving right along.)

Kirwan's departure from union ranks comes at a particularly damaging time for the 15-man code in New Zealand. Beneath the long white cloud, a rather bitter war is being fought for the hearts and minds of the sporting public, and Kirwan's donning of the Warriors' jersey is a huge moral victory for rugby league even before he plays his first game. If he can score tries for them too, that will be a bonus, but PR coups don't come much better.

'Ladies and gentlemen, in our corner, John Kirwan! A man who has played 63 Tests for the All Blacks, but who has recently seen the light just in time to catch the wave of the future—rugby league!'

Why would the former All Black winger do such a thing? (Apart from a reputed lazy $200 000 salary over the next two years, I mean.)

In part, because he had nowhere else to go in rugby union. Not only have his famous skills been a little on the wane in recent times, he also made the serious mistake last year of backing the wrong horse in the All Black coaching power struggle between Laurie Mains and John Hart.

Kirwan backed his mentor, Hart, Mains got up, and Irene said goodnight to Kirwan's All Black career. He was first approached to play for the Auckland Warriors shortly after he announced his retirement, and after some brief soul-searching, he declined.

Now he has obviously had a change of heart, perhaps hurried along by the painful silence that descends on many sportspeople when the glory days seem suddenly over. Where do I sign coach? Just get me back out there.

So he's gone, and for mine, it's more than passing sad both for him and the code.

Why? Because Kirwan has been revered for the past decade and a bit by the people who hold the All Black jersey dear; because he has risen to great fame through his feats in that jersey; and because such a magnificent All Black career required a far finer finish than a damaging departure when the code needed him most.

In the old days, the thought of such an esteemed All Black switching to rugby league wouldn't have been a thought at all—it would have been unthinkable. But it seems they're playing a different ball game in those parts these days, in more ways than one.

But to the battle royal between the World Rugby Corporation and the rugby establishment for the hearts and minds of the rugby players and public . . .

First up for the establishment was the task of extracting the money necessary to keep players onside from Uncle Rupert, by offering the television rights to a newly conceived competition. The following extract is from a book I wrote, called The Rugby War.

THE DONE DEAL

'Now remember,' Ian Frykberg briefed his companions, as they made their way to Sam Chisholm's apartment in exclusive inner London, opposite a particularly well-manicured green park. 'Don't waste Chisholm's time, don't say anything obvious, and keep whatever points you've got to make concise. He's always bloody busy, and he likes to get to the point,' said the CEO of TV brokerage firm Communication Services International.

It was eleven o'clock on the morning of 16 May 1995, and NSWRU chief executive officer David Moffett, in the company of a bevy of leading southern hemisphere rugby officials in Dick McGruther (Australian Rugby Union director), NZ Rugby Football Union chairman Richie Guy, and his deputy, Rob Fisher, was about to meet the head of News Corporation's international television empire for the first time.

In the business of selling the Super 12 and Tri-Series competition to News Corp, Frykberg's personal knowledge of Chisholm was going to be important. When you were dealing with Murdoch's main man, there were any number of landmines, dead ends and pits of verbal quicksand that could set you back if you didn't know where they were. And Frykberg was one of the few people who had a map.

So the door to Chisholm's apartment opened. Standing there was Bruce McWilliam, Chisholm's ever-present lawyer, and just behind him, Chisholm himself—a rather neatly compact sort of man, impeccably groomed and, for the moment, graciousness itself.

Chisholm, a charismatic chainsaw of a man, remained the perfectly polite host right up until it came time to get down to tintacks, by all accounts only a few minutes after entering. That was when the host stood up and rather peremptorily announced his rules of engagement. They went something like this:

Chisholm was to be News Corp's sole point of contact on this deal, while McWilliam would see to legal questions. He wasn't going to deal with any committee on this, and from their side of things would accept talking to only one person, two at most.

Everyone had to keep strictest confidentiality on this or the whole thing was off. If he read a single line about it in the newspapers, then forget it, and he meant *forget* it. This was a deal between News Corp and the three national unions of Australia, New Zealand and South Africa, and he didn't want anyone else knowing about it. If none of this was to anyone's liking, that was fine, because if News Corp didn't spend the money on rugby it would be happy to spend it somewhere else. All clear? Everything understood?

Crystal clear, Sam.

A discussion then ensued about the rugby model they wanted to sell, which Chisholm seemed to approve of, as near as they could reckon. There was some talk from the visitors about the fact that some of the unions already had commercial arrangements with other broadcasters, and whether or not these arrangements might affect their dealings with News Corp.

Chisholm, by all accounts, didn't want to hear it. It was for the unions to work out, he said, what it was that they were free to sell and what they weren't. Once they'd done that, he said, they could come back to him, and he would tell them what he was prepared to pay.

Fine. One minor hiccup though. One of the visitors ignored Frykberg's previous warning, and opined that rugby really could be a very valuable product if it was packaged properly, whereupon Chisholm cut him dead with a withering: 'Thank you for that penetrating glimpse into the obvious.'

No-one made any further pleasantries about the attractions of rugby. The meeting finished about an hour after it had begun, with Chisholm suddenly all bonhomie again.

'That was a pretty good meeting, wasn't it?' he asked nobody in particular. 'I behaved myself, didn't I?'

But of course, Sam. 'Well, I will tell you what,' Rob Fisher remembers Chisholm saying as they went out the door, 'there is no such thing in our organisation as good cop, bad cop. There is only bad cop and worse cop, and this is as good as it is going to get.'

Everyone laughed. 'He was right, of course,' says Fisher now wryly, 'but we liked him a lot.'

There had been no talk at this early stage of anything so gauche as money, but that would be broached in due course.

A phone call. To Kerry Packer's World Rugby Corporation director Geoff Levy at his office in Sydney's MLC Centre, situated in the very heart of downtown.

Did Levy know there was a rumour that some officials from the Australian Rugby Union had flown off to London to see Sam Chisholm and talk about some new competition they wanted to sell News Corp?

No he didn't, but he was certainly interested to hear it. As anyone would be who was even then heavily engaged in getting his own alternative international professional rugby competition up and running.

Finally, it was done. Frykberg had worked out the maximum price to which he thought Chisholm could be pushed; agreement had been reached between all three unions on all the fine points, and now Moffett found himself on another whirlwind trip to London.

This time he was in the company of South African Rugby Football Union chairman, Louis Luyt, and they were going to see Sam Chisholm to present him with both the refined version of the Super 12 and, more particularly, the price they were asking. The two were met by Frykberg in London. At Chisholm's offices at BSkyB—rather well-appointed, Moffett thought—they cut to the chase. Moffett opened his briefcase, and took out the document containing their proposal. He handed it to Chisholm and waited, watching carefully to see how he would react. Chisholm skimmed the first few pages, his eyes moving restlessly over the words, obviously looking for something, until *Bingo!* He found it.

There was the final price the three national unions were asking, at the bottom of the fifth page: $US650 million ($A886 million) for the rights to their competition over the next ten years.

With an air of mock theatricality, Chisholm gripped his chest and grimaced fiercely, feigning a heart attack.

'This is going to kill me,' he said with a long and hearty laugh, before abruptly continuing. 'And we're not paying that much.'

Luyt, an extremely practised business negotiator, said that was absolutely fine with him, and appeared entirely unconcerned. He left with David Moffett for Heathrow soon after.

Watching from London the World Cup semi-final between New Zealand and England (in which Jonah Lomu scored no fewer than four tries in astounding fashion), Sam Chisholm was delighted.

Given that the South Africans had beaten France the day before, it set up a South Africa v New Zealand final for the World Cup. This was a good result for Chisholm, in that he was getting very close to committing an enormous amount of his corporation's money to ten years of a competition which boasted those two teams.

Someone else was pleased. Chisholm was still trying to come down from the fantastic game when he took a phone call from the man he refers to as 'the boss', Rupert Murdoch. Murdoch was also delighted. Really delighted.

'Absolutely amazing,' is the phrase Chisholm remembers the chairman of News Corp using, as he realised, perhaps for the first time, just how enthralling rugby could be when it was played at its spectacular best. 'It's the most electrifying thing I have ever seen,' Chisholm recalls replying, 'and that was when Rupert said, "This is amazing, we've got to have that guy . . ."'

As it turned out, Murdoch was not Robinson Crusoe in wanting to have Lomu for his competition.

It was agreed. The unions would commit themselves to News Corp.

Luyt (representing the three unions) flew from South Africa and turned up at Chisholm's London apartment on 20 June. A business and legal neophyte would have thought for a massive deal, involving such enormous sums of money in exchange for a momentous allocation of rights over ten years, that the relevant document would have been drawn up by a battalion of lawyers on one side, and minutely examined by a whole army of roving legal beagles—*hunt, doggy! hunt!*—on the other.

But that was not the way News Corp did business, in this instance at least. When Luyt arrived that morning, there was no document in existence! Instead, it was to be drawn up by News Corp lawyer McWilliam on a portable computer perched on Chisholm's dining-room table and progressively printed out on a portable printer set up nearby.

As each page came off the printer, Luyt would read it carefully, making the request for a change here and there. Some were granted, some were declined. And so the document was drawn up over the next hour or so.

Entitled 'Heads of Agreement'—as in the broad brushstrokes of the deal which would later have its detail filled in—the emerging document gave News Corp wide powers.

As a sweetener, and after a little of the usual haggling, Chisholm had agreed to up the ante by another lazy $US 5 million—to bring the contract size to $US 555 million, 'so long as you sign today'. Luyt was agreeable. If the amount of money was to prove pleasing to the national unions concerned, it must be said that they ceded a lot of control to get it.

Clause 11 seemed more than generous towards News Corp.

> 11. For the next five seasons after the Term (as in at the conclusion of the 10 years), SANZAR shall negotiate with News in good faith in an endeavour to agree the terms for News obtaining similar rights as set out in this agreement and in any event shall not grant such rights (or rights included in such rights) to any other party . . .

A five-year option, no less, which if taken up would bind rugby with News Corp right through until 2011.

With the document ready, but still unsigned, Luyt (with his son) went off to lunch with Frykberg. Chisholm had a call to make—to Murdoch at his Los Angeles headquarters. Luyt and Frykberg, both men of healthy appetite, were tucking into their main course of massive ribs, when Frykberg's mobile phone rang. It was Chisholm. 'The boss has given the OK,' he said. 'Get back here now, and let's sign it.' Luyt was not happy about leaving the ribs half eaten, as Frykberg recalls, and inquired if the signing couldn't wait just a little while until they'd finished their meal. Frykberg, truth be told, wasn't too thrilled himself, but insisted they head back to Chisholm's apartment immediately.

So the job was done. Luyt initialled every page of the five-page document, with his signature on the final page and dated it. Sam Chisholm countersigned, and that was that.

Oddly enough, there was no hoopla, no fanfare, no air-punching from either side. A simple handshake all round. A broad smile from Luyt with a reflection to his son: 'You see how business is done at this level? Straight talking, and give your word.' And then the two departed with the men of News Corp's best wishes for a safe trip.

Oh. And one more thing.

'Make sure you get all your guys signed up soon,' Chisholm said just before the door closed. 'You've got to get those players signed immediately.'

The three most powerful national unions of the southern hemisphere were now formally and legally committed to the project, just as News Corp was committed to them, and all seemed set for a trouble-free dawning of the professional age of rugby union.

While this was going on, the 1995 Rugby World Cup was underway in South Africa. Together with Greg Growden, I covered the Cup for the Sydney Morning Herald.

THE END OF AN ERA

A golden period of Australian rugby came to an end today. At Newlands Stadium in Cape Town, the Wallabies were heartbreakingly beaten 25–22 by a rampaging England in the quarter-finals of the World Cup. The loss sees the end of a period of world domination by the Wallabies which began on 2 November 1991, at Twickenham when they won the William Webb Ellis Trophy, and it continued through series wins against New Zealand, South Africa, Ireland, Argentina and Scotland, among others.

It ended, effectively, just a minute before full-time yesterday, when the English five-eighth, Rob Andrew, launched a drop-goal attempt 40 metres out from the Australian goalposts. At that point the score was locked at 22–22, and the Australian team watched aghast as the ball sailed over their heads, and straight through the sticks.

With a three-point deficit, there still seemed some chance that Australia might be able to repeat what they famously did in Ireland four years ago—come back from the dead. With skinny, *starving* seconds remaining, the Wallabies retrieved the ball and launched an attack that moved through twelve pairs of hands, only to break down with the line in sight. The English halfback, Dewi Morris, gathered the ball and kicked it into the distance. Over the touchline, and out.

The final whistle blew.

Wallaby captain Michael Lynagh was gracious in defeat. 'We gave it our best shot,' he said simply, 'but we just couldn't get there. It had to end some time . . .'

While the Australian campaign sputtered and died, the New Zealanders were coming on strong like thunder, powered in large part by a young man named Jonah.

JONAH LOMU—THE FREIGHT TRAIN IN BALLET SHOES

Lomu. He's coming this way. Make way. Make way.

To a man, they make way, make way as, with the rest of the All Blacks, the 119kg, 195cm, 20-year-old winger makes his way to the bleachers on the edge of the practice field. *Fe fi fo fum*, he surely smells the blood of the media scrum.

Walkman firmly glued to his ears, he pretends not to notice the attention particularly, affecting the attitude of being entirely alone, not talking even to his fellow All Blacks changing their sandshoes for boots beside him.

This is the last of the 'open' New Zealand training sessions before the World Cup final, the last time to see Jonah Lomu close up before he disappears into the cocoon the New Zealand management has tailor-made for him. The photographers don't miss their mark. Their lenses drink in every image of the fellow from the moment he hoves into view, to his preparations, to his every move out on the paddock for the next hour and a half.

The bulk of the All Blacks' training on this day is a fast and furious game of touch. Every time Lomu has the ball in hand, the combined click of camera shutters sounds like handfuls of gravel being thrown on the roof of a distant tin shed. When at one point he makes a long, jinking run right by us, it is a large bucket tipping the gravel onto the roof in one long stream.

What is this all about? It's about someone who, only six Tests into his career, is being touted by the media, and by many serious rugby followers besides, as perhaps the most sensational player rugby has seen. It's not just that he has scored seven tries in the World Cup to date, and four in the semi-final against England alone, it's the *way* he has scored them—but we'll get to that.

There are famous people in this All Black side: Zinzan Brooke, who took over from Wayne Shelford at No 8 and dropped a field goal from 40 metres out in the semi-final; captain, Sean Fitzpatrick, who played his hundredth game for the All Blacks just three games ago; Walter Little, who is in the best form of his career and has been in the All Blacks since 1989—and is still only twenty-five. Nobody cares about any of these players, though—they have been reduced to mere supporting roles to Lomu's star turn.

And over there is Jeff Wilson, the winger on the other side who has also played international cricket for his country. Only an hour or so earlier he was what the media liaison officer had called 'today's Jonah spokesman' when he fronted 100 assembled members of the international press who were hungry for sight or sound of the giant Lomu, and who had been fed Wilson instead.

Wilson copes well with being asked a dozen questions about the winger who is his junior in terms of experience in international rugby. Eventually the question is put. Tell us, Jeff, tell us true, how would you stop Lomu if you were up against him? Quick as a flash, Wilson replies: 'Be on the same side as him, that way you never have to . . .'

We all dutifully note it down as some pretty good fodder for the How To Stop Lomu articles that are appearing all over the world. And did you hear, by the way, of the fax sent by the 8-year-old farm boy living just outside Christchurch?

> *Dear All Blacks,*
> *Remember, rugby is a team game. All 14 of you, pass the ball to Jonah!*
> *Yours,*
> *Jed*

Any story about Lomu is good at the moment, by simple virtue of his domination of this tournament.

Today's copy of the *Citizen* has seven, that's *seven* Lomu headlines. And here is the Afrikaans paper *Der Beeld*. It has an enormous article with a photo, about a female student from Cape Town who is claiming that Jonah is in love with her, that he rings her all the time, that he makes secret signs to her on the field.

Our guess is that the secret sign must surely be something like: 'Now listen, darling, when I score my *fourth* try in a row, that will mean I really, *really* love you.'

It's absurd, of course, to devote so much attention to just one player in a 15-man side, and it's surely conduct unbecoming for an enormous number of hardened journalists, who between them have seen it all, to be so atwitter about one young player. But this really is different. The feeling is that this guy is not just 'good' the way Zinzan Brooke was good when he first took over from Shelford, or 'great' the way David Campese was great in his early days.

Rightly or wrongly, the feeling is that Lomu is an absolute freak, the like of which we'll never see again. The feeling is that if you want to know what the absolute last word in wingers is, then we've just seen it—that you simply can't do better than score four tries against England in a semi-final of a World Cup.

Unless it's the same feat against the Springboks in the final.

Four years on and Jonah Lomu has had what might be described as a 'brilliantly chequered career' since. That is, he has continued to have many shining moments on the field, though he has been equally blighted by ill-health which has diminished his performance somewhat. At the time of going to press in mid-July 1999, he was listed as a reserve for the All Black Test side.

THE EVE OF BATTLE

It happened just a week or so from the World Cup Final. Sean Fitzpatrick, the All Black captain and man judged most likely to lift the William Webb Ellis Trophy above his shoulders at the conclusion of the final, was in a supermarket near the team hotel when a woman approached.

'She was a bit nervous,' Fitzpatrick recounts, 'but she asked would I mind signing a little rugby ball she had with her.'

No problem. The woman dug a pen out of her purse, and as he has done perhaps some 10 000 times over his ten-year Test career, Fitzpatrick began to write. 'I'd just written out "Sean",' he says, 'when suddenly she snatched the ball and the pen from me and ran up the aisle yelling.'

What was she yelling?

'JONAH!'

Jonah Lomu, the wing sensation of the All Black side, had just come into the same supermarket, leaving his captain standing, and Fitzpatrick laughs ruefully at the memory. Strange days indeed, mama, most peculiar.

He is a good fellow, this All Black captain, and if he is on edge about being on the eve of what he knows will be either his greatest hour or his most crushing disappointment, it doesn't show. Rather, like the team around him, Fitzpatrick comes across as relaxed and confident enough, though far from arrogant about it.

It is, of course, a marked change from the All Black side competing in the 1991 World Cup, famous for its snooty distance from the rest of the rugby world and what sometimes seemed its rather cold-blooded commercial outlook.

'In 1991,' says Fitzpatrick, 'we were focused on dollars, and in this team we just don't discuss it. It's just not an issue with us. This team is totally focused on rugby. We're simply enjoying it, and it's great.'

In a previous conversation, the hooker had mentioned that he felt instinctively that the Wallabies were not going to go far in this World Cup from the moment he saw them on television getting off the bus for their first game against South Africa. Can he expand on that now, with the tape-recorder running?

'Well, you know . . . the sunglasses, the *attitude*; it was exactly like we [All Blacks] were four years ago. We thought all we had to do was turn up and put the black jerseys on and we would win.

'I say that with the greatest respect for the Wallabies, because I still think they're a great side and will be tough in the Bledisloe Cup, but it is funny drawing the analogy from 1991 and seeing it so clearly now.

'You don't put in the same preparation as you did before, and you keep on telling yourself that everything is alright, even when you know it isn't.

'I'm sure they [the Wallabies] will look back in four years' time and see it happening to another team.'

The way back for his team, he says, was going back to the very basics of what the jersey was about—'just being All Blacks, we want to be All Blacks, and we want to be successful All Blacks'.

There was also some repairing to do in the relationship with their supporters.

'When we won the World Cup in 1987, the whole country was with us and it was fantastic. In 1991 it was more just us fifteen that we were focused on, and it didn't work.

'When [World Cup campaign manager] BJ Lochore came in last year, he said, "Look, before we go any further we've got to have the whole country behind us," and you can feel that at home now—the country is alive and buzzing, and the guys feel that . . .'

Not that it shows. There never seemed in all Christendom such a low-key All Black team as this one. Wherefore art thou, bragging, brouhaha, bravado?

'I suppose a big thing for us was the way our guys won the America's Cup,' says Fitzpatrick. 'They were very low-key, there was no big deal about anything, everybody just quietly went about doing their job, doing what had to be done to win and not going on about it.'

It is an approach that the captain himself enforces. In the semi-final against England, while standing under the goalposts as Rob Andrew took a final kick at goal in what was a crushing English loss, Fitzpatrick laid down the law.

'I said, "Right, that's it, shake their hands, change jerseys, do whatever you want to do but be humble—no nonsense."'

Nonsense, to Fitzpatrick's mind, would have been doing to England what England did to them when they beat the All Blacks in 1993, rubbing their noses in it.

'In 1993 they were terrible winners. For us you've got to be a good loser to be a good winner later on. We played it down.'

Medic! There's a serious problem here! This guy's a victorious All Black captain, on the edge of establishing world domination in just about as fantastic a fashion of rugby as has ever been seen, and he's coming across as humble as St Francis of Assisi. What gives?

'That's the way it is,' says the man with another smile.

As to the coming final, Fitzpatrick at least admits to a certain amount of hope that they might actually give a reasonable account of themselves.

'We've got a lot of work to do and we realise that the South Africans will come out like men possessed and play the match of their lives, but if we play like we can we'll go all right.'

(*Forget it, medic, I think we've lost him.*)

One more thing though, Sean, just between us Australasians. As the only man who will have played in two World Cup finals, as the captain of a side that's captured the imagination of the rugby world like no other in this tournament, do you never in the privacy of your own room do a few air-punches of exultation?

'Well, I'm enjoying it,' he says flatly. 'But all that stuff can wait till after the game—if we win.'

And so to the final of the Rugby World Cup, 1995.

THE PRAYERS OF A NATION'S HERO

They were emotions from opposite ends of the spectrum, side by side.

When the referee blew the game quits—for a South African victory in the 1995 Rugby World Cup—the Springbok captain, Francois Pienaar, sank straight to his knees, with his hands spread out on the ground before him. Other Springboks hit the field around him until they were all there, every man jack of them, doing exactly the same.

Hello? What is this all about?

'It was because we are all Christians,' Pienaar explained later, 'and we were praying, thanking the Lord for giving us the talent to play in the final, and the strength to win it.'

Riiiiight.

Meanwhile, the All Blacks turned their backs on the whole thing and walked resolutely away. Could it be that they had lost this World Cup final after being right on the razor's edge of winning it for a full 100 minutes (for the game had gone to extra time), and now it was over, now they had lost? Say it ain't so, Sam, sing some other tune but not that one.

They kept walking. Then some began to run for the dressing room and to hell with it, to hell with the whole thing. Not untypically, Richard Loe was first into that closed and comforting sanctuary, followed closely by Jamie Joseph and a couple of the other All Blacks. One of the New Zealand officials yelled after them, presumably to demand they have the grace to remain for the ceremony, but it was too late. They were gone with the wind, gone without the Cup that so narrowly escaped them.

Sean Fitzpatrick, the All Blacks captain, of course stayed, with ten of his men. He stood with his hands on his hips, a little apart from the others, watching proceedings. He stayed there as the stage was swiftly brought out onto the ground, as the security men set up a rope around the area, as the Springboks gradually made their way to it, as President Mandela and his entourage made their way onto the field and the crowd roared and began chanting, 'Nelson . . . Nelson . . . Nelson'.

Then, just when Mr Mandela was about to present the gleaming William Webb Ellis Trophy, the stadium and the southern scoreboard screen were filled with the sound and vision of Pienaar being interviewed live on the field by South African television.

Pienaar exulted about the joy of the victory, about how the Cup had been borne aloft not just by the fifteen of them, not just by the 60 000 of his countrymen in the stadium, but by all 43 million South Africans. Fair enough, and the crowd lapped it up. Fitzpatrick stood stock-still watching it all, surely replaying in his mind the three or four occasions when his team might have broken through for a win but *just* failed to do so.

Time though for the final act. Pienaar accepted the trophy from Mandela, raised it above his head in the manner Björn Borg made famous, and then left the stage to a rolling thunder of applause. The rest of the Springboks gathered around him, and they all joyously embarked on a victory lap, as the All Blacks were left there still, black shags on a lonely rock.

You mean that's *it*? No words from the All Black camp, no chance for Fitzpatrick to say a few words as Pienaar had only minutes earlier? Thanks for coming, and see you later? It scarcely seemed credible, but the New Zealanders realised that that was indeed the case and drifted off themselves—a few on a desultory walk around the field to thank their supporters, the rest to the tunnel.

Fitzpatrick left the field, alone and silent.

It all brought to mind, frankly, the rudeness of us Australians in not allowing Pienaar to speak at the conclusion of their three-Test series in Australia in 1993, and that rightly prompted a great outcry.

At least Pienaar, halfway through his side's victory lap, realised the untowardness of it all and ran half the length of the field alone to congratulate and thank the few All Blacks still out there. But that was it.

All up, it was an inappropriate ending to a game and a stirring South African campaign which deserved better. Pienaar has genuinely been a magnificent captain throughout, and his side did wonderfully well to beat a side which, by any measure, had so much more firepower than they did. It's just a pity that it ended thus.

Nowhere through any of it was the New Zealand coach Laurie Mains apparent. Whatever the devastation he must have been feeling, he may at least console himself that, by any measure, he has done well to mould this All Black side into an extremely formidable one that has played some fantastic rugby in this Cup.

But he will surely go to his grave with the waves of what-might-have-been still washing over him. What might have been on this day was a great All Black victory on the back of a straightforward Andrew Mehrtens field goal just three minutes from time, or a Lomu try a little earlier that was called back for a marginal forward pass, or any one of several occasions when the All Blacks threatened the Springboks' line, but just didn't get there.

In the end, though, the New Zealanders looked uncharacteristically lethargic throughout much of the match, as if they'd come onto the field straight out of a hot spa bath and simply couldn't get their legs moving no matter how they willed it. They were unrecognisable from the side which completely destroyed England a week earlier.

There was a rumour around that no fewer than nine of them

had picked up some kind of virus in the last forty-eight hours, but, true or not, none of the entourage was making excuses in the post-match press conference.

The verdict on this match overall? For mine, it was dissatisfying in the extreme. Partly because in the conclusive battle to prove who boasted the finest rugby team on earth, nothing conclusive was proved at all; and partly because no tries were scored in what was the most widely viewed rugby match ever held.

Mostly, though, I suppose it was that the occasion itself was so magnificent, the atmosphere so charged, that it was always going to be hard for any one match to live up to it. Whatever, the Boks are back!

While Rupert Murdoch's News Corp was putting together a ten-year $A770 million deal with the three principal unions of the southern hemisphere, Ross Turnbull and his World Rugby Corporation were busy on their own account, even while the World Cup proceeded around them. This is another extract from The Rugby War.

THE WORLD RUGBY CORPORATION

From 28 May to 11 June, Ross Turnbull and his partner, Michael Hill, had been travelling around South Africa making contact with key rugby people gathered for the World Cup. One of these was former Transvaal coach Harry Viljoen.

At one point, Turnbull, although he was not hopeful, wondered out loud about the possibility of meeting the Springbok captain, Francois Pienaar. Viljoen, to Turnbull's surprise, said that shouldn't be too much of a problem and he would make contact to check his availability. Perhaps Francois could come over to meet them in a few days time, on an afternoon, after the Springboks had finished their training.

Viljoen was as good as his word. On the afternoon of Wednesday 7 June, around three o'clock, there was a knock on the door of Turnbull's room. When he opened it, there stood Viljoen with not only his lawyer and close friend, Jennis Scholtz, but just over his right shoulder . . . a smiling Francois Pienaar himself.

Instantly, Turnbull was impressed. 'He had a magnificent sort of physical presence when he came into the room,' he recalls, 'with his multicoloured South African hat, his Springbok gear and obvious athletic prowess . . . he just looked fantastic.'

The two shook hands, with Turnbull also impressed by the Springbok captain's firm grip and clear-eyed gaze. Michael Hill, also in the room at this time, remembers equally strong first impressions.

'He just looked like a strong leader,' he says now, 'like somebody you could absolutely count on.'

And so they talked. With Pienaar sitting on the chair beside the desk, Turnbull for the next hour or so paced the room and set out the WRC agenda. His busy left arm carved out in the sweetly air-conditioned atmosphere a whole rugby empire that was just waiting to be formed, once players the ilk of Pienaar and his Springboks gave the say-so.

Pienaar was enthusiastic from the beginning, the way the Australians remember it, occasionally breaking in with quick comments like 'This is fantastic', 'I can't believe it', and 'Great!', as Turnbull continued to speak.

'But he didn't even have to say those things for us to know that he was keen,' says Turnbull. 'I mean, you could just see it in his expression and his body language as I talked. He was *in*.'

Turnbull still had one significant qualm, though. Both he and Michael Hill had the impression that of all the national union administrations they were attempting to outmanoeuvre, it was the South Africans who had been the most assiduous in finding their way around the amateur regulations to ensure that their players were well recompensed monetarily. Both Turnbull and Hill were expecting that it would be the Springboks who would be most reluctant to go against the desires of their officials.

With that in mind, Turnbull gently broached the subject of how Pienaar thought the South African Rugby Football Union might react to the WRC concept and if they were dead-set against it, how he thought his fellow Springboks might cope with . . .

Pshaw! Pienaar, in both Hill and Turnbull's memory, was entirely dismissive of whatever the South African officials might think about the matter.

'He just made it absolutely clear,' Turnbull says, 'that he and his team had absolutely no time for their officials whatsoever.'

The meeting broke up with Pienaar making a firm commitment there and then to approach his players on behalf of the WRC, and said he would get back to them with the answer, which he was sure would be positive.

After more warm handshakes, and even a little back-slapping at this early stage, the door clicked shut as Pienaar, Viljoen and Scholtz took their leave.

'That,' said Ross Turnbull firmly as he turned back from the door to face Michael Hill, 'is one of the better men I've met in my life. I feel privileged to have been in that bloke's presence.'

Hill did not disagree.

High in the Ernst & Young offices on Sydney's Sussex Street, three of Australia's best-known rugby coaches were gathered on the afternoon of Wednesday, 21 June 1995.

Bob Dwyer, Alec Evans and Bob Templeton sat around a table, jotting down various names. A couple of hours before, they had been briefed by Ross Turnbull in his office about where WRC was up to. They'd been joined a little late at the lunch by WRC director, Geoff Levy, and, at the lunch's conclusion, Ross Turnbull had asked the three Australian coaches to draw up a preliminary list of players in Australia who might be valuable to the cause. They'd retired to this room to do just that.

As Templeton recalls it, 'We had the meeting and then they just sort of said, "Write names down and see what players would be available". That was the whole scheme as far as I was concerned. Just to write down and say how are we going to get these squads [totalling] 120-odd players. Because there were four teams of thirty—one based in Melbourne, one in Perth, and one in Sydney and Brisbane.

'It was finding out who could play centre and the availability [of various positions] . . . It got very thin towards the end, if you can imagine.'

Templeton's presence there, particularly, is a measure of how seductive the WRC concept was at this point, at least to those who had been exposed to it and given time to think about it.

Templeton, long considered the grand old man of Australian

rugby—and a traditionalist with a capital T—had come to the meeting reluctantly, but felt there was simply no other option for Australian rugby than to throw in its lot with WRC.

'At that time we knew absolutely nothing about any Murdoch deal,' Templeton recalls, 'but what I did know was that the Wallabies would be absolutely decimated by players going to Super League if someone didn't come up with some money for them.

'The WRC fellows also wanted me to act as a recruiter for the Wallabies, in return for an enormous fee. I refused that, but did agree that I would at least pass on the message to the Queensland Wallabies about the basic concept of WRC, so they'd at least think twice before going to Super League.' (Templeton resigned from the whole thing straight after fulfilling that promise.)

Alec Evans, ditto. As the coach of Wales—easily the country most pillaged by the rugby league bandidos—he knew better than most that if rugby didn't get some big-time money flowing into it quick smart, then rugby at the elite level would be reduced to a Mickey Mouse affair.

Of his own involvement on that particular day, he remembers that, 'there was a lot of talk about me coaching in one of the franchises in Australia, but at that stage I felt my commitment was very much to Wales'.

He remembers being asked to compile the list, too, but felt that, 'for myself, after three and a half years out of the country, I didn't know enough about the players to do something like that properly, and I went in to Ross Turnbull and told him. Even the other two, with all their knowledge of Australian rugby, only really knew about the elite level of the game, so it was a very unsatisfactory exercise.'

Bob Dwyer acknowledges that such a meeting took place, but denies vehemently taking part in any drawing up of lists.

'My position at this time concerning WRC was that I continued to support their concept, while in no way forming an opinion about the financial viability of the project,' he says. 'I thought that it was in the best interests of the survival of the game, and of the continued presence of our players in the game.

'However, at all times, I presented the view that the concept should run under the control of the ARU.'

Rupert Murdoch's extraordinary deal was announced on the morning of 23 June 1995.

One would have thought that for the movers and shakers of the World Rugby Corporation, the bleeding obvious beckoned— that this was the end.

With Rupert Murdoch putting that amount of money behind the establishment competition, and with the three principal national unions 100 per cent behind it, surely it was obvious that the whole WRC vision lay lost and bleeding behind Ayers Rock? No chance, the way Turnbull and Levy tell it.

On the morning that the Murdoch deal was announced, Ross Turnbull was in the office section of Harry Viljoen's enormous compound, feeling pretty good about the way everything was going. He and Michael Hill had arrived in South Africa the previous evening with a dufflebag full of contracts; they'd already made further positive contact with Pienaar, plus other key rugby people in town for the World Cup final. As always with Ross, it was all systems go.

It was then that Viljoen's fax machine started rolling out the news, line by line. Turnbull tore it off, read it, didn't blanch.

'I thought, Mmmmm that's interesting,' Turnbull recalls, 'but when I thought about it, $US555 million might sound like a lot, but by the time you've taken out all the various commissions and divided it three ways it wasn't that much. I thought it was stupid that those national unions had sold themselves to Murdoch for such a long period of time and effectively put a salary cap on the code until well into the next century.

'But it made no difference to us. We had all the people we needed to make contact with, and our teams were in place in a highly organised fashion. They might have had the unions but I felt sure that we were going to have the players. For me it was full steam ahead, regardless.'

Michael Hill's observation stands: 'Ross's greatest talent is his ability to plough on regardless.'

Rupert Murdoch. Sitting right there. At the boardroom table. Super League executive assistant Michael O'Connor was nervous. He'd been rather suddenly summoned by Super League chief executive, John Ribot, to the meeting at News Corporation's

Sydney headquarters at Holt Street. He was asked to tell the half-dozen bosses gathered there—including *the* boss himself—what he knew about this Turnbull scheme he'd come across in South Africa, which clearly had the potential to scupper the deal with SANZAR.

O'Connor, sensing that with blokes like this he should be brief and to the point, got as far into the story as he could—130 South Africans signed, Turnbull and Packer involved, Francois Pienaar organising it, players signed all over the world—before he was interrupted by BSkyB chief executive, Sam Chisholm.

Chisholm said he had recently been talking on the phone to South African Rugby Football Union chairman, Louis Luyt, and Luyt had personally assured him that everything was fine. As a matter of fact, Chisholm recounted, he had recently received a warm letter from Francois Pienaar congratulating him on the SANZAR deal. Chisholm even produced the letter there and then.

Chisholm stuck to his guns, that Luyt couldn't possibly not know what was happening in his own union, and that Pienaar couldn't have written a letter like that if he'd signed with another organisation.

O'Connor backed down, way down. 'I didn't think it wise to go on with it,' he says now, 'because I think I was beginning to look like a fool.'

Rupert Murdoch listened, for the most part silently, though he did comment briefly that it would be a good idea to 'keep a close eye on it'.

The meeting moved on to other business, and O'Connor was ushered out the door.

The tables were set up in the defensive wagon-train formation in the spacious rooms at the top of the ARU's offices in North Sydney. The people around the table were trying to ward off the attack that had been launched by the World Rugby Corporation, and this meeting on Friday afternoon, 28 July, was to determine the scope of the attack, the damage it had already done, and how best to counter it.

Around the table sat Ian Ferrier, Richie Guy, Leo Williams, Louis Luyt, David Moffett and various other officials of the international Rugby Unions, while it was Communication

Services International chief executive, Ian Frykberg, who had the floor.

'Listen!' he said, once he had their full attention. 'We have a full-blown crisis on our hands. There's a few things you blokes have got to realise immediately. You've lost all the All Blacks, you've lost about fifty of your provincial players in New Zealand. In Australia you've lost all your Wallabies except maybe one or two, plus thirty state players! In South Africa you have lost 150 players!'

Consternation around the table. Disbelief. Replies that it couldn't possibly be as bad as Frykberg was making out, because such and such player, who they'd known for ten years, had looked them in the eye and told them that he hadn't signed and nor had the others.

'I'm telling you,' Frykberg remembers continuing, 'whatever they are saying to you, however long you've known them, they are *not* telling you the FUCKING TRUTH! We have got a crisis!'

Louis Luyt, who had flown in a couple of days before for further talks on SANZAR business, still didn't want to hear it. The way participants at the meeting remember it, the South African supremo simply couldn't believe even at this late stage that his Springboks, let alone so many provincial players, would ever have signed with Turnbull.

In the first instance, he refused to countenance Frykberg's contention that there was a crisis, and insisted upon making a phone call to South Africa to check. Whoever it was Dr Luyt called definitely had his or her finger on the pulse, because after a thirty-second conversation in Afrikaans, the chairman of SARFU snapped his mobile phone shut and said with a heavy affirmative nod: 'We have a crisis.'

He got that right. This ol' rugby war was heating up . . .

So were some of us rugby commentators.

IT'S THE END OF THE GAME AS WE KNOW IT

Think for a moment on exactly how you would destroy international rugby union if you could.

I reckon you'd have to proceed roughly along the following lines.

- Do everything possible to split the rugby union world in two. Start up a fully professional international circus, and hive the top players and coaches away from the rugby heartland, away from the rugby community. Get a donnybrook royal going between the 'rebels' and the 'loyalists' in the time-honoured fashion, and make sure the whole thing alienates the rugby faithful!
- Draw a line, using a very strong scalpel, beneath all sense of history and tradition of the international game. Organise it so that the best New Zealanders would no longer be the 'All Blacks', playing against the best that Australia could throw at them in the form of the 'Wallabies', and what they would be battling for would not be the 'Bledisloe Cup'. Forget the green and gold, forget jerseys as black as coal at midnight, forget the lot.
- Kill the ethos of the 'game for the game's sake' stone dead as quickly as possible.
- Change the status of players from chosen warriors of the tribe to highly paid employees. Make them sign contracts to the effect that if the circus ringmasters decide that they must go and play for a team in Malaysia, then it's there they must go, no questions asked. Top rugby players would no longer choke up the first time they donned the jersey of their childhood dreams, and play with passion unbridled because of what it represents.

Ummmmmmmmm, is any of this sounding familiar? Anybody else out there thinking that this is sounding uncannily like the mooted Ross Turnbull revolutionary rugby plan? Funny, I was thinking exactly the same thing myself.

Of course ruining international rugby is not what Turnbull is specifically setting out to do—he's just trying to make a buck, like the rest of us, albeit on a different scale—but for mine the ruination of rugby will be the inevitable result if his circus gets up.

Which of course raises the first question—will it?

Will Turnbull raise the $US100 million that he is apparently after, and, if so, will the rugby public return that in kind to the business backers so it's an ongoing proposition?

I strongly think not. While Turnbull may get the initial $100 million, my pound to your peanut says that we combined rugby nutters around the world won't do what the pinstripe brigade is counting on. That is, we won't throw cash at the circus simply because it boasts many of the players we've been admiring for so long. We'll make the men in serious suits understand that rugby followers are a different breed altogether, that rugby is a tribal game not to be messed with in this fashion.

We'll make them understand that if exactly the same game as tomorrow's Bledisloe Cup match was to be played between exactly the same players, but they were no more than highly paid entertainers wearing different jerseys, and we had lost all sense that they were representing us, then a lot of us couldn't give a rat's hiney.

None of this is to take a shot at the players, particularly. Personally, if anybody offered me $300 000 down for something like this, I'd grab it like a shot and to hell with the greater good of international rugby.

But as it happens, this is not a choice between an enormous amount of money and nothing at all. Instead, the way it's panning out seems to be a choice between a great deal of money from the traditional authorities, and a marginally more enormous amount from the circus. In that case, surely pride in the national jersey might be enough to make up the difference and hold them true.

(And incidentally, thanks to the anonymous caller who left a message yesterday saying he'd heard on good authority that I had signed with the David Lord circus, so where did I get off criticising the current shenanigans? You know, I think he might be *right?* Truth be told, I had a vague memory of once reading on the top of the back page of the *Herald* that I'd signed with Lord in 1983, so I looked it up and *hulloa!* The story was even *written* by me! Bloody hell, no wonder I always used to be the first ninny found in hide-and-seek when I was a kid.)

The Murdoch option, while still a soulless business deal done for purely business reasons without even an ounce of rugby spirit in it, at least is putting the money in the hands of the rugby administrators. At least that money in turn can be spread around the code as a whole, including the grassroots, and the code as a whole may profit.

Finally, there is this. Yes, rugby does have to adapt to the modern sporting world and go professional in some measure. But if they get it right, if it's done in a way that remains as true as possible to the spirit of the game, the game at the international level will retain some of the charm it has at the bottom. And that charm was never better expressed than in a letter to the sports editor, published in the *Herald* earlier this month. 'My father once gave me this reflection, from an unknown author, on a game I once knew,' one of our readers wrote.

> Rugby rests entirely on the enthusiasm of players and ex-players. Its gate is microscopic; its monetary return to players and officials is nil; it is fiercely and uncompromisingly amateur, the cult of free men who love their fellows with unparalleled ferocity. No other game permits men to plough opponents into the ground and then cheerfully help them to their feet to suffer like treatment in reverse.
>
> For boys it is the game for the sunshine of their lives, when the world is full and round and there is health and wonder in the air; a game of the mind as well as the body, and a test and source of character. Rugby football inspires all those qualities of skill and courage, magnanimity, co-operation and unselfishness that give the game its universal appeal to men of free spirit.

Sigh. What seems absolutely certain is that tomorrow's Test match is the last hurrah for the way things were. Win, lose or draw, tomorrow's game will be the last one in which the players are playing substantially for the pride of the jersey they wear.

Vale rugby as we knew it.

Oddly enough, right in the middle of all the hoopla about professionalism and rebels and all the rest, a single figure emerged who reminded everyone of what the game was meant to be about in the first place.

RISING FROM THE PITS—STEVE MERRICK

There is sleep, the sleep of the damned and the sleep of the dead. Finally, there is the sleep of a coal-truck driver in the few short hours between one 16-hour shift ending and another beginning.

In the middle of July Steve Merrick was sleeping thus—gone

for all money in the bedroom of his Singleton home—when he was woken by his wife, Rebecca, tugging on his shoulder, trying to bring him back from the land of Nod: 'Steve, Steve, there's a man who says he's Bob Dwyer on the phone and he wants to talk to you.'

Too tired to argue, or even think about why someone would pretend to be Dwyer at ten o'clock on a wet Wednesday night, Merrick staggered to the phone without a word and picked it up.

It really was Dwyer, wanting this unknown Singleton player to make himself available for representative rugby so the Australian selectors could get a better look at him. Well, Steve Merrick wasn't going to cop it, not by a long shot. Rebecca hovered in the living room doorway and listened to her husband's end of the conversation.

'No . . . *No* . . . I'm too old . . . I'm sure there are a lot of other players you're interested in, aren't there?' And so on. Finally Merrick put the phone down, and with a distracted air said to Beck: 'They're trying to make me play rep. I'm not going to play.'

Ah, but he would. As Merrick acknowledges now, 'I tried to say no to Bob, but just couldn't do it. He just wouldn't take "no".'

Dwyer wore Merrick down, and within a few days the Singleton man had made himself available for representative rugby and was making his debut for New South Wales against Otago, where he was judged good enough to be selected for the interstate series against Queensland.

A try apiece in those two victorious games for the Waratahs saw Merrick standing at the luggage carousel at Sydney's domestic airport two Sunday nights ago, when New South Wales manager, Dick Shaw, read out the Australian squad of twenty-one players to take on New Zealand.

'. . . Phillip Kearns, Daniel Manu,' Shaw read in that maddeningly neutral tone that managers always use when reading momentous lists, '. . . Ewen McKenzie, Steve Merrick . . .' In. He was *in*. Not that he was getting carried away with it all, mind, not by a long shot.

'What he said in the car on the way home,' his wife reports, 'was, "Just think, whatever happens I'll get all that Australian gear just for sitting on the bench."'

It was not to be. Three days later, from his Auckland hotel room, and still stunned, Merrick called his father on the cabin phone of his own coal truck to tell him. 'Dad. Steve. They've picked me in the Test team.'

And that was it. Up Singleton way, they reckon Merrick senior's feet haven't touched the ground since.

'I've tried to calm him down and tell him, "Dad, it's only football", but it doesn't seem to be working,' says Australia's new No 9.

Nor did it work in the rest of Singleton, which has been agog with Merrick fever since. The *Singleton Argus* has led the celebrations with no fewer than four front pages on the subject, including a superb 'Merrick to take on the All Blacks' headline. Which was true enough.

Andrew Avard, one of Merrick's clubmates from Singleton, was in the team clubhouse when the first Test started.

'It was just unbelievable,' he says. 'The whole clubhouse was chock-a-block with our people and with Mayfield East boys, who were playing us that day, and we all cheered every time he got the ball. It was fantastic.'

At Eden Park, Merrick made a few blues early but came good with a vengeance in the second half.

'I thought, "Right, I've gotta make the most of this. Gotta have a go and try a few things," Merrick said. He did just that, and for the most part they worked.

Not that the past few weeks have been without their problems for all that, not the least of which has been leaving Singleton and more or less using Sydney as his base.

'I hate it here,' he says flatly. 'I couldn't live here. I want to live in a place where you can play cricket out in the street and get twenty overs in before the first car comes.'

Is he at least glad that his entrance to top representative rugby has come at a time when a cyclone of change is about to hit it, a cyclone which one way or another will be bringing enormous amounts of money into the coffers of the top players?

'Mate, I don't know anything about that,' says Merrick, in a manner to make you believe him implicitly. 'And I don't really want to think about it. I'll tell you this, though—what is important to me is not losing my [trade union] ticket. That's where real financial security for me and my missus comes from and, whatever happens, I don't want to lose that.'

As soon as you lose that, he adds, you're stuffed.

Fair dinkum, no joking, they just don't make blokes like this any more. May we wish him well in the Test today. He is the last of his kind in a Test match that will be the last of its kind.

And so it proved. At the conclusion of the Test match, won by the All Blacks, the Wallaby captain, Phil Kearns, took the microphone and spoke directly to the crowd. 'Whatever happens in the future,' he said, 'we hope you and the Union support us.'

His words were taken as a clear signal that the whole rugby circus was fair dinkum on, and that the Wallabies had signed with the WRC. We didn't know the half of it. More from The Rugby War . . .

THE BATTLE WARMS

At around 6 p.m. on that Saturday night after the conclusion of the Bledisloe Cup Test, a 14-year-old schoolboy living in one of the most prestigious streets in Sydney's eastern suburbs looked out his bedroom window and saw something unbelievable. Truly, ruly, *unbelievable*.

Within moments he was on the phone to one of his school-mates whose father happened to have very close links to the Australian Rugby Union.

'The All Blacks!' he said excitedly. 'They're walking down my street and going into one of the houses. I promise you it's them. I saw Jonah Lomu and all the others!'

The news was out, as surely as if a telegram had been sent to every single Australian and New Zealand rugby official. After the Test match—and before the enormous post-Test dinner that was planned—the All Blacks had got straight onto the team bus and headed for the impressively opulent Vaucluse house of Kerry Packer's chief lieutenant, Brian Powers, to meet with WRC director Geoff Levy.

After the bus got stuck on the way down the twisting crescent where Powers lived, they got out and walked the last 100 metres, being ushered on arrival into the spacious basement of Powers's house. There, waiting for them, were a few drinks and nibblies,

Geoff Levy, Powers himself, David Leckie of Packer's television station, Channel Nine, and the lawyers from the New Zealand firm Davenports.

The reason for Leckie's presence was the same reason the venue was Brian Powers's house. Some of the All Blacks still had lingering doubts about the WRC's financial bona fides, and were not convinced that Kerry Packer was backing it.

'Geoff had said to us,' one of the individuals there that night recalls, 'that Packer *is* involved and to prove it, I will take you to the managing director's house and we'll have key guys there and you'll see them with your own eyes, flesh and blood.'

And, good as his word, there they were. To this point, there had been no solid proof that the Packer organisation was going to back the concept. The Packer name had not appeared on any of the documentation, the All Blacks had never sighted an official Packer representative, but you couldn't do much better than to be standing in the basement of the managing director's house for proof that the Big Boss himself was with the program.

The formalities were few. The Davenports lawyer made a brief but thorough speech about the legal implications of what they were about to sign, making it clear that they would be legally committed to WRC from this point, and then the All Blacks got to it.

A further inducement to the All Blacks signing was the guarantee for each and every signature. Well over $NZ2 million had been deposited in a trust account with Davenports, and Levy says his intention was for the players to understand that if they signed with WRC exclusively, they would get $100 000 whatever happened on November 22—even if the competition wasn't actually launched. If it was launched, they'd also get their $100 000, but it would be deducted from their contractual payments.

Even with an inducement like that, some four players declined to sign there and then. One of those was Jonah Lomu. The players who didn't sign had indicated earlier that they weren't going to, but coach Laurie Mains, in his own words, 'only agreed to let the players go provided we all went'.

And all did go, but not all went inside the house. The All Black coach had remained in the bus up the road with Colin Meads, talking quietly, and becoming increasingly agitated.

'I was very unhappy about it,' he recalls.

The problem was, where *were* they? It seemed to Mains his team was taking forever, and presently he could stand it no more.

'I actually did go into the house at one stage and pressed not the panic button, but I did say, "Listen guys, we have got to go, we cannot show bad manners".'

They left, and headed back to the dinner. In the darkened bus, with some players talking quietly while others were lost in thought, Mains pointedly did not ask anyone what had happened inside.

'I did not want to know at that time,' he says, 'It was only [the following day] before we left, that Sean, without giving me names, told me numbers who had signed. I didn't want to know names . . .'

If the All Blacks, Wallabies and Springboks were now convinced that the WRC was the way of the future, a lot of us rugby commentators remained unconvinced, and didn't mind saying so. I was one such.

AN HONOURED SOCIETY, HONOURED BY SOCIETY

Perhaps we should all calm down a bit, and look at this rationally. The fear is that the Wallabies are going to head out the door *en masse*, and sign up to play with the Turnbull Terriers or the Packer Pirates or whatever. Those who think this is possible simply do not understand, do not know personally, the key people involved.

Phil Kearns, for example, the Wallaby captain. Does anybody really think that Phil wants to go down in Australian sporting history as the man who had no sooner secured the most revered post in the rugby code, than he used it to rat on the Wallaby jersey and all that it represents? You think the heir to Mark Loane, Mark Ella, Nick Farr-Jones and Michael Lynagh wants that put on his record?

No chance. I know Phil. Phil is a friend of mine. He is an honourable man, a good man, and would never dream of doing such a thing. And I know, I know, the way he talked at the ceremony after the game made it sound as if it was all a *fait accompli*, as if he and the rest were heading off to different pastures, but that will prove to be a mistake on our part. We must have misunderstood because Phil would not do that.

Ditto, Bob Dwyer, the Australian coach. I have seen Dwyer *weep* on two occasions as he talked to Australian players before important Test matches about how sacred the green'n'gold jersey they wore was, of what it meant to Australian rugby supporters.

Dwyer didn't put those tears on for show; he meant them, he felt it. And no man with as deep a love of Australian rugby as he has could possibly be helping to steer the Wallabies in a direction whereby they wilfully destroy that heritage in exchange for the mere *chance* of more money than the enormous amount they're already assured. Not possible, not Bob. And I don't care what you've heard, it simply can't be true.

The same goes for the hard core of the Wallaby team. There are those who say that damn nigh the whole lot of them have already signed with the Turnbull crowd. Again, not possible. You can't know them if you think that.

Don't you realise that for the most part these are the same guys who covered Australia with so much glory in 1991 when they won the World Cup? And not just because of the fact that they won it. Long before that they were feted for the way they carried themselves—for their openness, uprightness and obvious integrity. They were the best advertisement international rugby could ever have hoped for, and so many of us felt prouder to be Australian because of them.

Are you really trying to tell me that only four years on, these same guys are going to abandon all that, and in one fell swoop turn themselves into the pariahs of the rugby community? You've got to be kidding.

What that would need would be for each and every one of them to look the ARFU right in the eye and say, in effect, 'I know you're now guaranteeing me more money than Mal Meninga was getting from the Canberra Raiders at the height of his career, but it's not enough, I want more.'

I'm losing patience with this, simply because it cannot be ridgy-didge. It's one thing to make a choice for bulk money against zero money—which might have been understandable—but altogether different when they are already assured of obscene money, and are greedy enough to go after still more. John Eales take that position? Totally out of the question. Tim Gavin? I'd sooner believe that Mother Teresa runs an illegal gambling den on the sly.

Despite all this, I am prepared to concede that just possibly one or two Wallabies have signed with Turnbull. To them, let me say this.

What can you be thinking of? Rugby is your *mother*, dammit. For the past two decades she's nurtured you, taken care of you, taught you, been proud to call you her own, and held chook raffles so that you could travel around the world.

She's allowed you to walk taller down George Street than ever you would have dreamed, and now that she has come into a large amount of money you are guaranteed to enjoy enormous amounts of her largesse as one of her favourite sons.

If you make a decision that that is still not enough, that instead you want her to whore for you, too—to earn the very last buck for you she can and to hell with the consequences—then you will be deserving of your fate.

And that may very well be that you miss out on the whole lot. The Turnbull thing will collapse as the rugby public rises as one against it, and your spot in the Wallabies will be taken by someone proud to wear the jersey.

I refuse to believe it will come to that, though. Rugby has always prided itself on being a character-forming game, and there will prove to be easily enough character in this team to do what they know is right at this most crucial of times.

It's just a question of which of the Wallabies will be the first to declare himself for Australia.

(In the meantime, let's hear it for Queensland coach, John Connolly. At a time when the easiest thing in the world would be to remain neutral and see which way the wind blows, he has expressed his repugnance at the whole notion of WRC. That will no doubt be remembered when the time comes to pick the next Wallaby coach.)

The only way WRC was going to collapse was if the establishment was able to drive a wedge between the players, and get enough of the stars to return to the fold. One who had been put under extraordinary pressure from both sides was the one who'd first held the World Cup aloft that year.

THE CLIMAX

It was at Harry Viljoen's house. Ross Turnbull could barely recognise Francois Pienaar. Here before him was the Springbok captain, sure enough, but it was an infinitely different man from the one Turnbull had met a little under two months before.

Then, Pienaar had been a 'magnificent looking man', whom Turnbull had felt privileged to meet. Now he looked almost as if he had wasted away, refusing to look Turnbull in the eye, sullenly refusing to speak to him, looking very jumpy indeed.

'He had transformed from a magnificent athletic business-type person to deal with, to a shaking bloody wreck,' Turnbull says. 'Like a frightened animal. Pathetic.'

The two were standing in the office of the Viljoen family compound with some of the other Springboks, making ready to head into the city of Johannesburg for a live video hook-up between the leading rebels in Australia, New Zealand and South Africa. There were a lot of things to discuss, but Turnbull's attention kept being drawn to Pienaar.

'I just couldn't work out what had got into him,' Turnbull recalls, 'but obviously somebody had got at him. He was breaking up before my eyes.'

But it was time. Time to head off to the city for the hook-up. 'Do you want a lift with me, Francois?' Turnbull remembers asking him.

'No, it's alright, I'll go with James [Small],' Pienaar replied, his eyes still averted from Turnbull's.

Pienaar, needless to say, never arrived at the studio, and Turnbull got the news shortly afterwards that he had returned to the establishment.

In Dunedin, way down on the far south of the South Island, Josh Kronfeld couldn't sleep properly that night, the same way he hadn't been able to sleep much for the previous few weeks.

The agony of wanting to make the right decision, without being quite sure what it was, was really starting to get to him.

Tossing and turning, the star new boy of the All Black forward pack kept going over and over in his mind the whys and wherefores of the whole WRC saga. The pressures on him were enormous. On the one hand, he desperately wanted to be with the other All Blacks. On the other, he wanted to *be* an All Black, first, last and always.

And to his way of thinking, there was no guarantee whatsoever of ensuring that other than by staying with the national body. In muffled, troubled conversations with close friends, he would say, 'I don't want to be just a seven-Test All Black, I want to be a *great* All Black. I want to play lots of Tests.'

In another suburb of Dunedin not too far away, his friend Jeff Wilson was in a similar position. They'd each had long conversations with their respective lawyers, but neither was still quite decided what to do.

It took them a week, but at last they were ready to put a couple of serious planks in WRC's coffin.

Wilson and Kronfeld had sat together on the flight from Dunedin to Wellington—in the company of their Otago team-mates— apparently still unsure about whether or not they were going to sign the contracts committing them to the establishment. They bided their time, going over every last little detail in their heads, even as their provincial team-mates signed their own loyalty contracts, albeit for much lesser sums.

They walked off the flight together, knowing that this was it. There, up ahead of them at the gate, was New Zealand's leading sports lawyer, David Howman, waiting for them. Every step took them closer to him. He had a briefcase. He had their contracts, ready for them to sign if they chose.

An emotive conversation ensued. It was all about timing, the players were told. Now was the time to do it. If they signed now they would be national heroes in New Zealand the following day. If they signed now, they would be helping to save New Zealand rugby. There was no doubt this is what the public wanted to see, and there was equally no doubt Wilson and Kronfeld were getting a good deal.

While it was one thing to have loyalty to a large group like the All Blacks, they also had to have loyalty to themselves, and there was no doubt that the NZRFU's offer was clearly the best one.

Finally, it was over.

After some twenty minutes of discussion, Kronfeld and Wilson looked at each other. Then, Kronfeld, trembling with a powerful but nameless emotion, reached for a pen. He signed. Wilson signed.

And it went from there. Pienaar had driven a wedge in the Springboks, Kronfield and Wilson did the same to the All Blacks, just as Tim Gavin and Jason Little had done by signing with the ARU in Australia. In short order nearly all the players flooded back to the establishment and the vision of WRC was left in smoking ruins.

Rugby quickly became fully professional, under the establishment umbrella, with the players enjoying untold riches. Not that everyone was happy.

STOP THE ITCH TO BITCH

No names, no pack drill. But . . . the word is that a lot of the players negotiating with the various Rugby Unions about their professional contracts are waxing furious that they bloody well want a whole lot more than the unions want to give them; that it better get up near $150 000 a year or they're going to bust a boiler. You just see if they don't.

Well, we never. One source within the union ranks has it that there really is a lot of bad feeling from players who feel they're being short-changed in having to live on sometimes as little as $100 000 a year, or worse, only $60 000 if you can believe it.

Apparently, their reasoning runs that this is not greed, this is simply a fair and equitable distribution of money that we have created, that we are earning through our skills. It is because of us alone that this money is being paid and we want that money.

One unconfirmed report has it that while the nascent Players Association at the time of the recent troubles with the World

Rugby Corporation was pushing to be guaranteed 100 per cent of all the monies generated by the Murdoch deal, the Australian Rugby Union was able to hold the line at guaranteeing it only 96 per cent.

Hmmmm.

One would have thought that this was no less than extraordinarily generous, but there are still rumblings of discontent.

Where do you begin? Perhaps like this: how come the city isn't resonating with a whole lot of whoopees at the moment? Where are the joyous shouts of 'you bloody beauty!' that should be drifting to us on every favourable gust of wind? Why, in all the pronouncements of all the players does there not seem to have been a single public expression of delight that for doing in the future what they have done in the past for nix, they will suddenly be receiving between two and fifteen times the average wage?

Before the bickering begins about not getting enough, shouldn't there at least have been a few celebrations about what they are getting?

Then there's this.

The reason the Murdoch crowd is paying so many hundreds of millions of dollars towards Australian rugby over the next ten years is because over the decades the exploits of players such as John Thornett, Ken Catchpole, Mark Loane, Mark Ella and Nick Farr-Jones have attracted an enormous number of loyal followers in this country.

Every time Loane broke the line and rampaged over opposing packs in his spectacular fashion, another hundred converts came to the game.

But Loane's monetary bonanza, now that many of those converts will be paying big bucks to Murdoch to watch rugby on his outlets, is—dot three, carry one, subtract two—nothing. So, too, with all the other players. Nary a brass razoo, and nor are they looking for it.

The fact remains, though, that the rosy state of Australian rugby is built on the efforts of dozens of generations of previous players, coaches, officials and voluntary workers. Given that only the current generation will cash in, any whingeing at all sounds a rather jarring note.

MILKING MILLIONS IN RUGBY'S PRO ERA—1996

And so into the brave new world of rugby union. It's been a week since professional rugby began in this country, and already you'd have to say that although it's still too soon to give definitive results, early counting indicates that the whole concept of a Super 12 competition will work.

The crowds have broken all records for provincial encounters and the media coverage seems way up on the usual. It is, after all, pretty much the only game in town. There seems to be an interest in this tournament far beyond any evinced in previous versions.

Why all of the above? Oddly enough, it's perhaps because the game is no longer anachronistically amateur in a professional sporting age.

In the words of Wallaby and ACT winger Joe Roff: 'I think one of the things, apart from the fact we take it more seriously, is that the public also takes it more seriously.

'Before, I think there might have been some sense that we were just a bunch of blokes running around on the weekends, but now there is a buzz around Canberra.'

There has been such a buzz, in fact, that in this past week Canberra Milk has switched its allegiance from rugby league's Canberra Raiders (*remember them?*) to the ACT Brumbies in a reputed $1.5 million deal over three years.

Is this, too, an indication of things to come, as the heavyweight corporate crowd gets in on the ground floor of a game that no less than Rampaging Rupert Murdoch has judged to be on the way up?

We'll see.

One thing, though. This wouldn't be a proper rugby article if there was not at least one clarion call for a return to some aspect of the good old days, and my choice for today is this. What about a simple, normal, unadorned celebration of victory?

This is archaic, I know, ridiculously old-fashioned I grant you, but what about it?

Take, for example, the situation the other night after the

Brumbies flogged Transvaal to within an inch of their lives, and then two inches.

No sooner had the game finished and the ACT players started giving each other bear-hugs and so forth, genuinely celebrating a great win, than someone handed them all sponsor caps with Canberra Milk on the front. The players looked sheepish, but mostly put the caps on.

It meant that a little bit of touching sporting theatre was instantly transformed into a jarring, 'orrible advertisement. If rugby union turns into a pale pastiche of what league was up to this year, it won't work. The magnetic charm of the whole thing will be gone, and the true believers won't believe any more. By all means find ways to milk the money from the sponsors, but can it be done in a more rugby kind of way?

Sigh. It wouldn't have done in myyyyyyy day.

For all that, while union was sorting itself out, rugby league continued to sink further into the abyss.

A VERY CIVIL WAR

The time is right. As sporadic cannon fire booms in the distance and the wind howls through the shattered citadels of League-Land, the streets clatter to the ceaseless tramp of straggling refugees, wearing bloodied beanies and heading west to where they know not. The civil war of rugby league sputters on, fought now by only those survivors with remaining blood for the battle.

The peace process ebbs, as all around calamity and confusion replace sureness and swagger.

The time is right I say. We of the union have almost got the numbers to seize control and form our own government. We can RULE the football world and rename it Union-Utopia! But at this crucial moment, we must move swiftly and surely, in much the same way as those great rugby forward Bolsheviks did in 1917.

Here is the blueprint on how to do it. Read it, commit it to memory, eat it, and then pass it on.

Activate our sleepers. Our people are all through the CBD, all through the media, on both sides of politics, and some are even acting as doctors during the death throes of League-Land. (Heh, heh, heh.) Pass the word to them all: 'When the sun shines off the oblong moon, heads are tails, and rugby will rise.' They will answer, 'Campese is King', and you'll know they are with us.

Knife between your teeth, belly-crawl your way out of there, and move onto the next target.

Gather the refugees. Treat them well—give them warm pies with real 'maty sauce when they are hungry, cold beer with a head when they are thirsty. Make them welcome and hold nothing against them because of their former residence in League-Land.

Point out to them the obvious similarities between their old world and our new one—'Look, it's still about running into other people at full pelt, it's not that different', and gently lead them to some further understanding of us and our ways.

Keep taking the game to everybody. We must steer away from concentrating all power, glory and resources only on the very pointy tip of the elite. The great glory of our world since forever has been that it matters naught whether you are short, tall, fat, thin, good-looking, ugly, fast, slow, good, bad—or all of the above from ages 5 to 40—union still has a game for you. This must continue full throttle, and it must be extended to the spectators, along the lines of it being irrelevant whether you are rich or poor, you can still afford to watch the game.

Remember. 'Universal access to the game', must be our buzz-phrase. The recent breakthrough in Union-Utopia is that it doesn't even matter now whether you are male or female, the code can still take care of you! (Look to the Australia vs USA women's Test match, as a curtain-raiser to Australia vs South Africa on Saturday.)

Avoid like the plague all those mistakes made by League-Land. In Union-Utopia we must resist the temptation to pave the streets with logos and sell everything that can't be totally nailed down to the highest bidder. We must do everything to preserve our soul, while admittedly raising a bit of money here and there to pay the rent.

Most crucial: we must never, ever forget that we are a game, and not a business. Our only act of venality should be to round up all administrators and business-heads who talk about rugby matches as 'product', and refer to rugby players as 'personnel'.

For them, the stinking sweatshops, where they can work their fingers to blood and bone knitting new jerseys for those who don't know any better. You get the drift.

Ready? At midnight, when the dingo howls, and the moon is oblong, we move, and the sun will rise again on Union-Utopia.

Go for it. Go for it like you used to when your five-eighth launched an up-and-under and you could see your dad sitting just the other side of the goalposts . . .

1996 also saw the ascension of a new man to the helm of the Wallabies on the field.

CAPTAIN PERFECT

Wallaby captain. Wallaby *captain*.

They are the two words that have been constantly recurring to John Eales over the past week, as he has endeavoured to wrap his head around the fact that when the referee knocks on the door before the Test this Saturday, it is he—having taken over from Phil Kearns—who will go to toss the coin with the Welsh captain, he who will run out onto Ballymore at the very head of fourteen other men dressed in green and gold.

'I'll get used to it,' says the man himself, now ensconced in the captain's room of his Brisbane hotel—a whole room all to himself—after completing another training session, 'but at the moment I'd still have to say that everything seems a little unreal. I haven't really had time to think about it too much'.

Such is the man. If ever there was a fellow whom the limelight has had a hard time convincing to come out from behind the curtains, it is him. By all reports he has been ever thus.

Growing up in Brissy as one of six children of devoted parents who liked their kids to play sport, but were equally keen that everything retain balance including the level-headedness of their progeny, sport was a fairly big part of his life.

'It was just all very normal,' Eales recalls, 'and nothing out of the ordinary.'

Actually not quite. Truth be told, in matters of sport Eales was always notable for being entirely out of the ordinary.

One of his high school teachers has recalled this week how, in the playground, with one stump-like stick a'hand, Eales was able to keep the rest of the kids at bay as they hurled tennis balls at his wicket.

Right then, the teacher recounted, he thought this kid had something out of the ordinary.

The story sounds, of course, Bradmanesque—the irony being that it wasn't cricket where Eales made his mark.

'I loved playing cricket,' he says, 'but the way things turned out, rugby sort of took over.'

It sort of did. Or, to be fair, it might be more accurate to say he sort of took over rugby . . . but we'll get to that.

Out of school, Eales joined the Brothers Rugby Club in Brisbane and captained their Colts side to victory in 1989, before making the leap to grade in 1990. On the field he took the opposition by storm, garnering enormous plaudits for not only the amount of ball he won, but also the extraordinarily un-second-rower-like things he did with it when he got it. Slotting field goals from 45 metres out was just a part of it. There were also the extraordinary passes, and innate sense of just where the play would be heading next, the last-ditch tackles he pulled off that turned the game around, and so on.

Off the field, though, he remained very much his parents' child.

The story is told of him that on his first pub crawl with the Brothers Club—traditionally a raucous affair involving a lot of drinking from pub to pub—Eales had to briefly abandon the drinkers, because he'd left his lunch box in one of the first hotels.

True?

'True,' he acknowledges with a laugh. 'Right through school and uni, Mum used to make me lunch—she makes great sandwiches—and she cut me this lunch to take on this pub crawl too. At one of the first pubs I asked them to put it into the fridge, and I forgot about it. Of course, I went back to get it.'

Of course. And the hell with the traditional reckonings of macho culture, which upon one neanderthal construction might think that the only thing more inconceivable than taking a lunch box on a pub crawl, with sandwiches made by your mum, is leaving the boys to go back and get it when you've left it behind.

At the end of 1990, he ran on as a late replacement for the Queensland side in the last twenty minutes of a game against Canterbury.

'I thought I could die happy,' he recalls, 'just for having worn the Queensland jersey in a game once.'

The following year he could die happier, after being selected to play for the Wallabies against Wales.

'I remember thinking, "Just let me play one Test, just one Test", and I was nervous about being able to play well.'

He did play well, very well. Did he have outside help though? For before that game, as with every game he plays in Brisbane, he must go through a reluctant ritual before leaving the Eales family home. Always, he must go to say goodbye to his Italian grandmother who lives with the family, and has done all his life. 'Nonna', he calls her.

'And I go to say, "Goodbye Nonna," and she says, "No you can't leave yet". Then she takes me by the hand and pulls me into the lounge room where she's got an altar, and in the middle of the altar is a big statue of St Anthony.'

At his grandmother's insistence, he must put his right hand on the statue, while she utters a prayer for both his safety and his good fortune on the day.

'It's an Italian thing,' he says simply.

As to that Welsh test, five years ago, 'It's funny, all you want to do is play that one Test, and after that all you want is to play fifty Tests!'

Eales is, of course, well on his way, having played 31 Tests at last count, including the victorious World Cup campaign of 1991.

And now he is captain. The honour came his way last Sunday, when he was still down in Sydney after the interstate game.

'Dick McGruther [the ARU chairman] called me, and said he wanted to have a bit of a chat. We had a drink, and then he said the selectors and the board had met, and they had decided they wanted to offer me the Wallaby captaincy.'

And your thoughts?

'Honestly, I was surprised at the way it was done. I thought something like that wouldn't be offered,' he says with a twinkle, 'because I couldn't imagine anyone would ever refuse it. I thought they'd just say, "We've picked a captain and you're it!" But when he offered it to me, I thought "Gee, I wonder if I should be thinking a lot about this before accepting it?"'

So he did think about it.

'For about a second,' as he recalls. 'It's something that I am very honoured to do, and I just want to do it as well as I can.'

For how long exactly? Eales considers a moment, before replying.

'At the beginning of the year my ambition was to be part of a successful team for a long time, and now I'm part of that team as captain my ambition is to be part of that successful team and hopefully captain for years to come . . .

I suppose as captain I'm even more keen that the team do well under my leadership.'

With the captaincy comes an attendant increase in the pressures upon him. The first of which, of course, is the much greater focus upon him personally. Already the interview requests are piling up, with most of us taking the well-trodden but true line that never a more modest man drew breath, etc.

How goes all the adulatory attention?

'It's embarrassing,' he replies, with a laugh. 'It almost makes me arrogant, with all the people saying how modest I am . . .'

The real pressure, though, will come as the rugby world takes a good hard look at whether or not he will prove to be a capable captain.

So can you do it, John? Can you read a game in the first place? It is reputed, for example, that one of your predecessors in the Wallaby second row had played for Australia before he was absolutely sure in his head about the difference between the loose-head side of the scrum and the tight-head. Are you like that, or can you read the changing tactics and strategies of the opposition, and change the Wallabies' own tack accordingly?

'Three years ago,' he replies, 'I suppose I was a bit like that in that I used to just run around like a madman, without ever having to think too much about it. But then I started analysing what was happening, why I was doing what I was doing, and what the team around me was doing, and the opposition. So I hope I've learnt a fair bit.

'What I most want to do is lead by example. I want to play well. I think if you're not playing well it's hard to tell other people to play well, and so I want to make sure my own form is good.'

(Under the circumstances, we may all safely assume that he's got that side of things taped.)

Next question though, counsellor. Have you. got enough nark in you to rip into a Wallaby team every now and then when the need arises, when one or other of them is out of line?

'Well it's been four days so far, and there hasn't been an occasion yet when I've had to do it, but I suppose I will be able to. And when it does come to being narky, at least I can say I've had plenty of practice with my sisters!'

But seriously. Let's just say that David Campese, for example, needs to be pulled into line over something or other. When Campo was making his debut for the Wallabies, you, John, were all of twelve years old. How will it be telling him to back off or back down?

'I can't see it will be a problem,' the new skipper says firmly. 'Campo is one of the experienced guys in the team who I'm very glad to have there and who I think will be a great support.'

And so on. The bottom line is that Eales does not know, just as the Wallabies don't know, how he will go in the role. They, and he, will have to see how things pan out. But, and this is crucial, he's off to a good start. He begins with the total respect of his fellow players as player and man, and in his only other two starts as captain—with the Brothers Colts in 1989 and the Australian Barbarians tour to Canada in 1994—the teams he led had conspicuous success.

And as the lunch-box incident illustrates, whatever else happens he's likely to remain his own man. John Eales. Wallaby captain. We wish him well.

Three years on John Eales has grown into the role, to the point where he is unchallenged as the natural skipper, whenever he is fit to take the field. His fitness is a problem, however, as at the time of going to press he is expected to be out for most of the year with a shoulder injury, though it is hoped he will return in time for the World Cup beginning in early October 1999.

While Eales had taken over the captaincy, Greg Smith had emerged as somewhat of a surprise victor of the four candidates to take over the Wallaby coaching reins from Bob Dwyer. I was one who didn't agree with some of the early moves made by Smith.

WALLABIES GIVEN A HARD LESSON IN GOOD MANNERS

It's about the All Black *haka*. While the words are in Maori, the rough translation is clear enough—'We're going to take yer */&†&† heads off!'

So how, as the opposing team, do you react? Certainly not the way the Wallabies did on Saturday. At the behest of the coaching staff, they retreated to the far end of the field to do some lovely little skill-drills while the All Blacks were going at it full cry on the halfway line. Thus, instead of standing and facing it, taking it full on and letting the gale wash over them that for better or worse the mother of all battles was about to begin, our blokes were removed far from all the ferocity.

Of course the message the Australian camp meant to send was this: 'You guys can do all your inane shouting and jumping around, but we are simply not interested and have better things to do with our time.'

Somehow the message that came out was: 'CRIKEY! that's just too intimidating to look at front-on, so let's fall back 40 metres and fool around with the ball.'

And what happened? Within 90 seconds of the kick-off the hyper-charged All Blacks had stormed over the top of the seemingly somnolent Wallabies for their first try. The game was effectively over, and things went downhill from there.

As for how an opposing team *should* face up to the *haka*, I refer once again to that most excellent book, the *June Dally-Watkins Rugby Manual*, where, under 'E' for 'Etiquette', it says among other things that 'rugby gentlemen should treat the *haka* much the same way they would an opposing team singing its national anthem. Stand back a reasonable distance, with your hands by your side, as the All Blacks let 'er rip. Do not stand so close that you risk a physical confrontation with the *haka* leader, and never practise your kicks with one of your team-mates while they are performing it.

'At least do them the honour of facing it—and in the process make it work for you—letting your own adrenalin build to the level of the ranters, before getting stuck in when the whistle blows and then tearing their heads off yourself.'

All up, it was a most unsettled time for Australian rugby, the more so because of strains brought on by the move to professionalism.

VOLCANO VOMIT ERUPTION HAS JUST STARTED

It's about the new Wallaby jersey the brutes have just unveiled . . .

OK, so maybe we are just a wheezing and messy mass of old fuddy-duddies. Maybe in the new age of rugby, people like me who hate with a passion this jersey are just a bunch of dusty antique cuckoo clocks in the attic that go off every now and then, long after they should have wound down and shut the hell up.

But we can help naught the way we feel. And that is this: to us, the new Reebok jersey looks like volcano vomit on a rag. Where there used to be a lustrous gold, there is now a runny yellow. Where there used to be one predominant rich colour all over, there are now harsh triangles of green and white colliding everywhere. Where there used to be a kind of holy sheen, there is now a commercial catastrophe. Where there used to be simplicity, there is now a jersey designed by committee—with something for everyone but the masses who loved the old jersey just the way it was.

We're annoyed that rugby's version of cricket's baggy green cap has simply been sold to the highest bidder, and dismayed that it has been done with such seemingly callous disregard for what the rugby public wants.

We know of no-one, and we mean no-one, who has seen the new jersey and genuinely liked it—apart from those in whose financial interest it is to toe the corporate line.

We are, not to put too fine a point on it, mightily pissed off. And sure, we're also woefully behind the times, and no doubt about it. We accept that we are incapable of understanding the imperatives of rugby doing this to survive in the modern age. We equally know that a lot of modern marketing logic goes clear over our simple little heads.

But this is the thing. There are so *many* of us antique cuckoo clocks, and we seem so united in our disgust, that we have not lost hope that sometime soon someone will come to their senses. Because in between bouts of wishing a raspberry on the houses of both the ARU and Reebok, we have got to thinking that if we all hate it so much then who is going to buy the brute of a thing? We may be cuckoo clocks, but there are an awful lot of us and we are the very same ones who have been the heart and soul of Australia's rugby following since pretty much forever—so we have to count for something, dammit.

And we think that after the fallout from this public relations Chernobyl for both Reebok and the ARU has abated the barest fraction, one or other of the CEOs of the said organisations will stagger out of the smoke—wounded but still stumbling—and say, 'I have the answer! We can neutralise the reactor and undo at least some of the damage by going back to the old jersey, and just whacking a couple of inoffensive logos here and there on it!'

Hurrah! Let's give it a go. And it will go from there . . .

The cuckoo clocks will be heard. United, our voices and paying power should easily be loud enough to make the ARU, Reebok and their entire mass of marketeering minions think again—just like Coca-Cola had to think again when it launched its 'New Coke' with great fanfare, and few sales. It had to recant, from rejection, and so will the ARU and Reebok.

Meantime, a raspberry on both their houses. Or did we mention that already?

Cuckoo! Cuckoo! Cuckoo!

If I was a cuckoo bird, there were nevertheless plenty of young eagles just then starting to get the full measure of their wings . . .

THE NATURAL

This then, is the portrait of the modern rugby union player on the eve of the battle royal. With the mobile phone beneath him softly winking, Wallaby and Waratah fullback, Matthew Burke, receives the ministrations of the New South Wales masseur in the corner of the team's amazingly sophisticated gym on the second level of New South Wales rugby headquarters at Concord Oval.

The still only 23-year-old Burke has already done three hours training this day, on top of twenty hours this week, and is starting to focus ever more fixedly on the opener of the Super 12 for New South Wales, against Waikato at the Sydney Football Stadium tonight.

Each kneading of the masseurs' hands is meant to make his muscles forget the strain they've been put through over the week, and remember only increased strength and vitality. Kneading, kneading, kneading, needing a result—out goes the bad air of fatigue, in comes the good air of freshness. Again and again.

Meanwhile, the posters on the far wall are there to more casually work on his mind.

WARATAHS TEAM VISION: *For the Waratahs to be the dominant provincial rugby team in the world.*

A TEAM THAT PLAYS AND TRAINS WITH RELENTLESS PERSISTENCE. *We want people who will never quit, people who will apply themselves relentlessly, who play one play at a time. The task is to focus on the moment rather than abstract notions of what might happen . . .*

Goodness, it all seems pretty serious these days, Matt?

'It's professional,' he replies with a soft laugh, 'so it probably is more serious; but it's good, too. [Our coach] Matt Williams has brought a very professional approach to everything and it's going well for us.'

In person, Burke is a very softly spoken, polite sort of bloke with still the whiff of impish humour always about him. Just a whiff, though. For while it may border on the trite to say so, there is also a strong sense that the Wallaby fullback would surely get 10 out of 10 on that scorecard most revered by our parents' generation, of being 'A Very Well Brought-Up Young Man'.

But football? 'Can play the game', is the summation of his team-mates in the ironic and understated vernacular of the moment, and on this count no-one in the New South Wales or Wallaby rugby fraternity would argue.

When Matt Williams had been asked minutes earlier, for

example, how Burke fitted into the team, his light-hearted response was immediate. 'It's more a case of how the team fits around him.' Indeed.

Such was Burke's form last year, in particular, so important was he to both the attacking flair and defensive grit of the side, that he appeared not only to be the first picked in the side, but also the one his team-mates looked to when the chips were down —as they often were in the 1996 season.

His rugby pedigree is as impeccable as it is traditional. Born the youngest of four sporting brothers, the sun never set on the family's big backyard at Carlingford or the nearby park, but that the Burke boys and their friends weren't trying to squeeze it for a last bit of light with which to continue their game-playing.

'Cricket, footie, touch, swimming, golf, anything and everything, we were always out there, always playing hard against each other,' Burke the Youngest recalls. 'Mum would call us in for dinner, and we'd always be going hard at it.'

At eleven he went off to board at that most famous of all rugby nurseries, St Joseph's College at Hunters Hill—which Burke calls even now 'the pinnacle'—and after a triumphant progression through the age teams, he made the revered First XV in year 11. By the end of year 12 he was in the 1990 Australian Schoolboys side to tour the British Isles and it was then that a moderately strange thing happened.

'It was through being with the Schoolboys that I guess I first realised what the possibilities of rugby were. Up to that point I was so focused on the St Joseph's First XV and all that represented, that everything else seemed pretty distant. The Wallabies were so far away we didn't even think about them.

'But then they had some dinners before we left, and they got some of the Australian players like Jason Little, Tim Horan and Simon Poidevin to come and talk to us, and I realised that the Schoolboys really could be a stepping stone to the Wallabies.'

Two other stepping stones were the Eastwood Rugby Club, which he joined in 1991, and then the New South Wales side, which he made in 1992.

For all the success that Burke went on to achieve in the representative ranks, though, he didn't actually take strong root and flourish like the very dickens immediately. From making his debut in the Wallabies in 1993, when he came on as a reserve in the third Test against South Africa, he was dropped from the side no fewer than four times over the next three years, and only made the Wallaby World Cup side to South Africa in 1995 by virtue of his versatility more than anything else.

'I was pretty glad to get the couriered letter saying I was on the plane, I can tell you,' says Burke with a wry laugh. 'All the other blokes got theirs at six o'clock in the morning, and mine didn't arrive until twenty past nine!'

He started the World Cup as a reserve, finished it as incumbent fullback, and played moderately well for the Wallabies for the rest of the year.

The 1996 season, though, bore the full Burke signature in the bottom right-hand corner of the painting. It was a year in which he broke the Wallaby point-scoring record with 39 points against Canada, scored a memorable 85-metre try against the All Blacks at Suncorp Stadium, Brisbane, and pulled off a try-saving tackle on Andre Joubert to beat South Africa. He finished the year as the winner of the Wallabies Players' Player of the Year—well in front of both runners-up, Michael Brial and John Eales.

So what was the change from journeyman Wallaby to consistent thuperstar?

'I don't know precisely,' replies Burke thoughtfully, 'but I think a large part of it was just maturity. After playing in and out of the top level for a while you realise what is really important, and how to go about things. I guess being around the Campeses and Horans and Littles helped me a lot, taking bits and pieces from those guys.

'For me, I think one of the most important things was realising that I had to be positive, to go out there with my head full of the good things I really wanted to do, rather than the bad things I had to avoid.'

Whatever. Nineteen ninety-six was a good time to come good, because while Burke had changed his approach, so had rugby. The end of 1995 saw the game go fully professional, and from earning a lazy twenty-five grand between friends from rugby in the year of the World Cup, some estimates put Burke's income last year at around ten times that.

The man himself will not say, as is his right, but he does grin widely at the mention of the subject and does acknowledge that when he first heard the number, it was 'mind-boggling'.

Not to get carried away, though—there is no collection of Porsches in his garage—'I've bought a unit and that's about it at the moment. Other than that I'm just concentrating on my football.'

Burke would go on to be, with New Zealand's Christian Cullen, one of the best two fullbacks in the world. Like Eales though, he too has struggled with injury—the most notable being a shoulder broken while scoring the winning try for the Wallabies in the last of three victorious Bledisloe Cup games in 1988.

TIM HORAN

In one day's time, Tim Horan will run out onto the turf at the Sydney Football Stadium, in front of about 40 000 people, playing at five-eighth: for the Wallabies, for glory, for contracts, for trophies, for international bragging rights.

Twenty-five years ago it was a lot different. He was still only three years old, living in Gympie in south-east Queensland, and his dairy-farmer father needed him to make up the numbers for the Gympie under-7 rugby league side he was coaching. Young Tim wasn't too keen, but anyway . . .

'But anyway, Dad said he would give me a bag of mixed lollies if I would play, because his team would automatically be disqualified if they didn't have enough players, so I said I would.'

And it went from there. With his bag of sweets in his hand, Tim would monitor what was going on up ahead and wait to see if anyone was likely to break through whom he would need to tackle, or at least get in the way of.

'Then I would carefully put down my bag,' Horan recalled yesterday with a laugh, 'run and make the tackle if I could, and then come back and get the bag and start eating again. I knew that whatever happened, every Saturday morning I would get 10-cents-worth of mixed lollies, and 10 cents could get you a lot of them back then.'

It would be two or three years before his father did not have to make such an offer to entice Tim to play, and by that time he was fully launched on what would become a glittering football career.

By the time he was sixteen or so, he was the star centre for the First XV of Downlands College in southern Queensland, and seeing a lot of another young bloke in the area by the name of Jason Little. Though attending different schools, the two were constantly thrown together in representative sides of cricket, athletics, swimming and rugby.

'I thought he was a very good player,' Horan recalls, 'and we became great friends.'

But the Wallabies? Forget it. In fact, the way Horan remembers it, as late as his last year of high school, he didn't really know there was a team called the Wallabies.

'I guess that was because right up until then, I really thought I was always going to go back to playing league, but then when a few people started telling me I might one day be a Wallaby— and I made the Australian Schoolboys team—I started to realise what they were about.'

It happened. Like the bloke who once famously said, 'Three years ago, I couldn't spell engineer, and now I are one,' Horan, at the still tender age of nineteen, in 1989 suddenly found himself making his debut for the Wallabies at Eden Park.

Against the All Blacks. In the middle of a fast and furious storm of thunder and lightning. And the weather wasn't too good either.

'It was hard, of course it was hard,' says Horan, 'but in a funny sort of way, because I was so young and naive I didn't really know enough to be scared and . . .'

And, oh gawd. Here's the famed All Black centre, Smokin' Joe Stanley, coming right for us, full pelt, ball in hand. Out of the way, everybody.

Arms wide, shoulders tensed, Horan swoops, hits, and knocks him over.

NEXT!

'I was able to stop him,' Horan recalls, 'and felt more confident after that. I came off at the end of the game, and thought, "Gee, that didn't seem like eighty minutes".'

And nor does it now seem like eight years and 48 Tests ago that that experience happened.

His finest moment in international rugby, lest we forget, came in the historic 1992 Test against South Africa in Cape Town, the first between the two nations in twenty-three years. With six minutes to go in the game, and the Springboks still with a sniff of coming back into it, Horan regathered a kick by the South African fullback, Theo van Rensburg, some 35 metres from the Wallabies' own line, and set off upfield, slicing and jinking all the way before sending a kick behind the South African defence.

Danie Gerber fielded the ball just inside his own quarter, but Horan just as quickly tackled him, got back to his knees, and somehow, amid all the churning feet and arms, picked the ball cleanly out of the muddy maelstrom without knocking on and got away a perfectly timed pass to . . . to . . .

'To this flash of a very gold jersey that I saw, while everyone else was muddy. It was Campo.'

Campo in for the winning try!

'Afterwards I went up to him and said, "Well done, Campo," and he said, "You still owe me a few".'

You know it? That really *was* Campo. But it was an account that would be paid in full over the next few years of international rugby, through all its ups and downs. Of the downs, he's had his fair share.

Two years later, Horan was again in South Africa, playing for Queensland against Natal, when late in the game he pulled off an extremely awkward tackle in which the full weight and momentum of an opposing player on the burst combined to turn his knee in a direction that it simply would not go . . . without breaking.

'I knew it was gone as soon as I went down,' Horan recalls with just the slightest of grimaces at the memory.

What he didn't know was just how much the inside of his left knee resembled a front-on car smash, with many fatalities. Three days later he was resting in his hospital bed in Brissy, after a bout of exploratory surgery, when 'the doctor just came in and said, just like that, "It's a lot worse than I thought, and you'll never play rugby again". I think he was a bit shocked by what he'd found, and that is what he said.'

Were this to be a film of Horan's life, we all know how it would go. After the doctor had said that, Horan would have shed bitter tears of anger and in the twilight of his quiet hospital room vowed to himself that he was going to prove medical science wrong. Cut to the next scene of Horan lifting tea cups on his knee at dawn, beginning the long and arduous process of turning himself into a champion again.

Actually . . . it was just slightly different.

'I questioned him about it, and didn't entirely believe it, but what I really was focused on in the first part was just making sure I could walk again, run around with my kids and live a normal life.'

And so it began. Not quite the tea cups at dawn, because even that would have to await more serious surgery, but Horan would indeed spend the better part of the next year focusing solely on rehabilitating his knee—first to ensure he could walk, and then to see if he could make the World Cup side that was going to South Africa in mid-1995.

He did indeed make the side—just—even if he now acknowledges that his knee wasn't really 'fully competent until the beginning of 1996'.

That brings us to the here and now, and the fact that tomorrow Horan will not be facing just another Test.

'It's also going to be a test,' he says, 'a test of whether or not I can play five-eighth. I must say, though, that even though a lot of people say I must be feeling the pressure, I don't really feel it. I think if I just play my natural game, I'll be fine. My natural game with just a few changes.'

And what is your natural game?

'Well, I always like to get my hands on the ball so as to attack as much as possible. But my number one priority, always, is never to miss a tackle. If I get that right, my attacking game usually falls into place after that.

'In terms of playing five-eighth, what I think you'd notice is there is not a lot of kicking done in that position now, because retaining possession is so important, and if you look at how good the players outside me are, if they don't get the ball it will be on me.

'So, I've got to get the ball to them. But on the other hand

I can't be shovelling the ball out every time I get it because it would be too predictable, so I'll have to mix it up.'

Looking forward to it?

'Of course I'm looking forward to it, because I'll be playing with the Wallabies; [that] is what I love to do, and I don't take it for granted. These days, I don't even take walking for granted.'

For all his confidence at the time, Horan did not last long at the position of five-eighth and in short order returned to his more natural position of inside-centre.

AS COACH, SMITH, YOU LET YOUR OWN PLAYERS DOWN

July 1997: which leaves the Wallabies where, exactly? In a very difficult situation unless all of us are completely mistaken. Halfway through the international season, the Australian team has already been thumped twice by the All Blacks and is about to face a rested, and desperate, Springbok side in Brisbane, before facing the All Blacks again in New Zealand.

There are injuries to key players; the usual game of musical chairs continues with the selection process—who's on first, what's on second, and God knows who will be five-eighth—and an overall feel that things are crook in Tallarook.

In the face of such disarray, a commentator is left with two essential options. The first is to wrap oneself in the flag and what is left of the national jersey, before hitting the journalistic ruck in defence of the national side—braying that everyone should get off their backs. The second is to rip in.

The first option is the far more pleasurable activity and no doubt the most rewarding, but the second is mighty tempting at the moment. You think not?

You think it's not right to have a go at the Wallabies and their coach when they are down? Granted on the former, but not necessarily on the latter.

Perhaps you'd care to look at these quotes from Greg Smith after the match, reported in the Melbourne, Sydney and national

press. They refer to a couple of mistakes made in the first half
by the Wallaby No 8, Michael Brial, which unfortunately proved
to be the catalysts for ensuing All Black tries.

'No-one told him to go out and do that, and when you play
against a team like that they'll exploit that,' he said. 'They were
certainly too good for us in the first half . . . and that was the
result of a person making two mistakes, and that's a bit of a
worry.

'Just elementary mistakes, too silly for words. I feel sorry for
Brially, but you can't pretend it didn't happen.'

Hello? Is there anyone else out there who reads the subtext
of those quotes as: 'Don't shoot me. I'm only the coach. Instead,
shoot Brial.'

Such public blaming of Brial seems outrageous in the circumstances. Those circumstances include the fact that Smith pushed
for Brial to be plucked straight out of playing for his club side,
Easts, for the past few weeks and into one of the toughest
cauldrons of football in the world. So he made mistakes? So it's
hardly surprising!

But professional era or not, this sort of approach from the
coach is not on. Of course the coach has to sometimes take a
player aside and have a go at him. And occasionally, very
occasionally, a coach has to have a go at a player in front of the
rest of the team. But to publicly pull down one of your own and
have it broadcast from coast to coast is the very antithesis of
that oh so crucial team approach. The ethic of 'we're all in the
same boat together and must row our way out of this together'
is not only the traditional one, but surely the only one with
which basic team harmony can be maintained.

Just what Brial thinks right now we can only guess, but it
would be a fair bet that the waters between him and Smith will
be poisoned more than somewhat for some time to come.

So in all those circumstances it maybe ain't too much to point
our own finger back at Smith and I'd like to quickly start.

Just what is going on with the selections, anyway? Can it be
a healthy selection policy when, after the first four Tests of the
season, there were only two Wallaby forwards who had been
allowed to remain at their posts? Any chance of some stability
settling on the all-too-nervous hides of the Wallabies?

And just what is happening with the Australian backline? Personally, I do not understand backline play and never really have, though even I could see one thing clearly on Saturday night.

That was that every time the All Black backs had the ball they seemed to have enough time and space to fill the Nullarbor, while our blokes seemed to be flat out filling a jar of Vegemite. The Wallaby backs were constantly running into a big black brick wall, while the New Zealand backs seemed to be dangerous damn nigh every time they touched the ball.

Precisely how all that is rectified I don't really know—but I imagine it has something to do with the way the coach sets the alignment of the backs, the 'game plan' and so forth.

Get on with it, Greg.

And enough already.

Let's hope that Smith can come up with the answers and that the Wallabies go on to great glory this season and beyond with him at the helm.

But if they don't, and Smith is eventually obliged to bite the bullet and recede, here's something else to chew on. His most likely successor is Rod Macqueen, the former New South Wales and Warringah coach as well as the ACT Brumbies coach. With each of those teams, Macqueen has succeeded in getting them to perform way above and beyond expectations.

If he does succeed to the Wallaby position, I suggest he not be obliged to leave the Brumbies behind. I suggest Australian rugby is not so flush with coaching talent at the moment that it can afford to take him out of the loop at any level he's available to coach.

Instead, he should be allowed, nay *begged*, to do the Brumbies first and then move onto the Wallabies. He should also be encouraged to pick a team, any team, and then stick with it.

Only a couple of months after this article, Greg Smith was indeed replaced by Rod Macqueen as national coach. A reason would soon emerge, however, to explain some of Smith's more erratic behaviour as national coach.

An hour from death, Greg Smith finds life

Good news.

Greg Smith is back. Not the Greg Smith of recent times—the surly, withdrawn and not always entirely coherent one—but the Smith of old, who Phil Kearns once described as 'the funniest bloke I know'; who had the wherewithal to rise to the position of Wallaby coach; who was highly regarded for his pure rugby nous.

'I feel like an entirely new man,' Smith said yesterday. 'And I think I've come a long way towards getting over the problem.'

As problems go, this one was about a nine on the Richter scale—a full-blown brain tumour.

'It was a massive one which was pressing down hard on the part of my brain that affects both personality and thinking,' Smith recounts.

The problem first came to light a fortnight ago, when Smith was doing a live cross to New Zealand's Sky Television to preview the Melbourne Bledisloe Cup Test. He was clearly struggling, both to complete sentences and to follow the line of questioning.

As soon as the show finished, he became even more flustered and told a fellow guest on the program that he felt he was 'going to explode'.

Insisting he was still alright to drive himself home, he went straight to bed with a blinding headache.

'The headache didn't ease, though,' he says in a voice now genuinely sparkling with renewed vitality, 'and my wife called a doctor very late that night.'

Only minutes after the doctor had examined him, Smith was on his way to Prince of Wales Hospital for a series of head scans.

He remembers being on his bed the following morning when the main medical man came in.

'I'm very pleased to meet you,' the surgeon said, 'but I'm sorry to have to tell you that you have a very large brain tumour that we must remove immediately.'

Smith sank back in the bed, stunned by the news but not surprised.

'I'd known something was wrong for a bit over twelve months,' he says. 'Basically, I was just not myself. I was very withdrawn, I was having blinding headaches that would last about twenty-five minutes, I would sometimes lose track of my thoughts—I was just not me.

'I remember last year doing a thing for Optus where I was trying to talk about rugby, and I barely had anything to say. I'm trained as an English teacher, and rugby is something I've talked about most of my life, and yet I had nothing to say.'

At five o'clock that Wednesday afternoon, Smith was wheeled into surgery with his wife, Janet, holding his hand, while their two young daughters were at home, waiting.

The anaesthetist cleaned an area of his arm in preparation for inserting the needle that would send him under—something which for most people in such circumstances would be enormously stressful.

About to leave consciousness, was this his last view of the world, ever?

'But I just didn't care,' Smith said. 'I just didn't care at all. I was not me, I was gone. That big thing pressing on my brain meant I didn't care.'

When he came to, late that night, Janet was there, and so was the doctor.

'The surgeon sat down next to me and said that the operation had gone well, but if they'd waited just an hour longer before operating I would have probably gone into a coma that I would never have come out of.'

The following morning, they waited for the pathology results on the tumour, and this time Smith cared passionately.

'Without the tumour in me I was thinking straight for the first time in ages, and of course I very much wanted the results to be good,' he says.

They were pretty good.

'There are three grades of tumour,' Smith explains. 'High, medium and low. My tumour was mostly low, with a bit of medium, and they think they got most of it.'

From here, Smith will undergo six weeks of radiotherapy to attempt to subdue whatever skerricks of the tumour remain.

'There is no way you can ever be sure about these things,' Smith says brightly, 'but at the moment things are looking good.

I'm a very, very lucky bloke, and I think I'll be OK. At the moment I'm just so glad to be feeling like my old self again. I can't tell you the relief.'

And where to from here, McDuff? More rugby coaching? Back to teaching?

'I just want to get through the radiotherapy, and then I want to get a job. What that job will be I don't know, but I'm very keen to get into it, whatever it is.

'Before, I just didn't want to do anything. Now I want to do everything. I'm back.'

Good news indeed.

A year on, and so far so good. It appears Mr Smith has made a complete recovery and he is now coaching the Eastern Suburbs First Grade side.

In the meantime, the new Wallaby coach, Rod Macqueen, had stamped his own authority on the side by quickly bringing on two notable younger talents.

YOUNG BOWMAN READY TO FIRE

Dawn.

Tom Bowman, twenty-one, up in Brisbane, will have woken around about that time this morning, with one thought in his head. Today is the day he will play his first Test match for Australia—in front of his parents, sisters and grandparents, who will be in the stands watching his debut.

That at least was his reckoning when asked about it on the eve of the battle against England, in the opening match of the international season for the Wallabies.

'Of course I will be thinking about it,' he said with a laugh, 'that's pretty much all I've been thinking about in the last few days. I've been a bit anxious about it, I suppose, going into the unknown, wondering what it will be like, how it's going to be. Whatever happens, I want to make sure I soak it all in when I'm out there.'

Bowman is from the country, up Barraba way, born and bred on a property called Tarpoly, and has the open, friendly manner of speaking you often find in people from those parts. (How are you, Tim Gavin, by the way?)

From those climes, Bowman has taken a fairly tried and true way into the Wallaby Test side. That is, he started dreaming of the possibility of wearing the green and gold in the late 1980s while boarding at Scots College, and started to realise that he not only enjoyed playing the game, but was also acquitting himself well at it.

He spent three years in the First XV, from year 10 onwards, under the tutelage of well-known former Randwick second-rower Warwick Melrose; then into the Australian Schoolboys side and the Easts club; which in turn launched him into the Australian under-21s; and last year he went on his first Wallaby tour, to Argentina, although he originally thought he'd be going on to England as well.

But there was a hitch. As the Argentina leg was winding up, the Australian Rugby Union announced that eight of the players would not be going on to England and, instead, would be returning to Australia. Cost, and all that.

'And I was one of those,' Bowman recounted. 'But before I left, Rod Macqueen had a word to me and said if I could play good, consistently good, rugby this year, I'd be a good chance of making the Test side.'

Cue, the phone. A couple of weeks ago, Bowman was doing his other job, at Barclays Menswear at Centrepoint, and lifted the receiver. It was Wallaby manager, John Mackay.

'Congratulations, Tom,' he said, 'you're in the Wallaby squad for the Tests, and we need you at a press conference tomorrow at the ARU.'

Still, there was no confirmation as to whether he was in the Test side, or a reserve, until the following day when, as the microphones picked it up and the cameras rolled, ARU chief executive, John O'Neill, read out the Test players.

'. . . John Eales, Tom Bowman . . .' he said.

In. Made it.

'It wasn't until I got back to the shop, though,' Bowman said, 'that it really hit home, when everyone was ringing with congratulations and everything.'

Other things have happened since . . .

'I went to the State of Origin [league game], with about 40 000 other people, all of whom were screaming, and I remember looking at them, and thinking, "Well, I guess in a few weeks I'll be in front of a crowd like this".'

Not necessarily against England, of course, but certainly if Bowman can consolidate his position beside John Eales in the second row, he has a good chance of being there for the biggest game of the season, at the MCG against the All Blacks on 11 July.

'All I want now, though,' Bowman said, 'is to play well against England. To be controlled, look around, assess the situation, and do my best.'

So that's him, and that's good. Good luck, God bless, and if in doubt, take 'em out.

Since that time Bowman has consolidated his Test spot to perhaps being second-picked in the pack, after John Eales. In the first Wallaby team of 1999, he was the sole New South Welshman selected in the run-on side.

ALL BLACK PUBLIC ENEMY NO 1

This is the Big One. Sure, there have been other rugby Tests already this season, and certainly Stephen Larkham has already played his fair share of Tests already—'about fourteen, I think,'—but this will be different. A lot different.

In the others, he was one of many players, in Tests that were themselves just one in a series. On Saturday night, though, at the Melbourne Cricket Ground against the All Blacks, in front of a crowd of 85 000, playing as the Wallaby five-eighth in a Test in which the Australian public has high hopes of victory, he will be the main man in what will undoubtedly rank as one of the premier sporting events in the Great South Land this year.

Not to put any undue pressure on you, Stephen . . .

BUT HOW ARE YOU COPING?!?!

'I'm not actually thinking about it that much,' said the slight one himself, earlier this week at the Wallaby base in Caloundra. 'There'll come a time soon, I guess, when I will really think about it a lot, but what I've been doing lately is relaxing and thinking about other things. In the last little while I've been missing a fair few interviews, trying to get away from it all, but I haven't had any sleepless nights.'

And as you see, the buzz around the bloke has not made the bloke himself vibrate at all. There is about him no obvious excitement, nor even the vaguest hint of trepidation.

Of course, the 24-year-old Larkham knows that come tomorrow night he will spend the entire eighty minutes as public enemy No 1 of an entire All Black back row sworn to do him down at every opportunity, so as to prevent him igniting the undoubted talents of the players outside him.

'But that doesn't worry me,' he says quite reasonably. 'If they get me, they get me, but I know I can take the hits.'

(And he can, having had his nose broken no fewer than three times this season.)

Cooler than this, he'd be an ice-box. Among the elite rugby fraternity, Larkham enjoys the nickname of 'Bernie', so called after that well-known thespian corpse that starred in the movie *Weekend at Bernie's*. Yet he is not from retiring stock.

'I think at the Brumbies games it's probably Mum and Dad who are the loudest ones there, always calling out, yelling at the referee and so on,' Larkham says. 'That's the way they are, and my grandma is also always passing on advice.'

The Larkhams have a 200-hectare sheep property just off the road between Canberra and Yass, and they are a well-known sporting family.

His grandmother grew up on a nearby farm with two brothers and three sisters and was an accomplished tennis player and cricketer, while his father, Geoff, played more than 300 games for the Wests rugby club in the ACT competition.

It was he who was Stephen's first rugby coach, for the Lyneham under-8s, and would remain in that position for the next seven years as his son pursued the only sport he would ever engage in seriously.

'I was super-keen to play,' Stephen recalls, 'because I knew all about Dad's rugby career, and of course I wanted to be just like him.'

'He was good from the beginning,' recalls Geoff Larkham, 'very athletic, with a great will to win, though he was always small for his age.'

That lack of size did not prevent his dad from putting his son in the front row at first—'because Dad told me I was the only one he could count on to push,' Stephen says—though it was not long before he made his way to the halfback position.

His time since in the backline has been extraordinarily peripatetic, in more ways than one. For not only was he nomadic, moving through each and every backline position over the years, but he also developed the happy knack of popping up, Terry Lamb-like, all over the field at times when he was most needed to keep the ball moving forward.

'A friend of mine started calling him the Phantom,' Geoff Larkham says, 'because, like the Ghost Who Walks, he would be here, there, everywhere, and then gone, before suddenly popping up again when you least expected him. Every rugby coach would like to think they might have a part in helping to shape a player who will become a Wallaby, but when that player is also your own son, well . . . well . . . it's just tremendous. I had a tear rolling down my cheek when he first ran out as a reserve for the Wallabies, in that Test against Wales in Sydney in mid-1996.'

In terms of his own rugby input into his son's make-up, Mr Larkham claims: 'I was always the world's worst loser, and always hated that bloke who said it was "only a game", so I think inside him Stephen probably has that same hate of coming off the field with a loss. But really, most of what he has I think he was born with. It was inbuilt, and I just helped guide it.'

Now, of course, the principal people trying to guide young Larkham's rugby instincts are Wallaby coach, Rod Macqueen, and his backline coach, Tim Lane.

'They've both put a lot of time into me,' Larkham says, 'and Rod tells me five-eighth is my natural position. He and Tim Lane want me to play the position more like [South African five-eighth] Henry Honiball, and mix it up a lot, sometimes passing and sometimes taking it up myself before off-loading to the forwards.'

In terms of the kind of game he intends to play against the All Blacks this Saturday night, Larkham is understandably less than forthcoming, though he does offer a candid assessment of his most direct opponent on Saturday night, All Black five-eighth, Andrew Mehrtens.

'I don't think he's such a good defender,' Larkham says frankly. 'He's good in attack, and maybe the best kicker in the game. He reads the game fantastically well and is a player you have to watch all the time, but I think he does have a weakness in defence because he doesn't commit himself to the tackles.'

(Memo: All Blacks. I've left a space there for you to put the thumbtack in when you stick this on the dressing-room wall.)

Dem's fightin' words, and bespeak a young man not at all lacking in confidence, notwithstanding his comparative lack of experience in this unaccustomed role. To this point Larkham has done very well against what has been generally viewed as sub-standard opposition. Tomorrow night we'll see how he fares against the best in the world.

At least that's what they are as this newspaper goes to press.

(No thumbtacks for me please, All Blacks. I just wrote that last bit because I thought you'd enjoy it.)

Larkham quickly justified his selection in the Test side in the position of five-eighth, but like Eales and Burke—is there a pattern emerging here, or what?—succumbed to a shoulder injury which has kept him out of most of the 1999 season, with the hope that he will return in time for the World Cup.

A MAGIC TRY THE MARK OF MACQUEEN'S WIZARDRY

Can I be the first to put it in print? Very well then . . . Rod Macqueen—master coach! In all the hoopla surrounding the Wallabies' extraordinary Bledisloe Cup win on Saturday— whereby the All Blacks were obliged to become the All Ordinaries in a manner that would make a brown dog weep with joy—some- where let it be noted that a large portion of the credit must go to the former Warringah, New South Wales and Australian Capital Territory coach.

Let the record show that in less than twelve months, Macqueen has taken a side that was only a couple of strewn stray bricks short of a rabble, and turned it into what is clearly, at the very least, one of the best two teams on the planet at the moment.

From being walloped by 40-odd points by the Springboks in August last year, in August of this year the Wallabies have beaten the All Blacks twice on the gallop, and they will, by God, give the Boks a very good run for their money later this month on the veldt.

Cue, movie voice-over man: 'They're baaaack, and this time, they're angry.'

Just how Macqueen and his team have worked this transformation is not yet crystal clear, but most obviously at its core lie greater organisation, more stability in selections, a greater confidence in abilities, a more coherent game plan and an enormous improvement in handling skills.

One doesn't want to get too carried away, of course, and say that John Eales already has his hands on next year's World Cup, but he certainly has at least his little pinkie around one handle, and only the Springboks could claim to have a slightly better grip a year out from the event.

If there was one passage of play that characterised the Australians' extraordinary dominance, it was the three minutes leading up to the wonderful try by Matthew Burke just before half-time. Did anyone count the phases that led up to it?

Phases, for the non-aficionados, are specific passages of play. A scrum, or lineout, is the first phase; the next ruck or maul is the second phase; the ruck or maul after that is the third phase, and so on.

In rugby, the cauliflower corps get excited about completing four phases of play without making a mistake which results in the ball being turned over to the other side, swoon at five phases, and simply disbelieve their eyes at six phases.

Burke's try came after the Wallabies had completed EIGHTEEN phases of play. Simply, they kept taking the ball forward into the teeth of the All Black defence, breaking or loosening a tooth every time, until the New Zealanders were all gums and Larkham was able to slip a pass inside for Burke to go over for a superb try.

The feat was a prodigy of control and fitness by the Wallabies and it was the try that seemed to spiritually break the New Zealanders.

A team capable of doing that without making a mistake was

never going to be beaten on the day, and the best the Blacks could hope for from that point was simply to try to limit the damage.

Over Auckland way at this very moment, there will be a lot of analysis of what has gone wrong in the past three Tests. Unless I miss my guess, the redoubtable All Black coach, John Hart, will have spent the past two nights staring at the cracks in the ceiling as he tries to work out just what is going wrong.

Humbly, I would like to offer two thoughts.

The Kiwis have in their team three of the most potent attacking weapons in world rugby in Jonah Lomu, Jeff Wilson and Christian Cullen. If they're not the best in the business, there's only Ben Tune and Matthew Burke who could seriously argue the toss with them.

And yet, and yet, somehow an All Black side that possesses such maestros of mayhem has managed in its past three Tests to go for about 200 minutes without scoring a try! From the time All Black lock Ian Jones put the ball down for a try with two minutes to go before the break in the first Test in Melbourne to when Cullen scored with minutes to go on Saturday, the only scoring had come from a bleak harvest of penalty goals.

Clearly, when Cullen, Wilson and Lomu are so under-used, while both the five-eighths tried in Mehrtens and Spencer have been shovelling the ball out often enough, there is a very big problem in the New Zealand centres.

Also, look to the possession on Saturday.

For most of the game the Wallabies had about 65 per cent control, while the All Blacks had to make do with the scraps of 35 per cent. Such dominance can only come when one back row is getting wiped out by another, and for whatever reason, the All Black back row is just not up to it at the moment. That reason may well be that they're already too exhausted in covering for a below par front five—but the back row problem remains, regardless.

(Giving well-meaning advice to the New Zealanders about how they can fix their game up—gawd, but I love this!)

While Hart addresses such issues, Macqueen will also be spooling endlessly through tapes to see what improvements we can make before taking on the Boks.

My suggestion would be the lineout. Somehow or other,

despite all the work, it is still not there. Maybe it just looks ordinary when compared with all the extraordinary that is around it, but there is still a lack of cohesion and co-ordination about it that resulted in three needless turnovers on Saturday.

Apart from that though, go you good things!

In late August 1998, the Wallabies beat the All Blacks once again, in the third Test of the Bledisloe Cup series . . .

STRAIGHT TO THE HART OF AN ALL BLACK FUTURE

And yea, verily, it was written. One day, the meek shall inherit the Earth, the poor shall be rich, and the All Blacks will lose five Tests on the trot.

Praise the Lord and pass the binoculars! As the result on Saturday night shows, there really is a God, Virginia, and though the Wallabies have a long way to go before their full debt of suffering to the New Zealanders is paid in full, major inroads have been made into paying that account.

One cannot really imagine just how badly the men in black are suffering at this moment, but hey . . . why don't we give it a burl anyway?

In just one season they have gone from being indisputably the best in the world to being only third-best and falling. Their new skipper, Taine Randell, has taken over the most revered position in New Zealand sport—actually, make that New Zealand generally—and started with five losses out of seven.

Coach, John Hart, has gone from being something close to the messiah of world rugby to lucky if he holds onto his job. Some players like Ian Jones have gone from being proud All Blacks of impeccable credentials to mere bench-warmers trotting on to replace the injured, while others like Michael Jones have simply moved off into history.

The aura of invincibility that the All Blacks used to have every time they took the field has now been shot to pieces and will not return any time this millennium.

Who is to blame for this state of affairs? That, unless I miss my guess, is the very question occupying the minds of the New Zealand rugby community—which is to say pretty much everybody—at this very moment. From their side of the ditch, there appears to be an answer, but none of them wants to say it out loud for fear of offending various sensibilities.

Over here though, we needn't worry and can repeat the scuttlebutt at will, while also disclaiming all knowledge of whether it's true or not.

Ahem . . .

What Kiwis with cauliflower ears all seem to be saying, including those quite close to the current team, is that the problem lies with John Hart himself. Rightly or wrongly, the strong undercurrent of feeling is that Hart is one of those particularly intense kinds of people who are able to achieve great results in a short time, but who quickly wear out their charges in the longer term.

To quote one Kiwi in the near orbit of the All Black team, whom I ran into after the game, 'When these blokes go on tour now, they can't drink, can't smoke, can't root, can't go out, and they're all just sick of it.'

(I know, I know, I thought it was unnecessarily vulgar of him to include one of those things too, but I can't help it—that's what he said.)

'Hart,' he said, 'is a schoolmaster type who has to be in control of everything, whereas a lot of the guys are used to running their own show, with a lot less input from the coach.'

True, or not? I have no idea, officer, and I was actually at home knitting a jumper with my mother at the time.

If it's not true, of course, then my mistake, and please excuse me Mr Hart for repeating it.

In September 1998, the Commonwealth Games were held in Kuala Lumpur, and rugby was included for the first time in the competition. The Australian side was captained by none other than David Campese.

CAMPO BIDS HEAVEN'S GAME FAREWELL WITH A BRONZE

'Ladies and gentlemen, this will be David Campese's last international match for Australia. Malaysia is very honoured that this should take place here.'

So said the ground announcer before the bronze medal match of the inaugural Commonwealth Games Rugby Sevens competition. The crowd roared, as all seemed to appreciate that it would be singularly appropriate for Campo to leave the stage with a shiny medal around his neck.

For the Australian team, too, it would be a worthy finish. At the end of a three-day campaign in which they had racked up five strong victories before falling to Fiji in the first semi-final, they now found themselves playing a Samoan side that had wowed the crowd in previous days.

Strangely, Campese did not start the game but sat quietly on the reserve bench as the opening whistle blew. It later transpired that he felt he had over-extended himself in previous matches, and it would be better to have fresher and younger legs on early.

At its best, sevens can be an exhilarating cross between basketball and 15-a-side rugby, with the ball flowing back and forth on the field . . . and this was just such a game.

The tide raged forward and back as the packed stadium cheered, stopping only at half-time, when the score stood at 12–12 with two tries apiece.

After the break, Brendan Williams broke through to score under the posts, and with nine minutes to go on the clock, Australia had a still very vulnerable lead of 19–12.

At last, though, Campese. With 4 minutes 30 seconds left on the clock, the famous Australian winger—now sevens captain and five-eighth—came onto the field to great applause, and perhaps one or two lumps in the throat among the large collection of Australians in the crowd.

With 90 seconds to go, Campese tried a chip-kick ahead, but was taken out by the Samoan defence before he had a chance to regather. Penalty! And easily kickable. Campese gathered it up.

(*No, Campo, don't do it. Ninety-nine captains out of 100 would take the kick so as to run down the clock and ensure victory, but not you, mate, not in your last minute on the international stage. RUN the bugger!*)

He ran it. And passed it, and Australia's Marc Stcherbina broke through for a try just seconds later.

Williams added another for good measure just 30 seconds later, and Australia won the game 31–12.

The Australians, superbly led by Campese on the field and Mark Ella off it, played above themselves to win their bronze medal. The players chosen did Australia proud, and the spirit in which they played was adventurous and clean.

And you, Campo? You've played good, done fine. In attack, none finer. We've had our differences, but if this is indeed the end—on ya. All of us who've been in teams with you over the years have been proud to play with you.

We'll tell our grandchildren.

Good taste prevails: well done, everyone

Eureka! They've done it! Let the Australian Rugby Union exist for another thousand years and men and women of the oval ball will still say that this was its finest hour.

I refer, of course, to the decision, quasi-official it seems, of the ARU to ditch the dreadful 'volcano vomit on a rag' jersey that the Wallabies have been running around in for the past couple of years and return to something that looks suspiciously like the old jersey, with simply a couple of bells and whistles attached to placate the marketeers.

Look, it has taken a lot of courage on the part of the rugby administrators to acknowledge the colossal error they made in ditching the original jersey—to say, in effect, 'There are stuff-ups, there is Chernobyl, and there is what we did to the jersey,'—but they have been big enough to do so and should be congratulated for it.

I mean it! How would you like to have spent the past two years stoutly defending the indefensible, resolutely insisting that there would be no change, that the new jersey was the new jersey, like it or lump it, and that was simply the end of it—only to find that everyone really was lumping it and everywhere you went people were having a go at you about it, writing letters, jeering, the whole catastrophe.

Wouldn't you just dig your heels in, refuse to budge an inch and try to take shelter behind figures you kept trotting out to show that it was a proven fact that kids between 10 and 14, living on the south side of Perth, with a slight impairment in the left eye, were buying the new jersey in record numbers!

I know I would. 'Bugger 'em!' I would say. Let those snivelling goats bray till their horns fall off and see if I care.

But no, the ARU has not done that. It knows that certain imbeciles in the rugby press will say that 'they've caved in to popular pressure and it bloody well serves them right', but they're prepared to wear it. (Who are those imbeciles anyway? Just wait till I get their names.)

The 'bells' of the new jersey are the stars of the Southern Cross on the right breast, the 'whistles' are the curious green and white stripes around the elbow—and the clanger, of course, is the tragic survival of the Vodafone lettering scrawled across the front of the jersey.

In sum though: goodo, you beaut, and for better or worse, for richer or poorer, let's hope the ARU stays with the substance of this new jersey for many decades to come.

National uniforms should not be easily trifled with, and our hope has got to be that this particular jersey will become as famous and revered as the All Black one. *Sans* the Vodafone lettering, of course, which simply ruins, my dears, the overall effect.

Now, if you'll excuse me, Yves St Laurent, Christian Dior, Giorgio Armani and I have to go and discuss the regrettable state of international fashion.

(Sniff.)

DAMMIT, THOSE KIWIS HAVE BEATEN US OUT OF THE CLOSET

Oh, he was old, and he was gnarled, and he was ruefully shaking his head in his beer—damn near crying in his pretzels, he was—in a bar at Darling Harbour a couple of weeks ago.

What, I asked, was the problem?

It stemmed from the 40-year reunion of his high school rugby team that he'd attended the night before, he said. One of the blokes who'd turned up hadn't turned up as a bloke at all, if I got his drift. He'd come in a dress! With real breasts.

None of the other blokes could believe it, but it was true. 'Johnny' had had one of them sex-change operations, apparently, and was now, like it or lump it, living the life of a female—except that he was still quite happy to see his old mates on such occasions. They had to accept 'her' as 'she' was, 'she' had told them, and he fair dinkum meant those quotation marks. For he wasn't going to accept it at all, and was still clearly struggling to wrap his head around it.

'Mind you,' he finished after some quiet reflection, 'I should have known it'd be him who'd do something like that. He was a *winger* . . .'

Of course!

A similar thing occurred recently, I'm told, at the 15-year reunion of the St Joseph's College class of 1983, where another former bloke turned up as a woman.

He, too, had been a winger . . . by of course the purest of coincidences. That generation of Joey's boys, by all accounts, had been more accepting of the change. And nowadays? The current generation of rugby players will probably have far fewer problems with those of differing sexuality, and I'm not just talking about the breakthrough engendered by Ian Roberts coming out and being accepted in the brother code of rugby league.

Far more important than that is the news out of New Zealand last week about the playing this Sunday of the first official interprovincial gay rugby match between Wellington's Krazy Knights and Auckland's Rainbow Heroes.

This follows the formation in Britain a couple of years ago of the first official gay rugby team, the Kings Cross Steelers, which now plays in a regular suburban competition.

One of the organisers of the Wellington gay team, Dean Knight, was quoted in a New Zealand Press Association story thus: 'The real victory is getting gay teams on the field and overcoming the barriers which dissuade gay men from playing rugby in mainstream competitions. It is simply amazing to see the gay rugby players, who played while in the closet, enjoying themselves playing in an open, gay environment together with first-time players who previously did not give rugby a go because of the homophobic attitudes which have been present in mainstream rugby.'

Another organiser with the Auckland side, Todd Martin, said: 'People still have some misconceptions about what a gay rugby team is like. In reality, you would not be able to tell a gay and a straight team apart by watching them play.'

And there it is, gay rugby starting to come to the boil. Good move or bad move?

I say great move. The glory of rugby has always been that it's inclusive, above and beyond all other sports. Whether you're fat, thin, tall, short, fast, slow, good-looking, ugly, good, bad, Russian, Moroccan, Chinese or American, rugby at its best will get you a game. You'll wind up with a spot as an athletic prop in the First XV, or as a slow-as-a-wet-weekend five-eighth in the Sixths, but you'll end up getting your shorts muddy, and that's what it's all about.

In recent times this voracious appetite of rugby to accommodate all comers has seen it storm the barrier of gender, to the point where it is now exploding in popularity among females of all ages the world over. And if it is now forcing a breach in the Berlin Wall of sexuality, all the better. (There has been a well-travelled Checkpoint Charlie through the Wall for a long time now, but to this point it's just about all been under the cover of darkness.)

So where is Sydney's first openly gay rugby team? You call this the largest gay city in the southern hemisphere, and yet we're behind Auckland and Wellington when it comes to making gay sporting history? It sounds embarrassingly pissant on our part.

Inquiries yesterday revealed that there is at least a gay touch football team in Sydney, calling itself the POOFTAs, short for the Proud Openly Out Football Touch Association, but this isn't good enough, dammit.

Get on with it Oxford Street. The New South Wales Rugby Union is awaiting your call, and will no doubt find a spot for your team in the Sydney subbies rugby competition.

After that, the world!